Boston Architecture

1975–1990

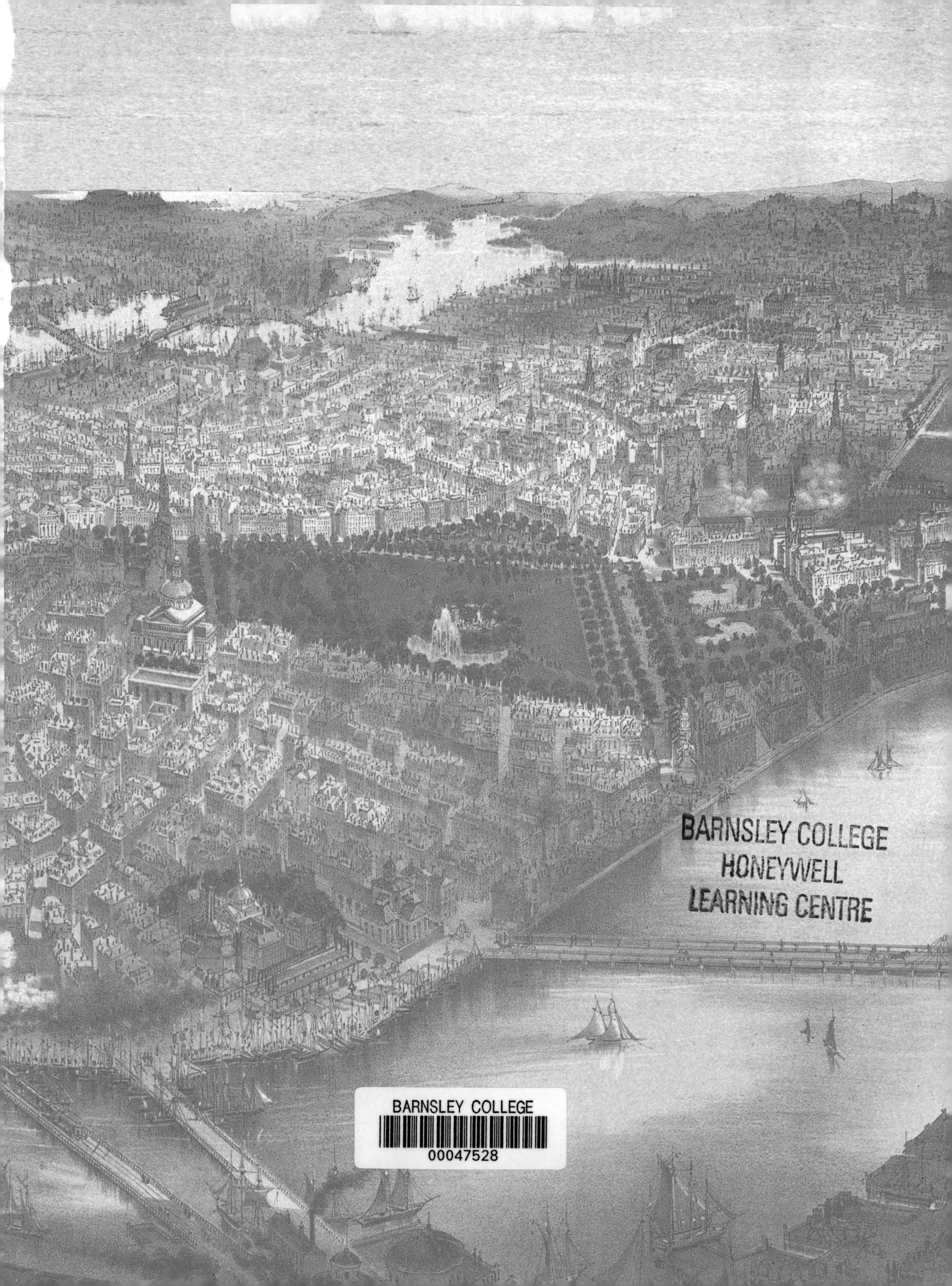

Naomi Miller · Keith Morgan

BOSTON
Architecture

1975–1990

Prestel

© 1990 Prestel-Verlag, Munich

Photographic Acknowledgements: p. 248
Map by Michael E. Brown, Streetwise Maps Inc.

Cover: John Hancock Tower. Photo: Steve Rosenthal, Auburndale, MA
Frontispiece: Quincy Market with Faneuil Hall; International Place and
75 State Street in background. Photo: Steve Rosenthal, Auburndale, MA
Endpapers: (front) View of Boston, 1877, courtesy the Geography and Map Division,
                        Library of Congress
                   (back) Boston, aerial view, 1989. Photo: Alex S. MacLean Landslides,
                        Boston, MA

Prestel-Verlag, Mandlstrasse 26, D-8000 Munich 40, Federal Republic of Germany
Tel: (89) 38 17 09 0; Telefax: (89) 38 17 09 35

Distributed in continental Europe by Prestel-Verlag
Verlegerdienst München GmbH & Co KG,
Gutenbergstrasse 1, D-8031 Gilching, Federal Republic of Germany
Tel: (81 05) 2110; Telefax: (8105) 55 20

Distributed in the USA and Canada on behalf of Prestel-Verlag
by te Neues Publishing Company,
15 East 76th Street New York, NY 10021, USA
Tel: (212) 288 0265; Telefax: (212) 570 2373

Distributed in Japan on behalf of Prestel-Verlag
by YOHAN-Western Publications Distribution Agency,
14-9 Okubo 3-chome, Shinjuku-ku, J-Tokyo 169
Tel: (3) 2080181; Telefax: (3) 2090288

Distributed in the United Kingdom, Ireland and all other countries
on behalf of Prestel-Verlag
by Thames & Hudson Limited, 30-40 Bloomsbury Street, London WC1B 3QP, England
Tel: (71) 636 5488; Telefax: (71) 636 4799

Edited by Ian Robson

Designed by Dietmar Rautner
Typesetting: Max Vornehm, Munich
Color separations: Gewa Repro GmbH, Gerlinger und Wagner, Munich
Printing and Binding: Passavia Druckerei GmbH, Passau

Printed in Germany

ISBN 3-7913-1097-6

Contents

Foreword

"Boston is the only city in America you could satirize. No other city has enough solidity, is complete enough. You couldn't write a satire on New York. Nothing is crystallized there. [The only] place static enough and finished enough to write a novel about is Boston." John Marquand, the novelist, spoke thus of the city in a 1937 interview. His explanation sheds more than a little light on the nature of Boston in a realm altogether distinct from that of the novelist, the realm of architecture and urbanism. More than half a century after Marquand made his remarks to justify the setting of *The Late George Apley* in Boston, his words still hold true, and concisely sum up what remains a fact about Boston: it is complex, yet comprehensible and definable, and it is a place unto itself.

Most American cities lack really potent identities or, like New York and Los Angeles, they have powerful identities that are simply too complicated, too vast and contradictory, to be easily understood. Boston has a presence, a sense of itself; it is not like other cities, and yet it is neither so vast geographically nor so complex historically and culturally that it defies any attempt to characterize it.

In *Boston Architecture, 1975–1990* Naomi Miller and Keith Morgan have summed up the essence of this city, and understood that it is one of the few large American cities in which history plays a strong, even a controlling, role. This does not mean that Boston is guided constantly by the preservation impulse, though it does loom large in the city's culture, not only safeguarding some of the nation's most admired historic districts, such as Beacon Hill, but also inspiring a strong inventory of inventively designed adaptive re-use projects. But to say that history is crucial to Boston is emphatically not to suggest that it is some kind of northern version of Williamsburg, that with all its tourist-luring old buildings it has come to function as a colonial theme park, for even a casual contact with the reality of the Boston landscape, or the most cursory reading of local newspaper headlines, makes clear that this is as profoundly real a city as exists in the United States, an urban environment as fraught with economic, racial, and political tensions as any.

But these dramas play themselves out on a stage that is different from most other American stages. Boston is relatively small, complicated in layout but by virtue of its scale not difficult to understand. It is at once relaxed and intense, and if that seems not to make sense, imagine lingering in the Public Garden, perhaps taking a leisurely cruise on a swanboat, then walking rapidly through Beacon Hill, past the State House,

and down to the waterfront: in a few minutes one can go from a genteel and gracious urban park to an extraordinary living eighteenth-century neighborhood, a government center, and a financial district, finally arriving at a harbor now filled with new kinds of urban activity.

In Boston there are models for almost everything, although a better way to say this may be that the models for almost everything are in Boston. Perhaps that is the thing: that it is all here, tighter and more concise than in other places, densely packed and manageable in scale. In Boston we see not only architecture but whole urban patterns work themselves out, as if on a trial for the rest of the country. Copley Square is a model for the cultural districts of a later age, possessing two of the greatest public buildings in America, the Boston Public Library and Trinity Church; Commonwealth Avenue and the Back Bay are models for planned urban neighborhoods, more successful, surely, than almost any others of the late nineteenth century. City Hall by Kallmann, McKinnell & Knowles, not to mention the Government Center around it, is a showpiece for the hubristic ambitions of the public realm of the 1960s, ambitions that failed as much as they succeeded, but which stand today as a poignant reminder of an age that at least wanted to do *something*. So, too, with the Boston Redevelopment Authority's sweeping schemes, with the sad loss of the West End neighborhood (here, Boston taught by negative example, as chronicled in Herbert Gans's *The Urban Villagers*), and with the ghastly Prudential Center complex by Charles Luckman on Boylston Street, perhaps the worst piece of corporate-sponsored late-1960s urban renewal in the country, and a project that is now being substantially rebuilt in the hope that it can become another kind of model, a model of 1990s rescue of 1960s mistakes.

So the examples, the models, in Boston are both negative and positive. There are many others that can also stand as symbols, as types: Henry Cobb and I. M. Pei's extraordinary Hancock Tower, the glass slab with a troubled history but a majestic visual presence, is surely the premier example in the country of a minimalist building enriching a cityscape. Rowes Wharf, by Skidmore, Owings & Merrill—a triumph of urban design, a reminder that well-meaning contextualism can yield monumentality as well—, Tent City, by Goody, Clancy & Associates, and several housing complexes by William Rawn together prove not only the inventive possibilities of contextualism but the continued commitment of Boston as a city to a housing policy, to public benefit, and to a sense of visual wholeness, of completeness.

This is what it comes down to in the end: in Boston there is a sense of wholeness. Buildings are not objects apart; they are emphatically and completely parts of larger wholes. This is the real gift of history to Boston: an ethos of urbanism. Even where Boston's urban fabric has been blown apart, as at Prudential Center, it struggles to knit itself back together, like a body healing itself naturally after a wound. And many buildings that might appear to stand apart, like Hancock does at Copley Square, in fact do acknowledge what is around them; they merely eschew connecting in a literal way.

So this book is really a paean to urbanity, for that is Boston's gift. Naomi Miller and Keith Morgan are properly critical of numerous buildings that fall short of Boston's standards (it is somehow endemic to Boston that many of its buildings fall short of its standards, but Boston's standards remain its standards nonetheless). Yet the overall sense one gets from these pages is an encouraging one, if only because this cityscape is so enriching. In Boston, the impulse toward architectural innovation, which has always been strong, exists in a kind of balance with the moral presence of history—a balance more profound, surely, than in any other city in the United States.

Paul Goldberger

Acknowledgements

This book had modest beginnings, namely as a catalogue to accompany an exhibit to commemorate the fiftieth anniversary meeting in Boston of the Society of Architectural Historians. That it grew beyond these limits was the result of a Research Seed Grant from the Graduate School of Boston University in the summer of 1988. We should like to express our sincerest thanks to former Associate Dean William Carroll for his support and encouragement of the project. Our deepest gratitude is due to Kimberly Shilland, our graduate assistant, who has been an indispensable part of this undertaking from the start. At Boston University, we should also like to thank Professor William Vance for conversations on literary Boston, and members of the Art History Department who have assisted in various stages: Arlene Arzigian and Pat Kelliher for providing photographs, and Cecilia Hanley and Megan Gardner for cheerfully unlocking lost computer codes. We owe a great debt to Lillian Lambrechts and her staff at the Bank of Boston for the beautiful installation of the exhibit, and, above all, to the architects, planners, developers, photographers, and staffs of the Boston Redevelopment Authority and the Boston Landmarks Commission for their generous contributions to the exhibit and the book. And, finally, our profound appreciation goes to Prestel Verlag, who made the entire enterprise possible and, what is more, enjoyable.

Bibliographical Note

History, indeed, with its long, leisurely, gentlemanly labor, ... is the ideal pursuit for the New England mind.
Elizabeth Hardwick, "Boston," *Harpers*, 1959

Considering the penchant of Bostonians for history, the number of guidebooks to the city is remarkably small. Historical sources abound, but writing on the architecture of Boston is limited. The interested reader is referred to the *Blue Guide: Boston and Cambridge* (New York: W. W. Norton & Co., 1984) for a selective bibliography on matters pertaining to the city: chronicles, biography, history (social, intellectual, maritime), and also architecture.

Our concern, however, is with recent buildings and their impact on the urban fabric. Hence, in preparing this book, our greatest debt has been to current guidebooks. None is more useful than that of Michael and Susan Southworth, *AIA Guide to Boston* (Chester, CT: Globe Pequot Press, 1987), whose copious illustrations and up-to-date entries were essential for exploring the city. Our admiration for Donlyn Lyndon's *Boston: The City Observed* (New York: Vintage Books, 1982) grew with every reading; restraint was needed to avoid quoting passages at length, for few authors on architecture combine such a fine understanding of building with judicious criticism and elegant writing. Our swift journey through the first 350 years of Boston's history was enhanced by Walter Muir Whitehill, whose *Boston: A Topographical History* (Cambridge, MA: The Belknap Press of Harvard University Press, 3rd ed. 1975) is the most succinct and authoritative introduction to the city. Mention should also be made of such basic books on Boston as: Bainbridge Bunting, *Houses of Boston's Back Bay* (Cambridge, MA: The Belknap Press of Harvard University Press, 2nd ed. 1975); Margaret Henderson Floyd, *Architectural Education and Boston* (Boston, MA: Boston Architectural Center, 1989); Donald Freeman (ed.), *Boston Architecture* (Cambridge, MA: MIT Press, 1970); Jane Holtz Kay, *Lost Boston* (Boston, MA: Houghton Mifflin Co., 1980), Kevin Lynch, *The Image of the City* (Cambridge, MA: MIT Press, 1960); Douglass Shand-Tucci, *Built in Boston* (Amherst, MA: University of Massachusetts Press, 1988); The Boston Society of Architects, *Architecture Boston* (Barre, VT: Barre Publishing, 1976); Cynthia Zaitzevsky, *Frederick Law Olmsted and the Boston Park System* (Cambridge, MA: The Belknap Press of Harvard University Press, 1982); and the maps in *Blueprint of the New Boston: A Guide to Recent Architecture* (Washington, DC: National Building Museum, 1984). Not least, we have profited from the architectural criticism of Robert Campbell in *The Boston Globe* and Paul Goldberger in *The New York Times*. The issue of *The Boston Globe* devoted to "The Livable City" (11 November 1984) proved to be invaluable.

Boston waterfront

Boston Architecture
1975–1990

To our students, who pose the problems
To architects, who search for solutions

Prologue

And did not indeed the small happy accidents of the disappearing Boston exhale in a comparatively sensible manner the warm breath of history, the history of something as against the history of nothing?

Henry James, "Boston," *The North American Review,* March 1906

Boston is history, and the history of Boston is built in brick and granite. From the dome-capped State House to Faneuil Hall, cradle of liberty, and the red brick townhouses of Beacon Hill to the planned development near the harbor, Charles Bulfinch—first native-born American architect—set the tone. And, despite the enormous transformations in the "city on the hill" during recent decades, much of old Boston remains intact. Its past glories continue to delight visitors, but a goodly number will wish to learn more about the new Boston, whose towers now dominate the horizon and, paradoxically, have returned the city to the sea.

The purpose of this book is to introduce students, architects, planners, tourists, and local residents to the architecture that has appeared since 1975. By so doing, we hope to show how Boston has been transformed, and to encourage a better understanding of the idiosyncrasies of the city's plan and a better appreciation of its particular beauty. It is the relationship of the buildings to the street network—the emphasis on an urban quality—that imparts the unique character of this city. In fact, the individual buildings are subsumed under overall vistas, for the pleasures at ground level give way to unexpected configurations upon turning a corner. The lack of orientation in the winding old world streets in the Central Business District complements the perfect grid of the Back Bay. Where the former is pervaded by stone and glass facades, the latter is characterized by Victorian townhouses on tree-lined avenues that are punctuated by church steeples and towers, now overshadowed by a new, fragmented skyline.

Center of a broad urban agglomeration, Boston itself is a medium size city, whose population, according to the 1980 census, numbered about 563,000 inhabitants. Prosperity peaked in the 1980s and is due to factors indigenous to the city together with a particular set of circumstances. Here is the capital of Massachusetts, the seat of its government. Here is the business center of New England, its financial hub, and its transportation center for air, sea, and rail. Here is the nation's most prestigious hospital network, with a plethora of medical facilities. Here is the college town par excellence, with over thirty institutions of higher learning within the area. Here is the gateway to Washington at the northern end of the Boston–New York–Washington corridor. And, above all, here is the nexus of a high-tech post-industrial economy: the development of computer-based technology and communications has been a prime factor in the metamorphosis of the three-square-mile area, an area with few equals among American cities, long blessed by its proximity to nature and the fertile countryside.

Today's Boston began in the late 1950s when the Boston Redevelopment Authority initiated a massive urban renewal scheme for Government Center. Down-and-out but lively Scollay Square was a picture of blight and decay. In those distant days renewal was equated with removal, and I. M. Pei's master plan practically obliterated the West End. Modernity arrived with certainty when Kallmann, McKinnell & Knowles won the competition to build the new City Hall as a fulcrum of the entire complex. Still, compared with other cities, the past persists with greater tenacity in Boston, delaying the arrival of the new, except perhaps for the traffic arteries that brutally truncate the city at a number of points.

Boston seems at first to have been impervious to the radical changes in the urban skyline that transformed the American city during the decades following the Second World War. Whereas tall buildings and dense housing complexes altered the nature of the American townscape, "new" architecture in the Boston area appeared to be selective, almost experimental. Not so the buildings since the mid-seventies, which almost without exception have followed the mainstream of architectural developments elsewhere. In an era of inequitable affluence, Boston had risen to occupy a place near the top of the table in terms of real estate prices and average income. Although some might welcome the lavishness and the scale of the new building as the opening up of a once restrictive society, one must also acknowledge the decline of the values that were until recently reflected in the urban fabric—the understated air of refinement, the moderation in all things, the dourness even.

A reorientation towards earlier times was signaled with great fanfare at the dedication of Faneuil Hall Marketplace on the occasion of the nation's bicentennial in 1976. Preservation and adaptive re-use now moved to center stage. That wonderful world of Disneyland evoked here at Faneuil Hall, where the pedestrian is king and every view is picturesque, is being recreated in Charlestown and around the harbor. (Surely this "festival marketplace" cannot be the city of the twenty-first century!) By the mid-eighties, facadism had arrived. As land values rose and air rights soared, towers were tacked onto the low-rise fronts of another era, under the guise of preservation. Architects turned from people and streets and the city itself and immersed themselves in history—all the history of all nations, but above all Palladio, as witnessed in the excessive fenestration at International Place.

The year of the Orwellian nightmare, 1984 was the year marked by the most extensive regeneration. Looking back, we see that this peak of the boom coincided with the end of Kevin White's term as mayor. The cautionary and optimistic tale told by the Hancock Tower, completed in 1975, was one factor in postponing the appearance of Boston's modern skyline, a silhouette which by then had proliferated in every major American city. But this is Boston, ever conscious of its historical legacy.

Slow to start, Boston's development accelerated. Pluralism and eclecticism have replaced the basic tenets of modernism. Not surprisingly, recent building reflects the consumer society of the eighties and the growth of international capitalism. The predominance of style over substance is frequently apparent in the appalling details and shoddy workmanship. Entrances are either overblown or overdiscreet. Rationalist principles have been reversed, for notwithstanding obvious complexities there is little attention to integral structure. Materials are more frequently veneer than natural, their usage artificial rather than logical, just as public spaces are often privately operated. Terms like glitter, clutter, and terminal trendiness, common in high fashion, are unfortunately applicable to much of the new architecture. Most disturbing of all is the lack of vision concerning future environmental problems. Hardly a building for offices or dwellings is constructed without a parking garage, and automobile space in these is at a premium. Legal and ethical issues are coming to the forefront, and will undoubtedly become a major factor in architectural developments.

The buildings that in their mannered ostentation, eclectic pomposity, and grandiose scale show a disregard for the very substance of architecture will in the future serve as a backdrop to the true innovations of recent years—the preservation and enhancement of the city's cultural heritage, and the renewed awareness of the public realm (in theory, if not in practice). Less visible, but just as significant, is the rebuilding of the city's infrastructure, and soon, it is hoped, the cleaning of Boston harbor.

No area has witnessed a more dramatic metamorphosis than the downtown business district; but buildings that have radically transformed the urban vista are also found outside the city center, in adjacent areas such as the Back Bay, the South End, Cambridge, and Charlestown, neighborhoods that are very much a part of the overall city. Space limitations have led us to focus on the most prominent new architecture, which may not be up to par in an aesthetic, structural, or urban sense. So overwhelming is the amount of recent construction that much has been omitted, especially buildings of quality in

surrounding districts. In the city of Cambridge, only the most notable and monumental projects have been included, such as the development of an impressive science and technology center around Kendall Square, the mixed-use enterprises of Charles Square and Lechmere Canal, and a few individual institutional buildings. Major projects in Charlestown and along the piers are discussed, as these constitute the principal thrust of Boston's boom, namely the renewal of the entire waterfront. The South End, too, is worthy of deeper study, being both contiguous with and separate from the Back Bay: housing and rehabilitation activity here is undoubtedly gentrifying the entire area. Although our focus is on the individual building, our main purpose is to convey an idea of its context, both immediate and overall: that is, its relation to the street and to the entire city. Even today, Boston's street pattern is the principal determinant in a building's design. In fact, the most visible of the new buildings—75 State, 99 Summer, 125 Federal, 101 Arch, 53 State—are inserted into an irregularly shaped streetscape, thereby adding to the interest of the structure and perpetuating the rich perspective at ground level. Moreover, the lobbies of these buildings constitute a network of well-appointed, indeed opulent, indoor concourses directly connected to the streets they border.

In tracing the developments of the period, we have naturally taken a critical look at the boom in commercial buildings and, to a far lesser degree, in housing, and we have focused special attention on schemes for the preservation and adaptive re-use of our historic patrimony. Because biomedical technology and related health care services will be crucial economic factors in the coming years, space alloted to the buildings that house these facilities seems to be justified. Though one may question the energy devoted to planning more traffic lanes and parking accommodations, a far-sighted transportation policy is essential if the city is to continue as a viable entity: we look at the schemes and structures that have been taking shape in this context, and consider their repercussions on the open spaces so vital to urban life. Boston's acknowledged assets in parks and waterfront may be further enriched by the private developer, as well as by the public authority, who may provide thoughtfully planned passageways, shopping malls, atria, and meeting-places for people.

The strength of Boston has always been the amenities at street level, and despite a few negative developments the inner city remains an area where the pedestrian rules. Competitions enhance the architectural debate, which is marked by a significant degree of citizen participation along with that of such professional organizations as the Boston Civic Design Review Board, the Boston Landmarks Commission, the Real Estate Board, and the Boston Society of Architects. It was the latter who sponsored the competition for "Boston Visions" of the twenty-first century: the winners among the nearly two hundred entrants proposed a waterfront town at Logan Airport with a new shoreline for the harbor, and the extension of Boylston Street west through the Fens thereby making fuller use of the legacy of Olmsted's nineteenth-century park schemes that created Boston's "Emerald Necklace." It is this level of citizen involvement that has had a marked impact upon major projects—the lack of affordable housing for minority groups from which Tent City arose, the community decisions at Villa Victoria, the popular competition for improving Copley Square, and the creation of such an organization as Friends of Post Office Square. By transferring a garage from above to below ground, the latter group has created a brilliant light-well midst the steel and glass canyons—though it may turn out to be a mixed blessing, a park that will encourage the flow of downtown traffic. Even such grand commercial enterprises as Copley Place were generated by open discussion. Not only has this development completely transformed the barrier between the Back Bay and the South End, but it has served as a catalyst for the creation of such public areas as the Southwest Corridor Park, among the most exemplary of recent designs. The tracks of the old elevated transit system have been shifted and the site converted to a multi-use connective link, a veritable green belt that joins formerly separate districts and acts as a perfect antidote to high-density development and parking wastelands.

Who are the architects of the new Boston? A few established local firms continue to make their imprint upon the city: Kallmann, McKinnell & Wood, The Architects Collaborative, and, not least, Hugh Stubbins, still the apostle of modernism. Offices like Goody & Clancy, Notter, Finegold + Alexander, Stull & Lee, and Jung/Brannen (the largest firm in town in 1989) have moved to the forefront. There are a host of newcomers: Childs, Bertman, Tseckares & Casendino, Ellenzweig Associates, and—most visible of all—Graham Gund Architects, a firm that is playing a major role in both adaptive reuse and the creation of new structures. There appears to have been a quantum leap in the sheer number of professionals involved in the building process. Just two decades ago, a handful of architectural offices dominated the scene. This is no longer the case: a new generation of architects has joined forces with developers to collaborate on major schemes.

Increasingly, it is the name of the developer that tells the main story, be it the Chiofaro Company, Olympia & York, The Beacon Companies, Renaissance Properties, or Cabot, Cabot & Forbes. Big projects are more and more being financed by out-of-state corporations, such as Gerald Hines of Texas, Urban Investment and Development Corporation of Chicago, and Prudential Property Company of New Jersey, the latter projecting a major overhaul of the Prudential Center. The corporate image has superseded individualism, as represented by those pioneers of modern architecture—Gropius, Le Corbusier, Aalto, Sert—who built in Cambridge and Boston. But the new architecture is a logical consequence, if often a distortion, of the ideas propagated by the leading lights of an earlier generation.

From "Massachusetts miracle"—a slogan used by Massachusetts Governor Michael Dukakis in his presidential campaign of 1988 to describe the prosperity of the state—to "welfare magnet"—a phrase recently employed to indicate the declining economy! Both pronouncements are writ in the language of hyperbole. Still, there is little doubt that the boom of the eighties has now crested, thereby permitting a more rational assessment of the present stateBosaffairs. Combined with the movement for a humane ambiance, there is a tendency towards more comprehensive planning in the city, a type of planning that focuses on urban conditions. While they no doubt enhance the quality of building, it is important that restrictions such as those imposed by the Boston Redevelopment Authority do not prevent growth. For example, the development of the waterfront and improved overall transportation are considered to be vital components of future economic prosperity. Current solutions, however, are often envisioned in accord with today's technology rather than with future possibilities, but at least a dialogue is now in progress.

At the beginning of the nineties, an international outlook has superseded provincialism, and the perspectives of local architectural offices are national and global. Mayor John Collins (1959–67), whose reduction of the infamous Boston property tax generated the economic and building resurgence, has long since gone; so too Edward Logue, the talented administrator of the Boston Redevelopment Authority, whose program to revitalize the downtown area was begun in 1958. Under Kevin White, mayor from 1968 to 1984, plans for growth and development peaked, whereas the current administration of Mayor Raymond Flynn has initiated "linkage," a program defining long-range goals and taking into account affordable housing, job training, and social services. "Linkage is a social contract between the city government, the development community and residents. It provides opportunities and builds bridges between Boston's booming downtown commercial economy and the people in its neighborhoods. It shares the benefits of prosperity with those who have been historically left behind."

Rhetoric? Time will tell. Stephen Coyle, the head of the Boston Redevelopment Authority, has instituted new zoning that puts limits on growth and tightens controls through review boards. Common sense and community consciousness may challenge the swelling ranks of real estate developers and individual entrepreneurs. However, a new breed has emerged, no longer shackled by the proverbial New England resistance to innovation, but willing to compromise in order to maintain and salvage a rich architectural heritage—as witness recent landmark cases revolving about the Stock Exchange Building or 101 Arch Street. Once more, there is an attempt to rediscover the city's primary contours and to enhance them, stressing, for example, the balance of winding narrow streets and broad open spaces. Contemporary Boston is at its best where the new dissolves into the old, and the old—whether it be a Greek Revival doorway, a Richardsonian church, a French Renaissance townhouse, a Victorian factory, or Olmsted's Emerald Necklace—retains its charm alongside its modern neighbors.

Boston has not led the way in the introduction of the new or in the creation of modern buildings of notable quality. Rather, it is in the process of preservation, the rehabilitation and conversion of older, largely nineteenth-century buildings, that her record is commendable. Urban values seem once again to be taking priority over strictly architectural ones. Certainly, the transformations of large portions of the Back Bay, Charlestown, and the South End point in that direction, as does the dramatic revitalization of the waterfront.

Past and present harmoniously coexist in Boston. The coherent fabric of the older areas may be compared with the fragmented, idiosyncratic configuration of some recent developments. An astute observer may indeed be conscious of how successfully the older distinguished districts have adapted themselves to the exigencies of modern living, of how the complex street network has inspired often unconventional solutions in building and planning, of how far Boston has progressed towards becoming the "livable city" that her politicians promulgate. The inquisitive pedestrian, for whom this book is written, will find feasts for the eyes and exercises for the mind while wandering about the city.

1   "A Plan of Boston
in New England with its environs."
Copperplate engraving
by Henry Pelham, London 1777.

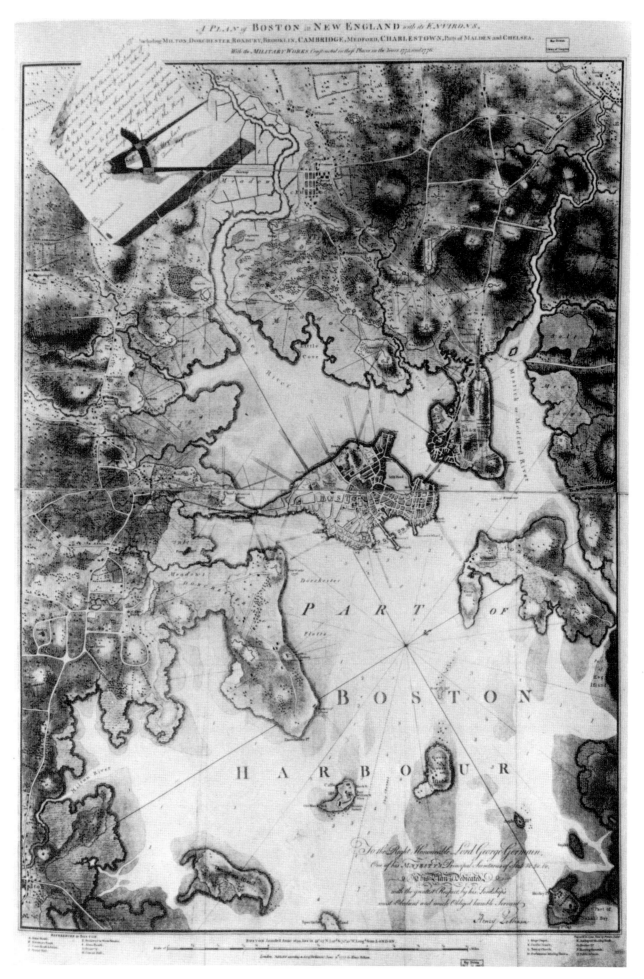

PAUL REVERE HOUSE AFTER RESTORATION

2   Paul Revere House (after restoration), ca. 1680.

3   First Town House, 1657–1711. Reconstruction drawing by Charles A. Lawrence, 1930.

Drawn from the Original
Specifications for
Thomas Joy and Bartholomew Bernard
1657

BOSTON'S FIRST TOWN-HOUSE
1657–1711

Charles A. Lawrence – 1930

Looking Backward

All thoughtful men agree that the present aspect of society is portentous of great changes. The only question is, whether they will be for the better or the worse. . . . [This book] was written in the belief that the Golden Age lies before us and not behind us, and is not far away.

Edward Bellamy, *Looking Backward*, Boston 1888

The Beginnings of Colonial Boston: The Seventeenth Century

The Metropolis of the whole English America.
Cotton Mather, 1698

Water has been the essence of Boston, from its beginnings on the hilly peninsula that was first settled in 1630 by the Massachusetts Bay Colony (Fig. 1). In the 360 years since, two of the three largest mounds that constituted the Trimountain have been leveled and bays have been filled, but the prospect of water – ever more distant – remains. The Reverend William Blaxton, the first English settler, who built a house near a spring at the foot of Beacon Hill in 1625, had access from the peninsula to the mainland on the south (now Roxbury) by a narrow isthmus surrounded by mudflats and marshes. And, as Walter Whitehill has pointed out, "the inexorable encroachment of land upon water that has marked Boston's history" began with the building of the wharves to facilitate commerce. As early as 1634 Boston was described as "fittest for such as can Trade into England, for such commodities as the Countrey wants, being the chiefe place for shipping and Merchandize." The Puritan colonists were determined to rebuild on this newfound soil the life they had been forced to abandon when they fled from England. Street names, only fixed in the early eighteenth century, bear witness to the English origins of the settlers.

Towards the end of the seventeenth century, Boston was a thriving seaport and the leading commercial town of the American colonies, with a population estimated at 7,000. "In tide-encircled Boston each street led down to the sea," and none was more prominent than King (now State) Street. Wharves (and later fortified breakwaters) lined the harbor, which bristled with the tall masts of the sailing ships. Against this was set the gentle sloping panorama of the town, where church steeples rose majestically above the pitched roofs of the clapboard wood-framed houses. Beyond were the fields of Beacon Hill and the Common, the 45 acres bought by the town from Blaxton in 1634. Here cattle grazed by day and people strolled towards evening.

Accounts of the seventeenth-century building fabric are few. Material evidence is virtually limited to Paul Revere's house in the North End (ca. 1680; Fig. 2), built on part of the site of the Reverend Increase Mather's house, the latter destroyed in the fire of 1676. Much rebuilt and restored, the wooden structure features casement windows and an over-hanging second story. By the end of the century, more clapboard dwellings had appeared with leaded casement windows. Meeting houses seemed akin to large barns. The average building was half-timbered, simple, and strictly functional, as befitted a town that the later revolutionary leader Samuel Adams would call "Christian Sparta."

A reconstruction drawing of the first Town House (1657–1711), a most important public and commercial building, shows its location at the principal crossroads of the meeting house square (Fig. 3). Providing protection from the elements and such amenities and necessities as library and armory, this two-story structure served as a central market and a gathering place for local merchants. Here they heard the latest news from the London exchange and the major coastal ports.

Meanwhile, the Boston area's most renowned institution, Harvard University–founded in Cambridge in 1636–was already grooming the future leaders of the colonies.

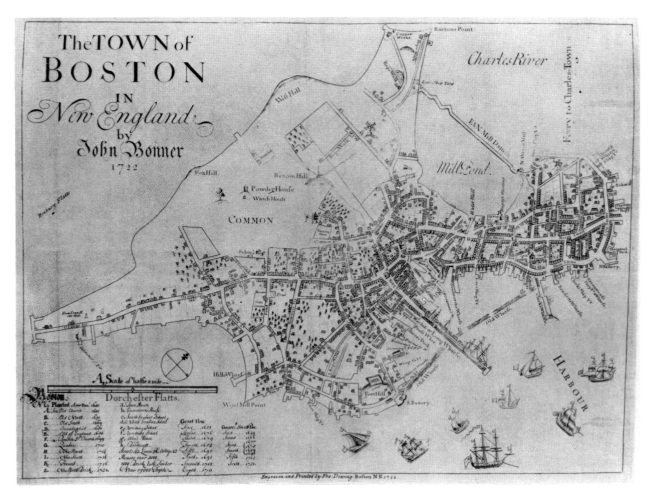

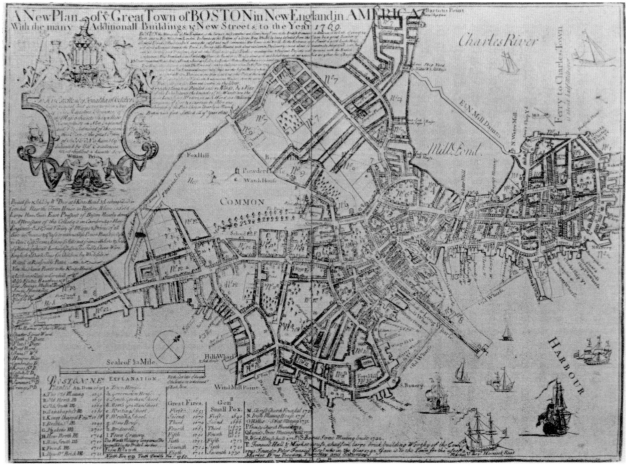

Pre-revolutionary Boston: The Eighteenth Century

March 21, 1775 – . . . After breakfast, being a fine day, went to the Common & got upon the top of the High hill at the back of Mr. Hancock's fine house. Upon the top of this hill is a large flag Staff with a Vane; & here I enjoyed the finest prospect I have seen in America. All the Bay of Boston, with the many Islands, & the Harbour with the Shipping & the water round to the Neck, with Boston neck & the fortifications on it; the whole Town lying below & on all sides, & the country on the other side of the Bay & Harbour to a considerable distance; which from this place makes a very agreeable appearance, being entirely cleared & open; consisting of gently rising hills & valleys, thick planted with Churches & country seats.

Dr. Robert Honyman, *Colonial Panorama*, 1775

4   "The Town of Boston in New England." Map by Captain John Bonner, 1722.

5   "The Town of Boston in New England, with revisions and additions." Map by Captain John Bonner, 1769.

6   "Panorama with Long Wharf. . . . A view of part of the town of Boston in New England and British ships of war landing their troops." Engraving by Paul Revere, 1768.

Prevolutionary Boston prospered. A bustling seaport, it was still isolated from the mainland. By mid-century its population had more than doubled to about 17,000, but shortly afterwards it was overtaken by Philadelphia and New York.

A series of maps and printed views enable us to trace the growth and transformation of the city. None are more revealing of the seaport's growth than the maps of John Bonner: the first, dated 1722 (Fig. 4), cites "houses near 3000, 1000 brick, rest timber." Compared with earlier maps, we note an increased density in the inhabited areas. Revised editions in 1733, 1743, and 1769 (Fig. 5) clearly depict the monuments of the city, as also changes and additions of individual structures.

Approaching Boston from the sea, we would have been struck by the proliferation of wharves, none more prominent than Long Wharf extending from King Street (Fig. 6). Built in 1710, teeming with shops and warehouses, it was a key to the town's maritime prosperity. Church spires dominated the panorama: Christ Church (now Old North Church), built in 1723, is the oldest surviving church in Boston (Fig. 7). Here Cotton Mather preached, and here the revolutionary patriot hung the signal lanterns—"one if by land and two if by sea"—immortalized in Longfellow's poetic recapitulation of Paul Revere's midnight ride. On the downtown side is the steeple of the Old South Meeting House (1729; Fig. 8) on the site of the original wooden church, built in 1669. Nearby, the gambrel roof of the brick house and apothecary shop built around 1711 for Thomas Crease remains as a distinctive example of

7   William Price: Old North Church, 1723. Engraving.

8   Joshua Blanchard: Old South Meeting House, 1729.
From photograph ca. 1895.

9   Thomas Crease House: Old Corner Bookstore, ca. 1711. Engraving.

10 Peter Harrison: King's Chapel, 1750. Engraving.

eighteenth-century domestic architecture (Fig. 9). Converted to the Old Corner Bookstore in 1828, it later became a publishing house; restored in the early 1960s, its ground floor, marked by the generous expanse of windows that once provided natural light for readers, now serves as part of the downtown office of *The Boston Globe*. Steps away on School Street, outside the Old City Hall, is the plaque marking the site of the first Boston Public Latin School.

Most significant of the mid-eighteenth-century churches is King's Chapel, designed in 1750 by Peter Harrison of Rhode Island (Fig. 10). Replacing the first Anglican church, founded in 1688, its site is next to the town's oldest burial ground, dating from 1631. Whereas the dark gray granite mass and wood Ionic colonnade (added decades later) strike a reticent note, the interior pays homage to its English ancestry in the disposition of the boxed pews, the paired colossal Corinthian columns framing the balcony, and the impressive organ. Only the steeple, designed in the English tradition of Wren and Gibbs, was never built.

"Faneuil Hall and Market House, a handsome, large, brick building worthy of the generous founder Peter Faneuil Esq." Thus is the two-story building given to the town for use as a market in 1742 (Fig. 11) described on Bonner's 1743 map. Above the market, designed by painter John Smibert, were offices and a town meeting hall. Destroyed by fire, it was rebuilt in 1762. In 1805 Charles Bulfinch doubled its width and added a third story for the Artillery Company, thereby maintaining the earlier Doric and Ionic articulation.

Throughout this period, the town center remained at the crucial intersection of King and Cornhill (now Washington) streets. The old wooden Town House on an uneven slope was reconstructed in brick after being destroyed by fire in 1711, but in 1747 the new building also went up in flames and was subsequently restored many times over the next two hundred years (most notably by Isaiah Rogers in 1830 and by George A. Clough in 1882), remaining always at the heart of the city. Today, set against the lofty skyscrapers of the financial district and close to Government Center, the gilded lion and unicorn on the gable of the red brick Old State House, as it has long been known, recall British rule and the site of the Boston Massacre on the eve of the Revolution (Fig. 12).

11 John Smibert: Faneuil Hall, 1740–42. Copper engraving by S. Hill, *The Massachusetts Magazine*, 1789.

12   "The Boston Massacre." Engraving by Paul Revere, 1770.
Old State House, 1712; rebuilt 1748, 1830 (Isaiah Rogers), 1882 (George A. Clough).

The Boston of Bulfinch:
1789 to 1818

Post-Revolutionary Boston was marked by relatively little population growth. The maritime trades pervaded all sectors of life and were especially vital for the increasing development of Charlestown, which became the home of the nation's leading shipyards. Whereas the city towards the south and west was still largely bordered by open fields, its boundaries expanded to the Charles River and the Common. Still, Boston's island character yielded slowly, and it was only in 1786 that the 1500-foot-long Charles River Bridge (Fig. 14) connected the town to the Cambridge mainland, followed by another bridge six years later.

Our architectural heritage from the Federal period includes civic and religious buildings, but is still permeated by domestic brick structures. To reduce the number of devastating fires, wood was prohibited, and an edict of 1803 required that all buildings over ten feet high be constructed in stone or brick and covered with slate or tile. Stone houses remained relatively scarce, due to a shortage of skilled stonemasons, but soon the material appeared in civic and commercial architecture.

Post-Revolutionary Boston belongs to Charles Bulfinch (1763–1844), who epitomizes the cultivated gentleman-architect. Boston born and bred and Harvard educated, Bulfinch set forth on a two-year Grand Tour of Europe in 1785. As with his contemporary Thomas Jefferson, then ambassador to France, this experience led Bulfinch to view his native land

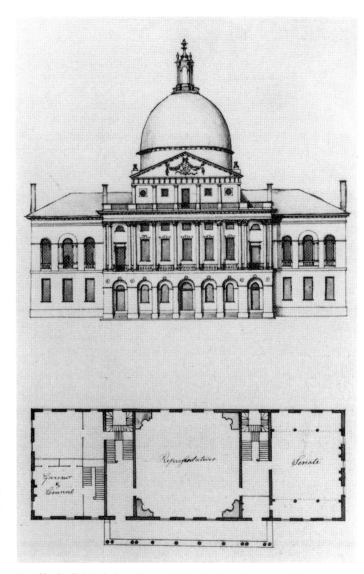

13 Charles Bulfinch: State House, 1795–98. Front elevation and plan.

14 "Charles River Bridge to Charlestown, 1786." Copper engraving by John Scoles, *The Massachusetts Magazine*, 1789.

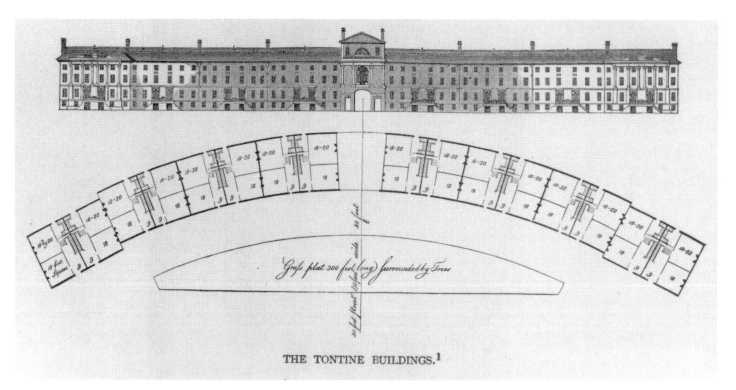

THE TONTINE BUILDINGS.[1]

15 Charles Bulfinch: Tontine Crescent, 1793–94.
Elevation and plan,
The Massachusetts Magazine, 1794.

16 Charles Bulfinch:
Second Harrison Gray Otis House, 1800.

with fresh eyes – that is, as decidedly provincial in the light of European Neoclassicism. He was impressed above all by the English and French architecture and town planning of the day. The ex-colonies soon began to reaffirm their commercial ties with England, and it is little wonder then that the Neoclassical Somerset House, built for government offices in London, was chosen as the prototype for the Boston State House (1795–98; Fig. 13). The gleaming dome rising from the Palladian facade sited at the apex of the Common seemed to reinforce the words of John Winthrop, first governor of Massachusetts Bay State Colony: "We must consider that we will be a city on a hill. The eyes of all people are upon us." Bulfinch would have preferred to use stone, but circumstances dictated that the state capitol be built in brick and wood. And while the Adamesque influence is particularly evident on the interiors, such as the ceiling of the original legislative chamber, the whole is simpler and more severe than its English antecedents. In no small measure the State House owes much to the magnificent site it occupies on the crest of the Common. But, above all, its use of a classical language made the building a paradigm for capitols in the United States and led to Bulfinch's call to Washington in 1818, where until 1830 he assumed the role of Architect of the Capitol.

As a model citizen and a dedicated public servant, Bulfinch was determined to improve his native city. To this end he virtually transformed Boston from a provincial colonial town into a truly urbane center. Best remembered for his monumental public buildings, Bulfinch pioneered in almost every conceivable genre. To him we owe the first theatre in the city, on Federal Street (1794), the first pavilion of the Massachusetts General Hospital (1816–23), and wharves, schools, markets, warehouses, alms societies, banks, and insurance buildings. There were churches, too, though the only surviving one in Boston is the New North Church (today's Roman Catholic St. Stephen's), a brick building on Hanover Street, restored in 1964 by Archbishop Richard Cardinal Cushing. However, it is as architect-developer that Bulfinch perhaps made his greatest contribution, for his ideas were pivotal in the development of the areas around the State House. It is he who bestowed on Beacon Hill and the immediate surroundings the wonderful brick mantle it still wears, marked by an elegance, a sense of perfect proportions, and a refinement unequaled in the city's fabric.

Speculative projects and private commissions set the stage for the dignified and disciplined urban vernacular of old Boston. Viewing the elegant housing on Tontine Crescent (Franklin Street, below Hawley Street), built in 1793–94 (Fig. 15), architect Asher Benjamin astutely remarked that Bulfinch "gave the first impulse to good taste and to architecture in this part of the country." In a city still predominantly built of wood, these attached three-story brick buildings facing an oval park echoed the recent developments of town plazas in Bath, as also terraces and squares in London. Was Bulfinch thinking of the entry to the seventeenth-century Parisian Place Royale in the central arch, which gives Arch Street its name? In Tontine Crescent the proportions of window to

wall, the fine craftsmanship of the brickwork, the simple and almost severe articulation of building elements, and, most importantly, the attention to scale contributed to the enhancement of the city. Bulfinch was surely the principal author of this regional Federal style, which echoed the reserved Neoclassicism of eighteenth-century London. Just witness the three fine homes, still extant, that Bulfinch built for the Federalist party leader Harrison Grey Otis: 141 Cambridge Street in the West End (1795–96, now the headquarters of the Society for the Preservation of New England Antiquities); 85 Mount Vernon Street (1800; Fig. 16), on the land of the Mount Vernon Proprietors bought from artist John Singleton Copley; and 45 Beacon Street (1806), facing the Common. Little wonder that a local inhabitant returning to Boston after a thirty year absence was able to remark: "I am really astonished at the appearance of Wealth magnificence & taste thro'out the town."

Only the Park Street Church, built by Peter Banner in 1809 on the corner of Park and Tremont streets (Fig. 17), has

17   Peter Banner: Park Street Church, 1809. One Beacon Street (Skidmore, Owings & Merrill, 1972) rises behind the church.

assumed a landmark status almost equivalent to that of the State House. Its site at the foot of the Common and steeple in the finest Wren-Gibbs tradition have conspired to create a powerful yet graceful monument. On the site of the old granary and next to the Old Granary Burying Ground (1660; its tombstones read like Who's Who of colonial America), the church joined the elegant line of houses designed by Bulfinch that extended up Park Street towards the State House, all gone now but for the completely restored and altered Amory-Ticknor mansion. In 1852 Thackeray would note that this row "could hardly be surpassed, for elegance and the appearance of comfort, even in London." If the rows of houses bordering the Common have been demolished, Bulfinch's legacy survives in the privately developed houses that the Mount Vernon Proprietors built from 1826 to 1848 around the cast-iron-fenced green oval of Louisburg Square.

18   Alexander Parris: Quincy Market, 1825. View from waterfront.

19   India and Central Wharves in 1857.

20   Isaiah Rogers: Tremont House, 1822–29. Photograph, 1870.

The Early Nineteenth Century

We dined the other day at Mr. Sear's. He has a fortune of five or six millions, his house is a kind of palace, he reigns there in luxury.
Alexis de Tocqueville, *Democracy in America*, 1831

In 1822 Boston, no longer governed by town meeting, adopted a city charter and elected its first mayor. This change was necessitated by the rapid growth of the community, which surpassed 43,000 inhabitants in 1820, more than double the population in 1790. The departure of Charles Bulfinch for Washington in 1818 had signaled a major turning point in the evolution of Boston architecture. While brick continued to be used, stone architecture emerged as the carrier of a new image. First granite, quarried in nearby Chelmsford and Quincy, then a range of sandstones—Connecticut brownstone and various limestones—and later the conglomerate Roxbury puddingstone became the materials of choice. This development coincided with important changes in the scale and character of Boston architecture over the next quarter-century.

Alexander Parris was heir to the mastery of Bulfinch, if indeed a single architect or builder can actually be said to have taken his place. Trained in Maine, Parris worked with Bulfinch on his final design in Boston, the Massachusetts General Hospital (1817–23), built of Chelmsford granite. The rational forms of Greek-inspired Neoclassicism were well suited to the blocky, sculptural massing to which granite lent itself. Parris also experimented with this species of stone in his David Sears House (1819–21), where a pure cylinder emerges from the entrance facade. But the most remarkable of his granite designs was Quincy Market (Fig. 18), a product of the renewal and reorganization of commercial activity on the waterfront (Fig. 19). Under the patronage of Mayor Josiah Quincy, Parris designed a 555-foot-long market building with temple facades at the ends and a central domed rotunda. Flanking this building to the north and south are two three-story brick warehouses with granite revetment on the sides towards the central market. The severity of these designs is in keeping with the hard nature of granite, a material which proliferated throughout the financial and commercial core of the city. Boston's first modern hotel, the three-story Tremont House (Fig. 20), was designed by Isaiah Rogers (1822–29) and built in granite, as were such churches as St. Paul's (Parris, 1825), whose Greek temple portico faces Boston Common, and Solomon Willard's vaguely Gothic Bowdoin Street Congregational Church (1831–33). And across the harbor in Charlestown, Parris designed engineering structures and industrial buildings in granite for the Navy Yard, while Willard oversaw the erection of his granite obelisk (Fig. 21) as a monument to the Revolutionary War battle of Bunker Hill.

Not all buildings of this period were granite temples, however. Italian palaces were the models for the city's new cultural institutions, such as Edward Clark Cabot's Boston Athenaeum (1847–49; Fig. 22), C. Kirby's old Boston Public Library (1859), or Hammett Billings's so-called Boston

21 Solomon Willard: Bunker Hill Monument, 1825–43.

22 Edward C. Cabot: The Boston Athenaeum, 1847. Second floor reading room.

23 "Map of the City of Boston and Suburbs...," 1878.

Museum (1846), a lavish theatre fronted by a lobby filled with paintings of dubious quality. For the commercial architecture of the period, granite remained the popular choice, as seen in the warehouses along the waterfront and the shops on Washington Street. Boston rarely experimented with new methods of construction, so that cast-iron-fronted commercial structures, popular in New York and elsewhere at mid-century, were infrequently built here.

Expanding the Landmass:
The 1850s and 1860s

By the 1840s, Boston's major problem was a lack of space. The original boundaries of the Shawmut peninsula had been gradually expanded throughout the eighteenth and early nineteenth centuries in response to the continuous, if modest, increase in commerce and population. The town sought new land through the filling of the waterfront with earth transferred from the tops of Boston's hills. And expansion to adjacent areas increased with the construction of bridges to South Boston in 1805 and 1828, and of new bridges to Cambridge and to Charlestown, and with the building of railways north, south, and west from Boston in the first half of the 1830s.

By mid-century, more drastic measures were needed. The problem had suddenly intensified in the late 1840s, as the first of several waves of immigration washed into Boston harbor. This caused the population to increase rapidly, from over 93,000 in 1840 to nearly 137,000 in 1850. The Irish potato famine of the late forties brought to Boston poor rural immigrants, who poured into the deteriorating neighborhoods of the North End, the South Cove, and the West End. By 1855 there were approximately fifty thousand Irish inhabitants in Boston, almost as many as the entire population of the city thirty years before. Urban congestion inspired the earliest of efforts to create suburban communities, beginning in the Cottage Farm and Longwood sections of Brookline, across the Back Bay. More important was the formation of large new districts on landfill within the city (Fig. 23).

Two new residential areas were created around the middle of the century—the South End, built from the 1840s onward on land north and south of Washington Street under the control of the city and private developers, and the Back Bay, constructed from the late 1850s onwards directly west of the Common and the Public Garden to plans developed by the Commonwealth of Massachusetts. Both districts were intended to fill the needs of new housing for the middle and upper classes. The two developments soon took different courses, however.

In the South End, the Washington Street spine that had been the narrow connection to the mainland was enlarged to the south and north in a series of disorganized streets and squares. Three-bay, four- and five-story brick townhouses with characteristic bowed fronts were arranged around landscaped private parks (Fig. 24), following a pattern that Bulfinch had introduced in his designs for Tontine Crescent a

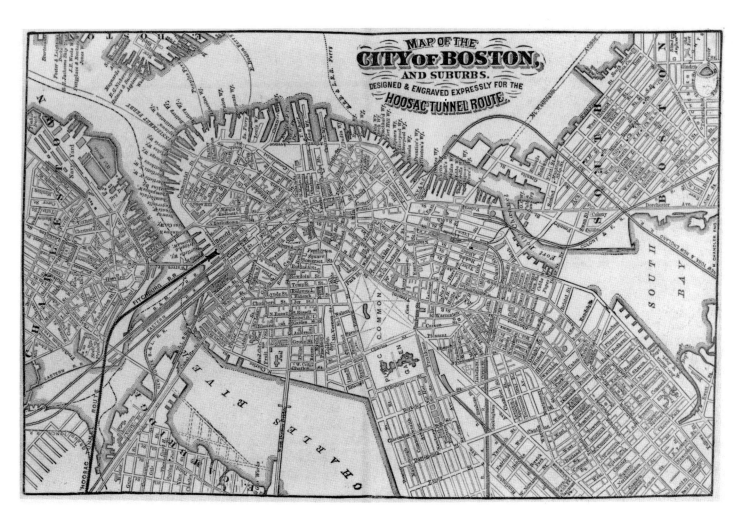

GLEASON'S PICTORIAL DRAWING-ROOM COMPANION.

DEVOTED TO LITERATURE, ARTS, AMUSEMENTS, NEWS, &c.

MUSEUM BUILDING, TREMONT STREET.   F. GLEASON, PROPRIETOR.   THREE DOLLARS PER ANNUM, SIX CENTS SINGLE COPY.

VOLUME I.   BOSTON, SATURDAY, NOVEMBER 15, 1851.   NUMBER 29.

BEAUTIFUL BLOCK OF BUILDINGS IN BLACKSTONE SQUARE, BOSTON

24   Blackstone Square. From *Gleason's Pictorial Drawing Room Companion*, 15 November 1851.

25   Commonwealth Avenue. Engraving by James S. Conant, 1882.

26   Boylston Arlington Streets: View of Arlington Street from the Public Garden in the early 1860s.

half-century before. The inauguration in 1856 of horsecar transport by the Metropolitan Railroad improved access to the new district. Very soon, the immigrants also began to invade the South End, as is reflected by the buildings designed by Patrick C. Keeley for the Roman Catholic church, namely the Church of the Immaculate Conception (1861) and the Cathedral of the Holy Cross (1875). The financial panic of 1873 destabilized the rapid development of the area, and by 1885 the South End had become predominantly a lodging house district. At the end of the century, the South End was synonymous with congested tenements, alcoholism, prostitution, and general urban decay.

Contributing to the further decline of the South End was the inauguration of the second major landfill effort. Directly west of the city, the Back Bay was the area where industrial activities had been pursued with no great success throughout the first half of the century, using the tidal flow of the Charles River as the source of power. With the filling in of the area, the Back Bay became the site of elegant townhouses, churches, and public institutions, and the most important district for the city's architects throughout the second half of the nineteenth century. Planned as a unified whole, the Back Bay was controlled by the Commonwealth of Massachusetts and by a development corporation that specified lot size, building height, and a generous allocation of open space and parkland. The new district was joined to the Common and the city core by the Public Garden, a picturesque pleasure ground designed by George Meacham in 1859. The swan boats that soon plied the still waters of the serpentine lagoon became the lovable symbol of genteel, bourgeois Victorian Boston. From the Public Garden, the tree-lined esplanade of Commonwealth Avenue (Fig. 25) became the thoroughfare of the new district and the location of the city's most sumptuous mansions. In architecture, city planning, and the arts in general, mid-century Boston patterned herself after the model of Second Empire Paris. This is particularly evident in the pavilions and mansard roofs of the earliest houses to rise along the Public Garden and Commonwealth Avenue (Fig. 26). Simi-

27   William Gibbons Preston:
Museum of Natural History,
1862 (*right*), and
Rogers Building, 1863 (*left*).

28   Ruins of Pearl Street
after the Fire of 1872.

29   Arthur Gilman and
Gridley J. Fox Bryant:
Old City Hall, 1862–65.

BOSTON CITY HALL, SCHOOL STREET.

The Boston of H. H. Richardson: 1868 to 1886

The things I want most to design are a grain-elevator and the interior of a great river-steamboat.

H. H. Richardson, as cited by M. G. VanRensselaer, *The Architecture of H. H. Richardson*, 1888

The 1872 fire coincided with the return to Boston of an architect who was destined to leave his mark on American architecture and, indeed, the architectural profession. Born in Louisiana, Henry Hobson Richardson (1838–1886) was educated at Harvard and graduated just before the Civil War

30 Henry Hobson Richardson: New Brattle Square Church, 1872. Tower.

larly, such public buildings (Fig. 27) as the Museum of Natural History (1862) and the Rogers Building (1863, home of the newly created Massachusetts Institute of Technology), both designed by William Gibbons Preston, reveal his debt to the Place de la Concorde, laid out by Jacques-Ange Gabriel in the mid-eighteenth century. This francophilia was not restricted to the expanding Back Bay, but can also be seen in the Old City Hall (Fig. 29), Arthur Gilman and Gridley J. Fox Bryant's 1865 homage to the new Louvre, or in the United States Post Office (1867) by the architect of the US Treasury, Alfred B. Mullett.

The process of reorganizing the central district and of pushing the city outward was further accelerated by the disastrous fire of October 1872, in which much of the inner city was destroyed (Fig. 28). Rebuilding was at first thwarted by the financial panic of 1873. However, after the fire this area became (and has remained) the financial and commercial center of the city. New construction followed older patterns, and commercial palaces of five or six stories were built in brick and granite. The chaotic street patterns inherited from colonial Boston by and large survived the fire, and continue to make the financial district a labyrinth for visitor and native alike.

31 Henry Hobson Richardson: Trinity Church, 1872–77.

32 Trinity Church. Interior.

erupted. With divided loyalties, Richardson left for Europe to become the second American to study architecture at the École des Beaux-Arts in Paris. After initially practicing in New York upon his return, Richardson soon found his Harvard connections provided opportunities in Boston. He was chosen 1869 as the designer of the New Brattle Square Church (now First Baptist Church; Fig. 30) on Commonwealth Avenue, one of his earliest exercises in a Romanesque Revival vocabulary that he soon transformed into a personal design mode much admired and imitated by his colleagues.

Richardson's most important work in Boston was the result of winning the competition for Trinity Church (1872–77) on Copley Square in the new Back Bay. The highly polychromatic mixture of granites and brownstones on the exterior (Fig. 31) only partly prepared his contemporaries for the explosion of color and form on the interior (Fig. 32), where he contracted with friends and colleagues to provide mural, sculptural, and stained glass embellishments. His reputation—local, national, and soon international—was established by this building, and the frequency of his Boston-area commissions now convinced him to relocate his home and office from New York to suburban Brookline, Massachusetts. In the remaining decade of his life he designed for Boston and its suburbs distinctive libraries, railroad stations, and such institutional buildings as Sever Hall and Austin Hall for Harvard University, which became models for similar building types throughout the country.

The years of Richardson's practice paralleled the period in which Boston architects consolidated their position as professionals. In 1866 the first school of architecture in the United States was established at the Massachusetts Institute of Technology under the direction of William Robert Ware, modeled on the system of the École des Beaux-Arts. A decade later, *American Architect and Building News*, the country's first significant architectural journal, was launched in Boston. Further architectural activity was generated by the founding of the Boston Society of Architects in 1867 and of the Boston Architectural Club in 1889. The Richardson era in Boston was the time when the architect clearly separated himself from the builder and took his place among the city's professional class.

The Greening of Boston: The Late Nineteenth Century

If possible, it is more impressive even than the crowded largeness of New York to trace the serene preparation Boston has made through this [Metropolitan Park] Commission to be widely and easily vast. New York's humanity has a curious air of being carried along upon a wave of irresistible prosperity, but Boston confesses design. I suppose no city in all the world... has ever produced so complete and ample a forecast of its own future as this Commission's plan of Boston.
H. G. Wells, *The Future in America*, 1906

Richardson was not the only important New Yorker to choose Boston as the location for his practice. His close friend, the landscape architect Frederick Law Olmsted (1822–1903), also moved his practice from Gotham to the suburban community of Brookline in 1883, in part to be near his friend and occasional collaborator. Olmsted continued to lay out the interconnected chain of municipal parks, begun in 1879, that

33   Frederick Law Olmsted:
Muddy River Parkway. Under construction,
near Longwood Avenue, 1892.

34   Muddy River Parkway,
near Longwood Avenue, 1902.

35   Comparative maps showing public parkland
in 1892 and 1902 (before and after the establishment
of the Boston Metropolitan Park System).

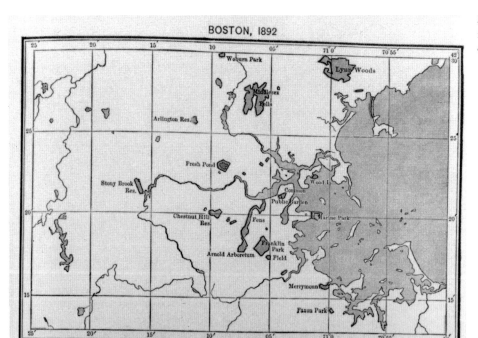

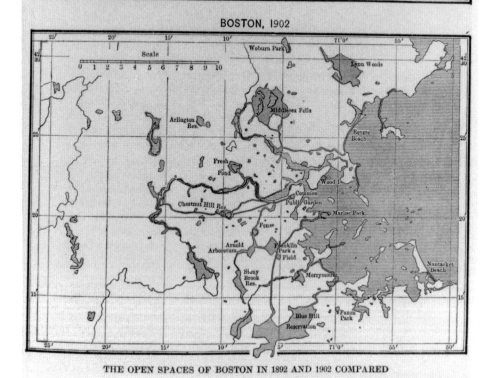

THE OPEN SPACES OF BOSTON IN 1892 AND 1902 COMPARED

is one of the major adornments of Boston, while maintaining a national practice as a landscape architect. Indeed, the Brookline studio became a proving ground for the next generation of American landscape architects and regional planners. In Boston, Olmsted began by solving the engineering problems of the Muddy River/Charles River juncture with the Back Bay Fens plan (1879) and proceeded to design a sequence of water-focused parks (Figs. 33, 34) and parkways that culminated in Franklin Park (1885), the green country park that Olmsted saw as the Boston equivalent of his plan for Central Park (1857) in New York City.

By the 1890s, Olmsted's health had seriously deteriorated, and his practice was taken over by his adopted son and nephew John Charles Olmsted, his own son Frederick Law Olmsted Jr., and Charles Eliot, the most talented of the designers who worked for Olmsted. John Charles and Fred junior maintained the firm's national dominance with work in regional and city planning, park design, and historic preservation well into the twentieth century. Eliot distinguished himself through the creation of the Boston Metropolitan Park System, that he had proposed in 1893. This plan for a regional network of open spaces (Fig. 35) included the maintenance and management of harbor islands, ocean beaches, the tidal estuaries of the three rivers emptying into the harbor, and large forest reservations strategically located throughout the Boston metropolitan area.

Reform Boston: The Turn of the Century

At my feet lay a great city. Miles of broad streets, shaded by trees and lined with fine buildings. . . . Public buildings of colossal size and architectural grandeur unparalleled in my day raised their stately piles on every side. Surely I had never seen this city or one comparable to it before.

Edward Bellamy, *Looking Backward*, 1888

The progressive reformist ideals that infused Boston politics in the final decade of the century were also embraced by architects, landscape architects and planners. The broad

vision of Charles Eliot in creating the Boston Metropolitan Park System, or that of the planners of the country's first subway system from 1895 onwards (Fig. 37), are excellent examples of this search for system and order. Among the architects, several distinct responses to the reform ethos emerged in the 1890s and continued to inform Boston architecture through the first two decades of the new century.

A vision of monumental, urban grandeur was proposed by Charles F. McKim in his design for the new Boston Public Library (1888–95) on Copley Square, with the proclamation "Free to All" engraved over the front portal between allegorical statues of the arts and sciences. Here, McKim skillfully combined images derived from the Italian Renaissance and

36   McKim, Mead & White:
Boston Public Library, 1888–95.

37   Park Street subway station.
Aerial view of construction, 1895.

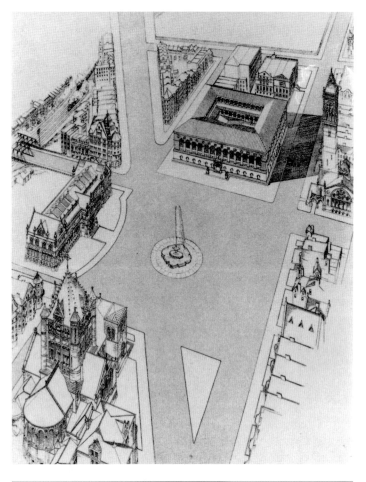

from the nineteenth-century Bibliothèque Sainte Geneviève in Paris to create a "Palace for the People" (Fig. 36) that would epitomize Boston's respect for knowledge and culture. A visit to the library was to be an ennobling experience, enriched by a monument replete with sculpture, ironwork, mosaics, and murals by the period's finest artists and craftsmen. Copley Square was now truly the cultural locus of Boston (Fig. 38): in addition to Trinity Church it also boasted the old Museum of Fine Arts (Fig. 40), constructed in 1870–76 following designs by John H. Sturgis and Charles Brigham in a style that reflected the South Kensington Museum in London. The Boston Public Library, however, demonstrated allegiance to a cosmopolitan Western culture, primarily grounded in the classical tradition. As such, the library came to represent for Boston the emerging vision of monumental civic grandeur that the Columbian Exposition (1893) in Chicago had helped to inspire, and it set the tone for the many cultural institutions that moved into new buildings in the next few years. Huntington Avenue, west of Copley Square, soon became a cultural axis after Preston built the immense exhibition hall and headquarters (1876–79; Fig. 41) for the Massachusetts Mechanics Charitable Association (founded in 1795). The Renaissance image that the Public Library had established became the basis for such Huntington Avenue landmarks as McKim's Symphony Hall (1900), the adjacent building for the Massachusetts Horticultural Society by Wheelwright & Haven (1901), and the same firm's Opera House (1908–09), sadly demolished in 1958. Other institutions were moving west because of the availability of new land, generated by the success of Olmsted's Back Bay Fens project. Fronting the Fens, the new Museum of Fine Arts was built by Guy Lowell (1907–09) on an ample site off Huntington Avenue; organized around garden courtyards, the museum exemplifies the classical vocabulary that was being used for art museums throughout the country. A few years earlier (1902) Willard T. Sears had built Fenway Court as the new residence of the dynamic patron and art collector Isabella Stewart Gardner. Known today as the Gardner Museum, the modest exterior masks a glass-roofed Venetian courtyard garden (Fig. 39) and a superb collection of art, particularly rich in Italian Renaissance painting. Educational institutions also felt the thrust of monumental classicism, as best exemplified in the Longwood Avenue group of buildings

38   Charles F. McKim: Proposal for Copley Square, 1888. Aerial view.

39   Left: Willard Sears: Isabella Stewart Gardner Museum, 1902. View of courtyard.

40   Sturgis & Brigham: Museum of Fine Arts, 1870–76.

41   William Gibbons Preston: Massachusetts Mechanics Charitable Association, 1876–79.

THE FOREIGN EXHIBITION AT BOSTON, MASSACHUSETTS.—[See Page 559.]

42   Shepley, Rutan & Coolidge: Harvard Medical School, 1906.

43   Arthur Little: Little House, 1890.

constituting the Harvard Medical School (Fig. 42), designed along a bisymmetrical axis by Shepley, Rutan & Coolidge in 1906, or the new riverfront campus in Cambridge for the Massachusetts Institute of Technology, designed by Welles Bosworth and occupied in 1916.

If the classical revival became the signature of institutional Boston, for other types of building local architects turned increasingly to the work of the colonial past, reveling in the New England tradition. Buildings surviving from the colonial and Federal periods, especially those by Bulfinch and his contemporaries, became sources of inspiration. Actually, Boston architects were among the first in the nation to redirect attention to the American heritage. Interest had arisen as early as the period of the Civil War, and soared in the years around the national centennial (1876), both in professional journals and in the work of local designers. A key figure was John Sturgis, who documented the John Hancock House before its demolition in 1863, perhaps the earliest American use of scale drawings for record purposes. Sturgis proceeded to use the Hancock House and other colonial survivals as models for his new designs, such as the A. A. Carey House in Cambridge (1875).

Arthur Little was another important early protagonist of the "Colonial Revival," first through his publication in 1882 of *Early New England Interiors*, and then through designs such as the 1890 house at 2 Raleigh Street (Fig. 43), which he filled with fragments salvaged from early buildings. Whereas domestic architecture was seen as the most appropriate transmitter for the colonial tradition, churches, schools, and commercial buildings in the central city and its suburbs also joined in the celebration of the American past. The Colonial Revival remained the dominant style of Boston-area buildings, especially for domestic architecture, until the mid-twentieth century. The vocabulary of the revival, already commonplace in private residences for the wealthy, proved adaptable to all levels of society; it was used in the modest single-family shingle or clapboard houses of the rapidly expanding Boston suburbs, and in the characteristic local tenement form, the three-decker, in which horizontal living units were stacked, often with shingled skins ornamented with colonially inspired trim. As late as the 1920s and 1930s, Harvard University was constructing its immense and elegant colonial revival "houses," dormitory complexes along the Charles River, according to the designs of Shepley, Rutan & Coolidge.

Another important influence on Boston architecture at the turn of the century was the establishment of the Boston Society of Arts and Crafts in 1897. Modeled on the English organizations that originated in the ideas of John Ruskin and William Morris on social reform and a new philosophy of design, Boston's Society of Arts and Crafts was the first such group in the United States. Local roots for the movement could be seen in the interior decoration of Trinity Church and in the embellishment of the Boston Public Library. Dominated by architect members, the Society of Arts and Crafts sought to foster a closer relationship between designers and craftsmen, without embracing the socialist doctrines of their British predecessors. Architects realized that the organization provided a means to direct and train craftsmen for their own projects. The Arts and Crafts movement facilitated an influential new phase of the Gothic Revival begun under the leadership of Ralph Adams Cram (1863–1942), who revitalized the Gothic vocabulary for Christian churches and other buildings from the 1890s onwards; he inspired a generation of talented architects, the most prominent being the firm of Maginnis & Walsh, who served as builders for the expanding Roman Catholic church in Boston and its surroundings. Except in commercial architecture, the Colonial Revival and the Society of Arts and Crafts were, along with the City Beautiful movement, dominant forces in Boston architecture from the late nineteenth century to the time of the Depression.

Boston in the Early Twentieth Century

The glimpse of red brick Boston and the state house with its gold dome beyond the slate colored Charles as the train came out into the air to cross the bridge looked like the places in foreign countries he . . . talked about going to.
John Dos Passos, *U.S.A. – 1919*, 1930

At the turn of the century, Boston's dominance in New England was assured. A functioning port and hub of an extensive rail network, the city gained a new "American Renaissance" monument in the South Station (Shepley, Rutan & Coolidge, 1899; Fig. 44). Financial and trade center of the region, Boston was also the nation's leading manufacturing city for the

44 Shepley, Rutan & Coolidge: South Station, 1899.

45 Tremont Street, opposite the Old Granary Burying Ground, 1895. *At left*, old Horticultural Hall (Gridley J. Fox Bryant, 1865).

46 Shepley, Rutan & Coolidge: Ames Building, 1892.

47 Summer Street and Downtown Crossing, with Filene's department store (Daniel Burnham & Co., 1912), and 101 Arch Street (*background*).

48 Peabody & Stearns: Custom House Tower, 1913–15. *At right*, Grain and Flour Exchange Building (Shepley, Rutan & Coolidge, 1891–93).

wool, shoe, and leather industries (Fig. 45). Old Boston continued to vanish, as the city's first steel-frame skyscraper, the Winthrop/Carter building (Blackall, 1893) rose on the Washington Street site of the Great Spring, a source of water known from the earliest colonial days. Established in 1834, the Boston Stock Exchange was rehoused in a new building (Peabody & Stearns, 1889–91) in the midst of banks and financial companies, now located in steel-frame buildings clad in stone masonry, eight to ten stories high, most bearing the marks of the Renaissance revival, American style. Standing tall among these structures, the Ames Building remains as a monument to masonry wall construction (Fig. 46). Designed by Richardson's successor firm Shepley, Rutan & Coolidge in 1892, the articulation of its colossal arches and the massive cornice bespeak its origins in the fifteenth-century Florentine palace. Retail and carriage trade was concentrated in the Washington Street district, where buildings were characterized by slim cast stone piers and glazed terra cotta spandrels, separating expanses of plate glass windows. Structures such as Filene's Department Store (Daniel Burnham, 1912; Fig. 47) remain but an austere echo of their more flamboyant counterparts in New York and Chicago.

Citizen participation has always been a way of life for the proper Bostonian. Recall that its civic-minded burghers were responsible for the first public library in the country, the Museum of Fine Arts, Symphony Hall, Horticultural Hall, and institutional buildings of Harvard University. Hence it is not surprising to learn that in 1909 a group of eminent Bostonians banded together to organize "Boston 1915" as an offshoot of the City Beautiful movement. In an effort to revitalize the city at social, economic, physical, and educational levels, this influential body tried to enlist business interests and prominent citizens in the drawing up of a plan that would encourage an enlightened concept of urban development. As frequently occurs in Boston, this impetus towards reform and improvement of the general welfare became known as a "noble experiment" but, not unexpectedly, it aroused the antipathy of the wealthier suburbs. Herein lies a geographical state of affairs that is still extant—a

city surrounded by ever increasing, ever more populous satellite cities.

Boston's economic decline was inevitable, particularly with the demise of the shipping trade. Moreover, Boston did not share in the venturesome commercial development of New York, Chicago, or San Francisco in the early part of the twentieth century, with the concomitant proliferation of the office tower. In fact, only the tower of the US Custom House (Fig. 48), built by Peabody & Stearns in 1913–15, was taller than the domed silhouette of the State House. As a federal building, the former was not subject to local regulations established in 1904 that restricted height in commercial districts to 125 feet; its 29-story tower rising to 495 feet above Ammi Young's Doric temple of 1837–47 was the tallest structure in town for decades.

In 1928 the allowable height was increased to 155 feet high, and the code included provisions for setbacks, thereby following zoning laws already in force in New York and Chicago. This new height ordinance led to the erection of skyscrapers, a mode stimulated by the building boom then in progress in New York. However, despite the application of "modernist" or "Art Deco" details, there is a marked reticence in the ornamentation of the Boston skyscrapers. As a group they may be distinguished by their massive structure, as witness the Batterymarch (Henry Kellogg, 1927), the United Shoe Machinery (Parker, Thomas & Rice, 1928, recently restored), the State Street Bank and Trust Co. (Thomas M. James, 1929),

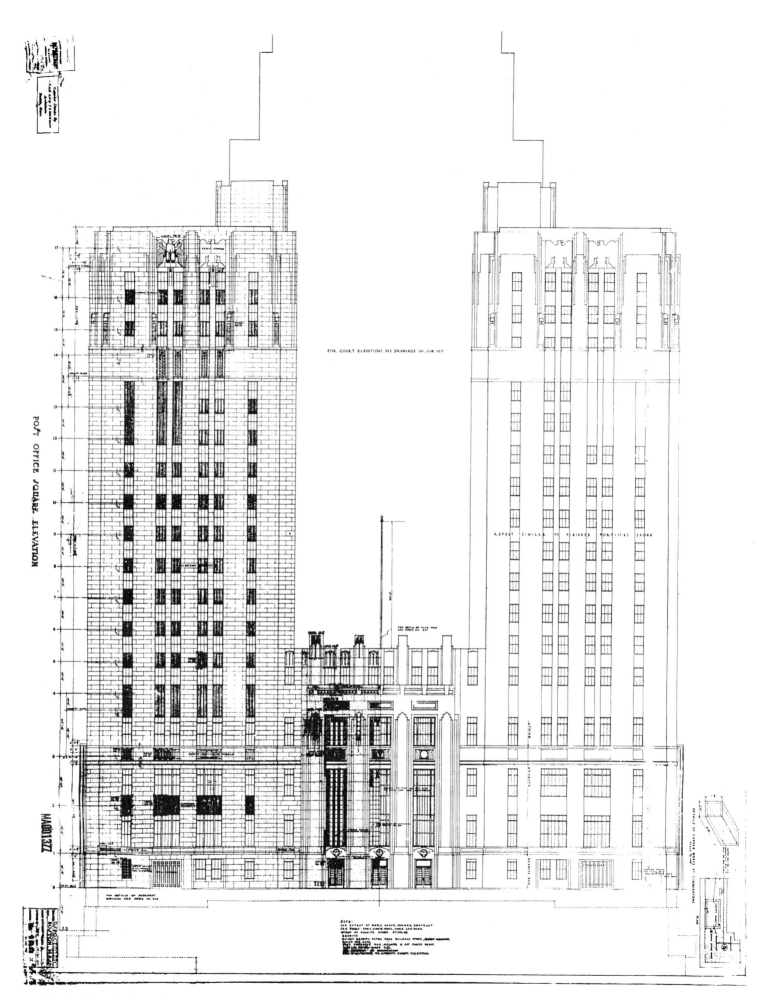

and the Boston Post Office and Federal Building (Cram & Ferguson with James A. Wetmore, 1929–31; Fig. 49). Little happened during the thirties and forties, but the AT&T Building at Post Office Square (1946–47) is a last gasp of the style, a late example of a type given international fame by the New York Telephone Company Building (or Barclay/Vesey) of 1926, which appeared as the frontispiece of Le Corbusier's *Towards a New Architecture* in 1927.

Two Boston landmarks were born in 1927. Facing the Public Garden, the Ritz-Carlton Hotel (Strickland, Blodget and Law) stood twelve stories high, and thus violated the height restrictions, and was out of keeping with the size of Back Bay buildings. Not so the Parker House (Desmond & Lord) on School and Tremont streets, an old Boston institution, that was well attuned to its propitious downtown site, where a tavern and a hotel (1856) were already occupants.

New construction virtually ceased during the depression of the 1930s. A notable exception was the BB Chemical Building, now Polaroid (Coolidge, Shepley, Bulfinch & Abbott, 1937; Fig. 50), on the Charles River in Cambridge, whose horizontal window bands and glass blocks introduce the language of the International Style, which is however tempered by classical principles.

49   Cram & Ferguson with James A. Wetmore:
John D. McCormack Federal Building and Post Office, 1929–31.

50   Coolidge, Shepley, Bulfinch & Abbott: BB Chemical Building (now Polaroid), 1937.

Boston after World War II

Boston's backwardness is its principal asset … If Boston avoided some of the economic prosperity of the years that followed the 90s, it also avoided some of the mistakes.

Lewis Mumford, 11 December 1957 (Boston College Citizens Seminar; cited in *The Boston Globe*, 11 November 1984)

Economic decline set in with the stock market crash of 1929 and lingered until the 1960s (Fig. 51). The gradual deterioration was accelerated by the flight of traditional industries like textiles and small manufacturing from the city to the South, where cheaper labor was available. There was little new building activity, but the Berkeley Street addition to the John Hancock Mutual Life Insurance Building (Cram & Ferguson, 1947) did manage to achieve distinction as the tallest structure in town. Still, stagnation meant a reprieve for the past: little occurred to destroy the urban fabric so characteristic of Boston's old historic center, namely, Beacon Hill and the Back Bay, and the tempo of modern life was not immune to their charms.

Signs of a major turnabout were seen across the river, where the genteel college atmosphere became transformed by the growth of a modern industrial landscape along Route 128, the first ring, albeit irregular, around an American city. Electronics and space technology thus made Cambridge the "hub of a new world," as author Christopher Rand observed in 1964.

From an architectural perspective, Cambridge had moved to the fore when Walter Gropius became professor of architecture at Harvard in 1937 (he was chairman of the department from 1938–52). In 1939, on the brink of World War II, Sigfried Giedion delivered the Norton lectures that resulted in *Space, Time and Architecture*, a seminal work that influenced a gener-

ation of architects by promoting the progressive ideals of the Modern Movement. Further, the presence of leading schools of architecture at Harvard and the Massachusetts Institute of Technology may partly explain why relatively few modern buildings assume so much architectural importance. In the immediate post-war decades the institutions of higher learning, then undergoing unprecedented expansion, became the chief patrons of the "new architecture." Alvar Aalto was visiting professor at MIT in 1947 when he received the commission for Baker House, whose serpentine brick facade is still a landmark on Memorial Drive (Fig. 52). Gropius, with The Architects Collaborative, designed the Graduate Center at Harvard (1950; Fig. 53), based on Bauhaus principles. Shortly thereafter, Eero Saarinen began a new plaza at MIT, where he introduced his daringly expressive and symbolic forms in the Kresge Auditorium and the chapel (1953–55; Figs. 54, 55), alien but exciting elements in the Beaux-Arts configuration of the Institute.

51   Aerial view of Boston from above Logan Airport, ca. 1960.

52   Alvar Aalto (with Perry, Shaw & Hepburn): Baker House, Massachusetts Institute of Technology, 1947–49.

53   Walter Gropius: Harkness Commons/Graduate Center, Harvard University, 1950.

54   Eero Saarinen: Kresge Auditorium and Chapel, Massachusetts Institute of Technology, 1953–55. *In background*, MacLaurin and Rogers buildings.

55   Kresge Auditorium and Chapel.

56   Le Corbusier: Carpenter Center for the Visual Arts, Harvard University, 1961–63.

57   Sert, Jackson & Gourley: Law School and Student Union, Boston University, 1964. *At left*, Chapel and Schools of Liberal Arts and Theology (Cram & Ferguson, 1947).

52

54

56

Rising architects were particularly receptive to the early twentieth-century concrete warehouses and to the possibilities of pre-packaged, prefabricated technology and the opportunity to weave pre- and site-cast concrete with the existing brick and stone texture of Cambridge and Boston. Concrete was poured in abundance over the old city as the Modern Movement was imported from Europe, producing Le Corbusier's Carpenter Center at Harvard (1961–63; Fig. 56) and I. M. Pei's Earth Sciences Building at MIT (1962–64). José-Luis Sert, when dean of the Harvard Graduate School of Design, grafted a Mediterranean aesthetic onto the "new brutalism" in the high rises that he built on the banks of the Charles River–from Peabody Terrace (1963), which provided housing for Harvard's married students, to the Boston University law and education tower (1964; Fig. 57)–before moving inland to construct the enormous Undergraduate Science Center (1970–73) at Harvard. Concrete even penetrated the brick-lined Back Bay when the Boston Architectural Center

58   Ashley, Myer & Associates: Boston Architectural Center, 1967.

59   Government Center area. Aerial view from north, ca. 1960.

50   *Looking Backward*

(Ashley, Myer & Associates) opened on Newbury Street in 1967 (Fig. 58), thereby giving new life to an old institution created to train architects.

Not until 1957 had the building boom then sweeping the nation finally arrived in Boston. It all began in the West End, whose center, Scollay Square, was infamous for the Old Howard and other burlesque houses, long the destination of merchant seamen, traveling salesmen, and Harvard students. An area of speculative building was reclassified as tenement housing, and shortly thereafter scheduled for renewal. The Boston Redevelopment Authority presented a plan for the 48-acre tract, whereupon much of the West End was brutally demolished and its inhabitants displaced (Fig. 59). But Mayor John Collins (1959–67) and Edward Logue, chairman of the Boston Redevelopment Authority, were determined to rebuild Boston by fostering an architecture that would emphasize beautiful civic design. To this end, they enlisted the aid of the Chamber of Commerce in rebuilding the waterfront area so that it would once more become Boston's "window on the world." In 1960, I. M. Pei & Partners were chosen to draw up the master plan "to delineate each disposition parcel and establish controls which would limit height, bulk, and setback, and establish a pattern of relationships between each

building." Kallmann, McKinnell & Knowles's award-winning design for the New City Hall competition produced a monument that became the "keystone" of the complex and, more, of the entire downtown area (Fig. 60). Here five principal districts of the city converge—the West and North Ends, waterfront, financial center, and Beacon Hill. Concern for the pedestrian and a public space belonging to the people set City Hall apart from all other structures of the new Boston. Various types of interaction between citizens and government and among the people themselves occur inside and outside this rugged concrete and brick building, designed to express a "celebration of government." Unlike the varied shapes of City Hall, which subtly convey their different purposes, the two connecting towers of the John F. Kennedy Federal Building (The Architects Collaborative, 1966) all too clearly bespeak their bureaucratic functions. The JFK Building epitomizes that corporate architecture which began to proliferate in downtown areas throughout the western world in the fifties and sixties. Of the old buildings in the area bordering the plaza of Government Center, only Sears Crescent (1848) and the adjoining Sears Block (1845) were saved. The convex facade of One Center Plaza, the office building opposite, acts as a perfect foil to the older brick building of Sears Crescent by

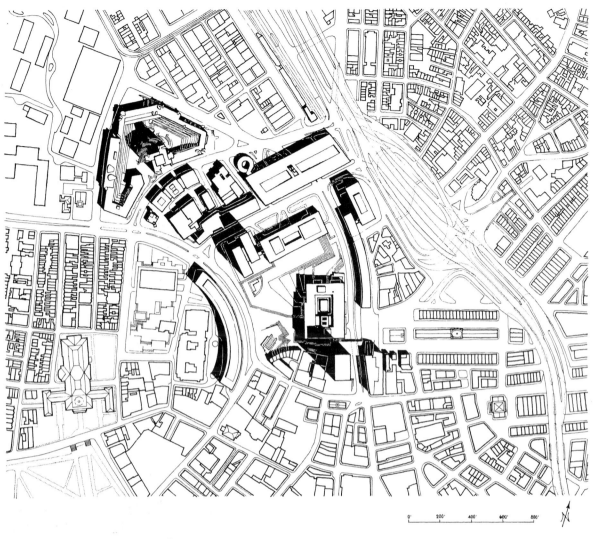

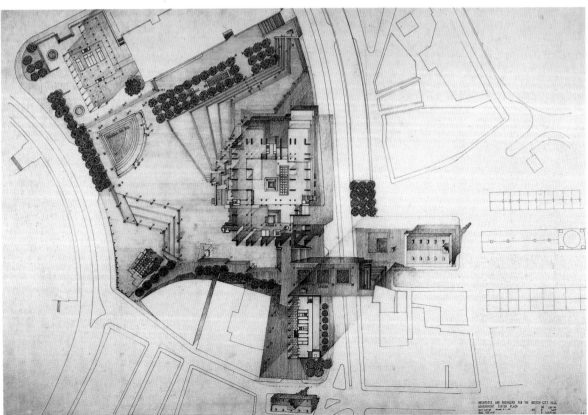

61 I. M. Pei & Partners: Government Center. Site plan, 1961.
Below: axonometric view of City Hall and Plaza.

62 Government Center. Aerial view towards west.

repeating its shape, albeit it on a larger scale; at the same time, it screens the Suffolk County Court House, and serves as a "propylaeum" to Beacon Hill (Figs. 61, 62).

While the parcels that constitute the Government Center complex remain separate entities, the strikingly handsome State Services Building amalgamates the departments of health, education and welfare in one megastructure (1970; Figs. 63, 64). Labyrinthine passageways and scenographic stairways lead to the cavernous center, which once harbored a chapel for mental health patients, whereas mounds of striated concrete flow down in wavelike motion to metaphorically return the city to the sea. In the words of architect Paul Rudolph: "I wanted to hollow out a concavity at the bottom of Beacon Hill, a spiraling space like a conch in negative relation to the convex dome of the State Capitol on top of the hill." All lines merge in the nucleus, which was to be crowned by a central tower until the money ran out, and weeds now

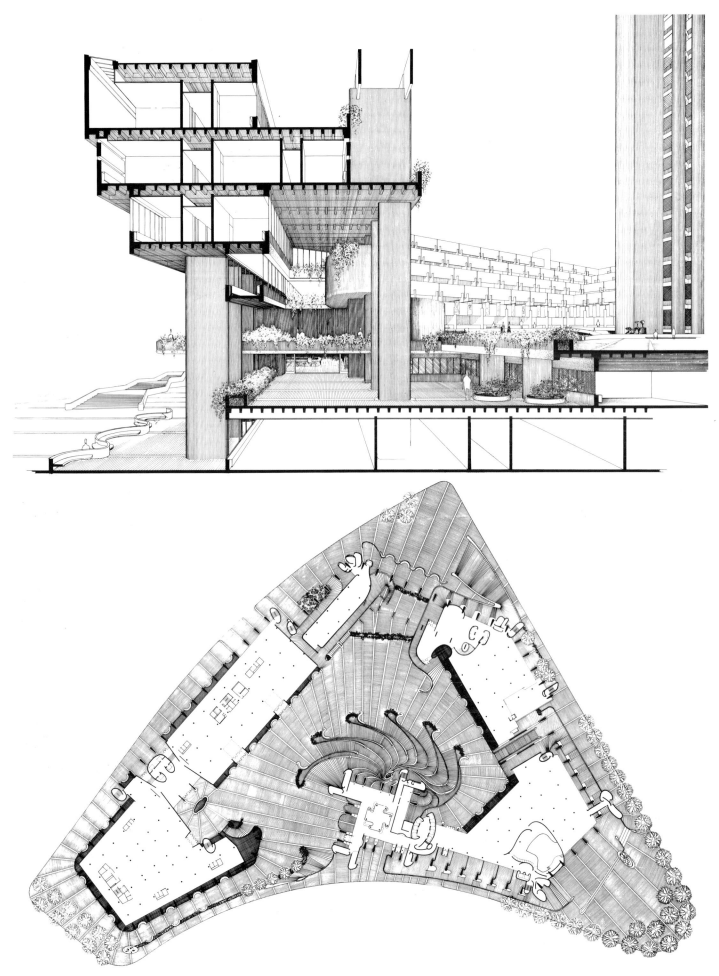

63 Paul Rudolph: State Services Center (Health, Education and Welfare), 1970. Perspective drawing of Mental Health Building; tower (unbuilt).

64 State Services Center. Plan.

65 Sert, Jackson & Gourley: Holyoke Center, Harvard University, 1965. Café as seen from Harvard Square subway station plaza.

66 Kallmann & McKinnell: Boston Five Cent Savings Bank, 1972.

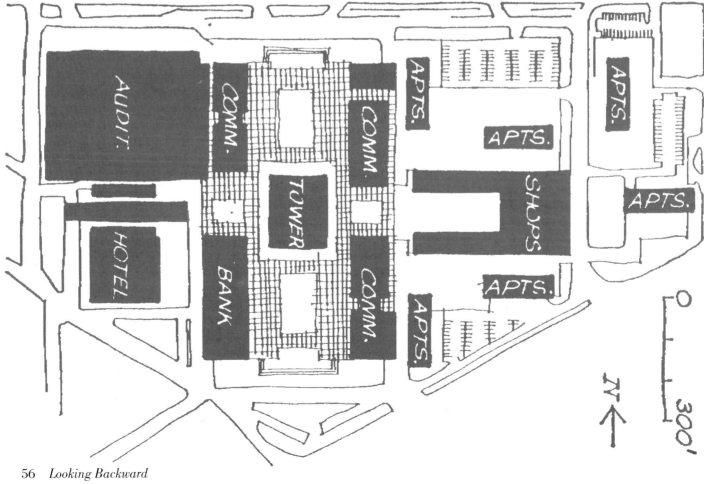

scramble over one of the few vacant lots in town. Dazzled by formal and symbolic brilliance, the observer may well question the appropriateness of the structure to its contents. Because user-needs do not appear to have been a fundamental consideration in the formulation of the program, the State Services Building has served as an object lesson to the succeeding generation of architects and planners.

In 1964, a move to further stimulate the economy resulted in the replacement of the 1924 zoning regulations by a system of "floor area ratios" and "planned development areas." These revised codes acted as incentives for the construction of new and taller banking establishments, government offices, and commercial buildings—those structures that have created the downtown corporate skyline (Fig. 63). At the same time, greater attention was given to light-filled interiors, to public spaces, and to communal aspects of design. Witness especially the open plaza before Sert's mixed-use Holyoke Center in Cambridge (1965; Fig. 65), which owes much of its free-wheeling "oratorical" and "performance" spaces to the student activism of the late sixties. In a similar spirit, the corner before the Boston Five Cent Savings Bank (Kallmann, McKinnell & Knowles, 1972; Fig. 66) can be seen as a public space belonging to the city. Actually, this plaza derived from a competition requirement "to cope with a site whose distorted and curtailed form is the by-product of a traffic adjustment."

Activity throughout the city accelerated in the sixties and seventies. In addition to the high-rise corporate structures, a move was underway to prevent the disintegration of downtown Boston as a lively shopping area. While the malling of American cities was proceeding with unprecedented speed from coast to coast, a committee was formed to preserve the Central Business District. Victor Gruen Associates drew up proposals to revitalize the city by improving public transportation and renewing the central business and theatre districts. Today, the traffic-free Downtown Crossing, with the pedestrian once more in control, is a testimony to their efforts, although the prognosis for the general vitality of the area remains uncertain.

Renewal of the Back Bay began with plans for the multi-use Prudential Center in 1959 (Charles Luckman & Associates and Hoyle, Doran & Berry; Figs. 67, 68) on the site of old railroad tracks. Dominated by the 52-story office tower, the com-

67 Charles Luckman & Associates and Hoyle, Doran & Berry:
Prudential Center Complex, 1959–68. View of Prudential Tower
from Copley Square, ca. 1970. Boston Public Library and New Old South Church
in foreground.

68 Prudential Center Complex. Site plan.

69 I. M. Pei & Partners, Cossuta & Ponte, and Sasaki, Dawson & DeMay
(landscaping): Christian Science World Headquarters, 1968–73. Site plan.

70 Christian Science World Headquarters. View of administrative tower
towards Sunday School, church center, and original Mother Church.

plex, which includes housing, shopping, entertainment and hotel, never became the predicted design success. Exaggerated concern for parking and security prevented access at ground level. This violation of an urban precept together with decidedly undistinguished architecture contributed to the Prudential's failure as a lively entity. For all the design defects, the building's tower, visible throughout the region, soon became the beacon of Boston. Not until the mideighties, however, did Boylston Street, which the Prudential fronts, begin to show signs of renewal. One monumental exception was Philip Johnson's addition to the Boston Public Library in 1971 (Fig. 71). Despite a somewhat forbidding exterior, the building was praised for its harmonious relationship with the adjoining Boylston Street facade of the McKim, Mead & White masterpiece (as also the engineering innovation by the LeMessurieur Associates on the interior). Twenty years later, the same architect is being censured for his New England Life addition 500 Boylston Street precisely because of insensitivity to scale and context.

At the southwest apex of the Back Bay, radical change came with the rebuilding and expansion of the Christian Science complex in 1968–73 (Figs. 69, 70). Displacing older housing along Massachusetts Avenue, the church built a new office tower, Sunday School, and administrative center on the banks of a long reflecting pool over underground parking. I. M. Pei, with Cossuta & Ponte, gave maximum visibility to the Mother Church, whose modern concrete aesthetic was unusual in the Back Bay, however, they tempered reminiscences of Le Corbusier's Chandigarh with the language of classicism in the admirably carved Corinthian portico that frames a convex glass-enclosed space on the Massachusetts Avenue facade of the church. Like many of Pei's designs, the abstract geometric layout of its site plan is dazzling, especially when viewed from above. But the most important aspect of the Christian Science center is that it paved the way for a connection between the Back Bay and the South End, a link recently fortified by the creation of the Southwest Corridor Park.

No transformation in the city has proven to be more dramatic than the waterfront project initiated by the Boston Redevelopment Authority in the late sixties. Derelict wharves and warehouses have been demolished (including the beautifully proportioned India Wharf by Bulfinch, Fig. 72) or converted to luxury housing. Urbanization began with the new aquarium at Central Wharf (Cambridge Seven, 1969) and Harbor Towers, a pair of high-rise residential buildings designed by I. M. Pei in 1971. Towards the harbor, Faneuil Hall Marketplace stands at the beginning of the new Boston. Architect Benjamin Thompson (hitherto largely known locally as the creator of Design Research in Cambridge) seeking to bridge the new Government Center and the new waterfront set forth his proposal for the renovation of Quincy Market: "It looks at the past. It looks at the Boston Redevelopment Authority Master Plan. It looks at existing conditions. To create new life for an old place."

71   Philip Johnson:
Boston Public Library addition, 1971.
In background, Boston Public Library,
John Hancock Tower, and New England Life addition 500 Boylston Street.

72   Charles Bulfinch: India Wharf, 1805.
Photograph from the 1870s.

Old as New: Adaptive Re-use in Boston

I shall enter no encomium upon Massachusetts; she needs none. There is her history; the world knows it by heart. The past at least is secure.
Daniel Webster, *Second Speech on Foote's Resolution*, 26 January 1830

In Boston, as throughout the country, the recycling of older buildings for new uses has been a major component of architectural development during the past two decades. Possessing an especially rich heritage of historic structures, Boston has taken the lead in these activities. Not only has the city rehabilitated its own buildings, but it has become a center for architectural firms, developers, and consultants for rehabilitation projects nationwide. The extended use of older buildings and the more traditional restoration activities of the preservation movement have affected general trends in architecture and the position of architects in relation to their clients and to the public at large.

The reaction to the "demolition and new construction" mentality of the post-World War II urban renewal era set the pendulum swinging. After the virtual elimination of the old West End in the late 1950s, neighborhood activists, urban pioneers, and preservationists began to counterattack in the early sixties. Focusing on neighborhoods like the South End and the waterfront and individual complexes such as Quincy Market, the new enthusiasts for historic buildings began to question and oppose the city's renewal programs. The subsequent story, however, is not one of logical development or unchallenged success for the physical environment of Boston.

Locally and nationally, the political, racial, and social unrest of the mid-1960s focused on urban centers. The election of Kevin White as mayor of Boston in 1968 ushered in a sixteen-year period that might easily have been given over to indiscriminate development. However, the passage of the National Historic Preservation Act of 1966 had finally established a comprehensive federal program for the protection of historic buildings. Using private and public capital, local architects and preservationists demonstrated the value of pre-serving varied types of older structures and, more importantly, the appropriateness of changing the function of a building to meet specific modern needs and opportunities. Architects Tim Anderson and George Notter established significant models for rehabilitation, first in the North End's Prince Building, a warehouse converted for residential purposes, and in 1969 in Old City Hall, a surplus government building recast for offices and retail. The concept of adaptive re-use, long practiced in European cities, thus emerged as an exciting and rational alternative to the demolition of noteworthy buildings.

New interest in conversions came with the serious recession caused by the oil embargo in 1973. Arguing that adaptive re-use was labor intensive and energy conserving, and thus appropriate to the times, the preservationists set out to fight City Hall. New architects joined the cause, such as Childs, Bertram & Tseckares, who produced two exemplary rehabilitations: the Ames-Webster Mansion (Peabody & Stearns, 1872; enlarged by John H. Sturgis, 1882) on Commonwealth Avenue was restored and converted to offices in 1969, and the Record-American Building, a marble-fronted commercial palace (Fehmer & Emerson, 1872) was transformed into offices as One Winthrop Square in 1974. Most early rehabilitation projects retained modernist biases in the frequent elimination of detailing, the exposed interior materials, and the windows of single sheets of glass. Preservationists, delighted with their victories, did not immediately question the propriety of such architectural license.

The mid-1970s witnessed some accommodations between the White administration's development stance and the possibilities of adaptive re-use. In 1973, White appointed Robert T. Kenney as the new director of the Boston Redevelopment Authority. Two large projects soon came under his control. He selected Benjamin Thompson as architect-developer for the rehabilitation of Quincy Market. With marketing and financial expertise from James Rouse, Thompson turned the impressive, but gritty granite and brick produce markets into a successful district of chic eateries, fashionable shops and, not least, open, park-like spaces. Perhaps no other project was as important in changing the way Bostonians, and Americans at large, thought about old buildings and the possibilities that lay within blighted urban cores.

The second major initiative from the Boston Redevelopment Authority under Kenney was the rehabilitation of 110 acres and scores of historic industrial structures at the U. S. Navy Yard in Charlestown. Declared surplus in 1974, the

Navy Yard was transferred to the city and to the National Park Service. A new residential quarter with associated amenities has since been created. The adaptive re-use of large industrial structures and the building of attractive new elements have capitalized upon the Charlestown waterfront, with its spectacular views of the Boston harbor and skyline.

The legitimacy of these projects was significantly bolstered by the concurrence of events in 1976. The city at last established the Boston Landmarks Commission as the municipal agency for preservation planning, though its powers were restricted to the designation of individual buildings, not districts. Of greater significance, the United States Congress passed the Tax Reform Act of 1976, which removed the tax-code bias against old buildings and introduced substantial tax incentives for the appropriate rehabilitation of historic structures. President Carter increased federal funding for preservation from a level of $17.5 million in 1975 to $200 million by 1979. In 1975, the American Institute of Architects established the "extended use" category as a new division for their annual Gold Medal Awards. In 1978, eight of the fifteen AIA awards were given for such projects, two in Boston—Quincy Market and the Institute of Contemporary Art. With some architectural critics proclaiming the death of modernism, and with new financial, legal and bureaucratic tools at hand, the preservationists and their design and financial partners seemed to have entered the mainstream.

At the same time, however, cracks appeared in the preservationist mirror. Emblematic of the underlying problems was the proposal to demolish the 1889 Stock Exchange Building at State and Congress streets and construct a faceted glass tower, a scheme backed by Mayor White. Unsure of its political clout, the fledgling Landmarks Commission feared that the denial of the demolition permit would result in a veto from the mayor. Hoping to avoid confrontation, the commission proposed the retention of two facades of the building with the glass tower behind. Effectively labeled "prosthetic architecture" by Robert Campbell, architecture critic for *The Boston Globe*, the Exchange Building was soon seen as a design compromise of disastrous proportions. One important result of this fiasco was the establishment in 1978 of the Boston Preservation Alliance, a coordinating committee for scores of likeminded organizations throughout the city.

What did Boston learn from the Exchange Building debacle? Evidently very little. In fact, gutted older structures have frequently been the launching pads for historicizing skyscrapers, as a string of recent buildings on Summer Street demonstrates. Despite the Reagan administration's annual attempt to eliminate preservation funding from the federal budget, tax incentives remained, as amended in the Economic Recovery Tax Act of 1981 and subsequent tax law modifications. Thus, the rehabilitation market continued to flourish in Boston throughout the 1980s. The ability of the Boston Redevelopment Authority, the Landmarks Commission, or the Preservation Alliance to realize the dream of effective preservation planning is however still elusive. The absence of a comprehensive preservation plan has permitted incremental, ad hoc decisions on preservation and adaptive re-use versus demolition and new construction. During the eighties, the pressure of development caused the balance to shift towards intensive new construction.

It would be naively pessimistic to see the twilight of preservation and adaptive re-use as we enter the 1990s. In fact, the recent, drastic reversals in the Boston economy create a favorable climate for the preservation ethic. Whatever the future may hold, it is evident that adaptation—and the attendant political and financial framework—has shaped the character of Boston during the past two decades. The issue of contextualism, a watchword for recent urban planning and new architecture, is related to new uses for old buildings and the preservation spirit of the recent past. The expanded role of developers in shaping the character of the built environment has partially emerged from the partnership of preservationists, architects, and moneymen. And because the concerned public makes its voice heard in neighborhood organizations and preservation commissions, it is often the case that designs have to be approved by a committee before a building can be erected. Greater public participation in design decisions has not always produced better buildings, and has partly been responsible for the tendency of architects to become lobbyists and diplomats, attempting to please varied special interests. Still, the architect must be ever mindful that the purpose of his art is to accommodate and to ease the stress of life, and to do so by creating an architecture in harmony with nature and in the service of humanity.

Epilogue

I like collapsing civilizations. I'm a connoisseur of collapse and systems breakdown and bankruptcy – moral, ethical and financial. So Boston is perfect.
Ward Just, "About Boston," *Twenty-one Selected Stories*, 1990

Farewell to the limits of growth, to Puritan discretion, to innate restraint. Though imbedded in history, today's Boston is a city of our time, a city enriched, sometimes dubiously, by the excesses of the eighties. Under the auspices of the Boston Redevelopment Authority, the civic responsibility endemic to an earlier era survives. It is an ethos based on community participation and an obligation founded on democratic principles to promote the common good. For, here in Boston, municipal authorities work with public and private sectors, with developers and designers, with landmarks commissions and review panels. And, here, a new form of urbanity is being created, one that may be embraced by an essentially non-urban population. New spaces are being built as stages for common activities, harking back in some way to those late nineteenth-century institutional palaces that provided cultural functions for another era. But, of all urban schemes now underway, none is more radical, and, to a degree, more disturbing, than current plans for an enlarged transportation network.

We have witnessed the renewal and extension and even the enhancement (with such programs as "Arts on the Line") of the oldest subway system in the country, as also the re-opening of South and Back Bay stations and the extension of various branch lines. Work is now in progress on the third harbor tunnel, to be built of prefabricated steel tubes, connecting South Boston and Logan Airport. Even more revolutionary is the forthcoming depression of the Central Artery into a ten-lane tunnel winding its way through downtown Boston.

Whereas most urbanists are applauding Boston's foresight in planning such multi-billion dollar projects for the future, we should remember that the Central Artery was also a child of its time. Is it really the best way to prepare for the next millennium by encouraging the proliferation of a twentieth-century mode of traffic, the automobile, with all its concomitant environmental hazards?

We are certainly in a dilemma here: on the one hand, the new artery and tunnel are considered to be essential for the region's prosperity and development, while, on the other, economic expansion, urban growth, neighborhood revitalization, and a comprehensive program of public works are dependent on the creation of an efficient mass transit system. During this period of construction, the Massachusetts Bay Transportation Authority notes that we will have "to change our way of thinking" by using alternative means of transportation—subway and bus, the harbor ferry service, free park-and-ride lots at key locations. It does not seem to have occurred to the transit authority that these options might be the starting point for a genuinely innovative public transit system. The question is: Can the roles of private and public transport be fitted into an integral concept that will meet with general approval?

Architectural pilgrimages to icons of historic and modern building are still part of the grand tour in the Greater Boston area. Despite the changes, so much has been restored, and so much has been made more accessible, that the popular press may rightly proclaim that "Boston is fun!" And, for all our reservations, the new architecture does contribute to our appreciation of the old city, so redolent of America's past. We can enjoy our stroll backwards in time, through the Athens of America, occasionally glancing seawards to remind ourselves of Heraclitus's words, "All is flux, nothing stays still."

Prudential Center. View from Massachusetts Avenue with the Christian Science Complex in the foreground (Symphony Hall at far right).
From left to right: Back Bay, Downtown, South End. In the distance, Logan Airport and Boston Harbor.

Buildings

Downtown and Waterfront

Though Los Angeles presents the hugest example of large-scale urban demolition by incontinent expressway building, Boston is perhaps an even more pitiable victim, because it had more to lose, since it boasts a valuable historic core, where every facility is within walking distance, and a metropolitan transit system that, as far back as the eighteen-nineties, was a model of effective unification. As with current military plans based on nuclear extermination, Boston's planners are attempting to cover over their initial mistakes by repeating them on a wider scale.

Lewis Mumford, *The City in History*, 1961

Downtown Boston in the eighties was an immense construction site. As in other American cities, the core was being destroyed and developed, preserved and purified, renewed and revived. Soaring commercial towers seemed commensurate with rising costs in the Greater Boston housing market. New England was enjoying a wave of prosperity, with the nation's lowest unemployment rate, and the landscape of boom was taking shape throughout the region, but nowhere more visibly than at the hub. Downtown Boston may be defined as that area where the financial district almost imperceptibly merges with the new and old market areas, the shopping districts, and the waterfront, where the city began.

State Street retains its position as the heart of the city's financial center. Banks led the way in the transformation of the corporate skyline—the State Street Bank by Hugh Stubbins, F. A. Stahl, and Le Messurier & Associates in 1966, the New England Merchants Bank by Edward L. Barnes in 1969, the Boston Company Building by P. Belluschi in 1970, and The Bank of Boston by Campbell, Aldrich & Nulty in 1971.

A turning point was reached in the accelerating rate of development during the mid-seventies. While the recession caused by the oil crisis in 1973 prompted architects to return to their drawing boards, the Bicentennial celebrations of 1976 led to a giant step backwards. Not only was the past to be preserved, it was to be venerated as it had not been since the nineteenth century. Down on the waterfront and all over town, the battle cry was raised for recycling, adaptive reuse, and preservation. The old New England penchant for moderation, for maintaining and salvaging a rich architectural heritage, came to the fore. Modernism receded as landmarks commissions, architects, and planners tried hard to preserve the balance of narrow winding streets and broad open spaces. How to deploy new buildings to enhance the city's primary contours—this became the challenge. The Rouse Company joined forces with Benjamin Thompson to develop the marketplace at Faneuil Hall, a project underway since 1960. Here, with the beginning of the development of the nineteenth-century waterfront, came the striking rise in office construction and the gentrification of the urban core.

By the 1980s the era of foreign investment and multinational capitalism had arrived: the high-tech market was well ensconced throughout the region. Office buildings were part of the real estate boom. Together with the new, old warehouses, factories, and mercantile establishments were converted to condominium enterprises. Builders in Boston also participated in the suburbanization of the city by incorporating atria into hotels and business establishments. An attempt too has been made to foster a diversity of uses—commercial, residential, and public—in order to maintain the physical density characteristic of a major urban aggregation. New construction throughout the eighties was spurred on by the "Massachusetts miracle," but signs of warning began to appear beginning on Black Monday, 19 October 1987. A rise in vacancies now underlines the insubstantial aspect of these castles in the air, as does a fall in the number of architects employed in the big firms. Aesthetically, all is surface, with little concern for the basics of architecture, form and space. But high-style fashion is a passing fancy: all that veneer of marble, granite and brick can fade away. While welcoming the return to beginnings, to the European-type "historic center," one questions the *modus operandi* with which the program is being pursued. Old world cities always have been renewed, but rarely within the exclusive domain of real estate developers, who are seldom motivated *pro bono publico*.

No factor is more significant in today's downtown plan than the revival of the waterfront. Harbor Park is designed primarily to encourage public access along the wharves, and thus to assist in the creation of communities. Contingent on this development is the depression of the Central Artery, and the construction of a new tunnel to Logan Airport. Thus, one of the chief priorities of the Boston Redevelopment Authority is the reclamation of this seven-mile strip of public land extending from the old Charlestown Navy Yard via the North End and the downtown waterfront to the Fort Point Channel. Approval for most of the current activity was obtained during the administration of Mayor Kevin White. By now it is conceded that a need exists for a master plan that would provide a public policy document to replace the long outmoded general plan of 1965. Whereas the Boston Redevelopment Authority is supposed to regulate the design process, set standards, and review plans, the current scale of development has made close supervision and the enforcing of regulations difficult. Still, there is a tendency towards more comprehensive planning in the development of neighborhoods. There is also an increasing consciousness of the effects of scale on city life, prompted by the grand office complexes that have added millions of square feet to the downtown area and, in the process, endangered the human dimension of the city. A glance at reports on the projected Woolworth tower at 40 Franklin Street or the Prudential Center restoration give some idea of the magnitude of the current design review process.

With the increasing international concern for the environment, even city planners have been forced to take account of climatic conditions and ecological factors. Not surprisingly, the view on the nearest horizon shows a diminution of height in buildings now under construction. Commendably, renewed efforts are being made to accommodate the public realm, to attain a sense of urbanity, to integrate past and present, and to find the right balance of density and growth.

1

Faneuil Hall Marketplace

Original: Alexander Parris, 1825–26
Re-use: Benjamin Thompson Associates,
1976–78

Today's Faneuil Hall Marketplace was born in 1960 as part of an urban renewal scheme under Mayor John Collins and city planner Edward Logue, head of the Boston Redevelopment Authority. Appropriately, it opened in 1976, as part of the Bicentennial, thereby celebrating the city's architectural heritage. The first of the Rouse Corporation's grand urban schemes for renewing downtown waterfronts, Faneuil Hall Marketplace is to date the most successful. "More tourists per annum than Disneyland," it is said, and this complex does partake of some of the playland's marketable assets, most notably, richly diversified activities and a well-maintained pedestrian enclave.

The current appellation derives from Faneuil Hall, one of the city's oldest historic sites. This bastion of freedom was built by John Smibert in 1740–42 and enlarged by Charles Bulfinch in 1805–06. Mayor Josiah Quincy extended the markets in 1825–26 by commissioning the two-story domed granite building and the flanking warehouses named after him. Ships came right up to the markets, which constituted the earliest planned scheme for regularizing a chaotic waterfront on the Atlantic coast.

Architect Alexander Parris designed these markets on the harbor site in the Greek Revival style, but combined this with cast-iron columns and iron tension rods in post-and-beam construction. The central market is dominated by temple-like porticos at each end in a bold Tuscan order and a pavilion crowned with a copper-clad dome built of wooden ribs in the middle. It stands between the long three-story brick and granite faced warehouse buildings with their gabled roofs, dormers, and skylights. Additions to the clear structural framework are largely superficial. Still, the abundant lights, the greenhouses, the stalls and pushcarts, all distantly reinforce links with the original functions of the market.

At first, the glass-enclosed attachments and the endless eateries appeared to be excessive, but the mix of tourists, local population, and office personnel during daytime hours creates a happy and festive place, especially on the south. Here the cobblestone pavement, benches, and trees provide a lively setting on the sunny side of the street. The northern part, with its bars and restaurants, is the center of after-hours activity.

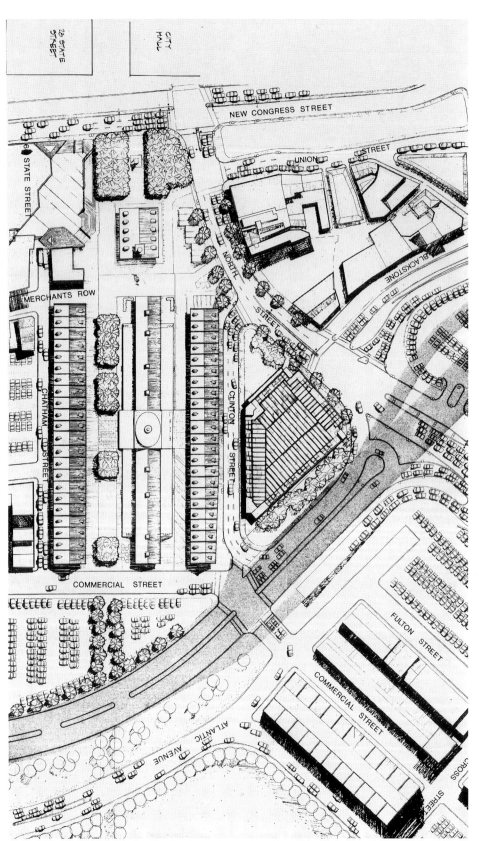

Opposite, top: Interior with Dome

2
Shawmut Bank NA

One Federal Street
The Architects Collaborative, 1975

Following the model for tall office buildings established by the New England
Merchants Bank (Edward Larrabee
Barnes, 1969), the Shawmut Bank is a
cement-colored tower with pronounced
horizontal fenestration. The structure
occupies an entire block and contains a
lower section on Franklin Street for a large
banking-hall with administration office
above, and a tower on the Arch Street end.
The pebble aggregate adds little interest
to the exterior of the building. A branch of
the Harvard Coop is situated on the
ground floor and the Downtown Harvard
Club at the top. The Architects Collaborative provided almost no space for exterior
public areas, thus creating street canyons
encompassing an inward-turning mass.

3
Fiduciary Trust Building

175 Summer Street
The Architects Collaborative, 1977

Sited on an irregularly shaped lot between
the financial district and the South Station
area, the Fiduciary Trust Building rises
like a bizarre urban flower. Plan and elevation are unusual, but not because they
have to conform to the lot-shape. Like the
nearby Bank of Boston (Campbell,
Aldrich, Nulty, 1971), the Fiduciary Trust
bulges out from a small base, overshadow-
ing the adjacent streets, especially High
Street. The building assumes a defensive
stance, like a cliff-dwelling without a lad-
der. The exposed black pebble aggregate
is punctuated with small windows and
ornamented with the vertical lines of
narrow steel I-beams.

Boston Waterfront Park

Sasaki Associates, 1976

In 1966, Sasaki, Dawson & DeMay established themselves as leading landscape planners with their winning competition design for Copley Square, which has since been replaced. Today, a more positive prognosis can be made for the transformation of this barren site on the waterfront, which will be an important element in the city's return to the harbor. Waterfront Park serves as the entrance to an intended circuit of harborfront promenades, not yet completed.

There have been competing interests for the dedication of this park. One monument states that the park is intended as a memorial to Frank J. Christian (1906–70), a Boston businessman who vigorously supported the opening of the waterfront. However, the North End community saw Waterfront Park as a local amenity for the abutting neighborhood: the cultural association with this district is signaled by the prominent statue of Christopher Columbus, erected in 1979 through contributions from Italo-American organizations and private individuals.

A mecca for sunbathers, children, and tourists, the park is zoned into a series of intimate spaces for active play, solitude, or conversation, with a large lawn facing the harbor. The two general areas are divided by a handsome granite and natural wood arched trellis that winds its way across the site. The perimeter is defined by serpentine earthen berms with evergreen plantings backed by sycamore trees, which not only enhance the landscape but also reduce the roar of vehicles along Atlantic Avenue. Located between the harbor and the heavily trafficked Quincy Market district, the park also provides a much needed respite for shoppers. Its role will become even more important with the depression of the Central Artery. The visual connection between the park, the main channel of the harbor, and Logan Airport in the distance ties the denser fabric of the central city to its historic maritime environment.

Neworld Bank

55 Summer Street
The Architects Collaborative, 1976

The glass grid facade is set at about a sixty-degree angle to Summer and Chauncy Streets, thereby creating a plaza dominated by a score of honey locust trees. Carefully arranged in asymmetrical clusters of threes and fours, the urban arbor on a fifty-foot setback is in harmony with the geometrically ordered street lights. Acting as a minimalist sculptural form, a solid triangular stele of polished marble bears the name of the bank, and two granite piers frame the entry. Integrating the plaza and the two-story banking hall is the overhanging angle of the ten-story facade, set between granite service cores. Within, the mirrored ceiling creates a theatrical effect when animated by customers and staff. Judging from the exterior, the office space must evoke the "fish bowl" concept to its daytime inhabitants.

Whereas the area before the building constitutes a welcome plaza opposite Jordan Marsh and Filene's, it does lack the presence of distinguished neighbors and the open sunlit space that contribute to the success of the plaza before the Boston Five Cent Savings Bank addition (Kallmann & McKinnell, 1972) on School Street.

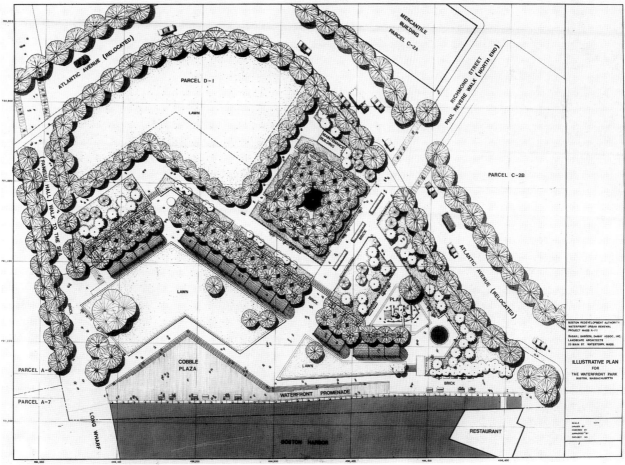

6
Mercantile Wharf

33–81 Mercantile Street
Original: Gridley J. Fox Bryant, 1856
Re-use: John Sharratt Associates, Inc., 1976

The tremendous power of this granite commercial building, one of the earliest commissions of Gridley J. Fox Bryant, was studiously maintained on the exterior in its conversion to housing and retail use. Inside, however, John Sharratt employed the images of shopping malls and hotels in the skylit atrium that forms the core of the building.

Organized in three-bay units marked by vertical lines of rustication, the five-story Mercantile Wharf originally stood at the water's edge. It now forms one of the boundaries of Waterfront Park, jostling for position with the Central Artery and the Long Wharf Marriott. Sharratt respected the powerful massing of the building and only altered the exterior at the roof level, where the plane was maintained but the surface was littered with skylights that indicate the two floors that have been inserted for apartments. As an adaptive re-use solution, the interior influenced the later Constitution Quarters reworking at the Charlestown Navy Yard. However, instead of the vacuous space of that atrium core, the central area of Mercantile Wharf is cluttered with overscaled brick planters that occupy most of the ground floor and with the traditional glass elevators rising from the midpoint of the atrium. Horizontal planes of white walls trimmed with blond wood and topped with planters of hanging philodendra conceal the corridors to the apartments.

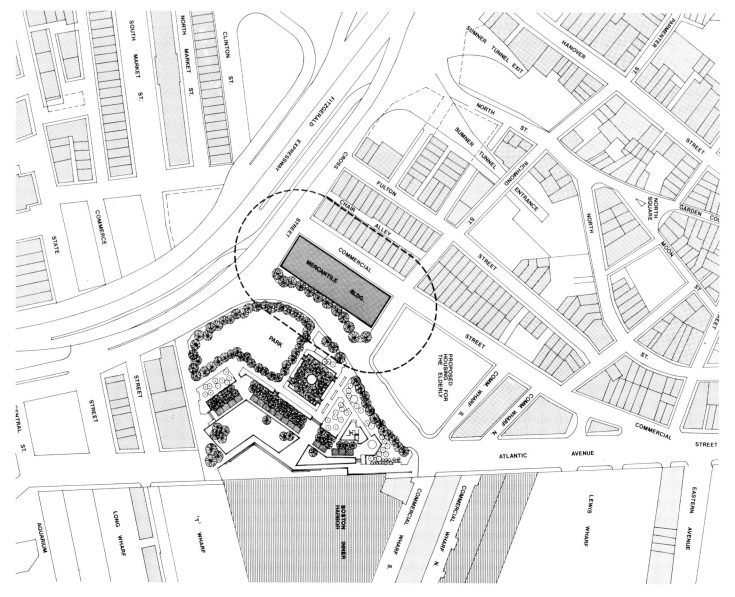

7

60 State Street

Skidmore, Owings & Merrill, 1977

The ground plan of this 38-story tower faced with rose granite is not easy to determine from its exterior massing. Composed of two attached faceted turrets with a rectilinear grid system of fenestration, the triangular piers provide a potential for depth that is never realized (compare Saarinen's articulation of the CBS facade

in New York). The beveled contours, angled on the skyline as well, form a stepped profile at the apex. In contrast to the rectangular solids of the sixties and seventies, the irregularities of this skyscraper reflect the aesthetic concerns of minimalist sculpture. Even the public amenities are subtle: at the plaza level, there are seats built into the wall and the formal element of a matching granite ventilation duct. However, the State Street passage leads to an extended plaza facing

Faneuil Hall, where curved wooden seats encircle trees bordered by cotoneaster. Because the plaza is located on a terrace above the markets, it is a less frequented place, but its relatively large area prevents it from being a quiet oasis. The climax of 60 State is reserved for the club and restaurant on the 33rd floor, the Bay Tower Room, which boasts spectacular views of the harbor.

8
South Postal Annex

25 Dorchester Avenue
Perry, Dean, Rogers & Partners, 1980

Overlooking the Fort Point Channel, the South Postal Annex is a giant aluminum-clad machine for processing letters. Following its function, the building's form and details also pay homage to its site. Windows are confined to a row of circular openings, much like the portholes of a ship. The nautical feeling is further perpetuated in the large projecting exhaust ducts that puncture the aluminum covering at three levels. Horizontal yellow stripes and yellow service bays provide a cheerful counterpoint to the two-tone gray treatment of the box. The brick extension at the southern end of the building represents the original scale and material of the section renovated by Perry, Dean, Rogers & Partners. The South Postal Annex was one of the first components of the South Station area rehabilitation plan to be completed.

9
Federal Reserve Bank

600 Atlantic Avenue
The Stubbins Associates, Inc., 1977–78

Here is a true landmark building in the modern mode conveying the power and poetry of high technology. The prominent aluminum-clad tower occupies 16% of its site; the other components of the building are arranged according to specific functions, clearly visible on the facade. The lower public part is separated from the offices constituting the tower, which is composed of two grand end pylons framing a facade of louvers, "windows" that minimize drafts; acting also as sunshades and reflectors, they mask an open-plan office space with panoramic views of the city and waterfront. Service equipment, including elevators and devices for wind bracing, are located within the piers.

Because the program called for maximum security, the banking operations are confined to the low-rise block. Administrative functions occupy the tower, and the connecting link, including an auditorium and an art gallery, is largely devoted to use by the employees and the public. Light pouring in midst the comfort of the tasteful blue and gray modular furniture of the open lobby creates an extraordinary contrast with the high-security world beyond. This difference begins in the elevator to the public banking-room on the second floor and continues in the specific functions of the Boston branch of the Federal Reserve, serving the New England states. Significantly, amenities for employees and public are built into the program. With a view of the Fort Point Channel, the restaurant for the staff also comprises facilities for outdoor terrace dining. At ground level, spaces provided for gallery, auditorium, lobby, and landscaping are generous.

On the exterior, the high-tech aluminum skin reflects changing atmospheric states, and its chromatic surface varies from an almost pure white to shades of gold and pink and rose. Functional as well as aesthetic, the skin reduces the effects of solar heat, while the angled spandrels act as wind-breakers. A monument on the horizon, this fortress-like structure is lightened somewhat by its protective sheathing. However, the grand expanse and lawn-like landscape at ground level lack sufficient enclosure to serve as a viable urban plaza. There are fascinating views of the Federal Reserve from different angles, though the louvers may be blinding in the late afternoon sun.

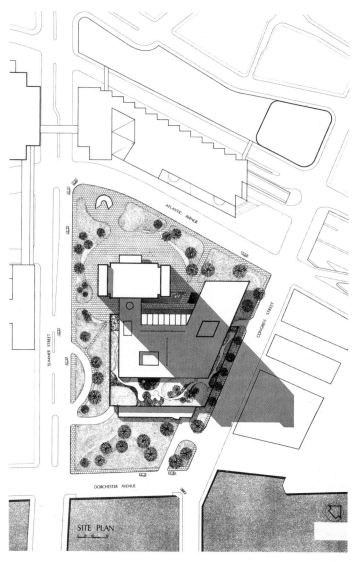

SITE PLAN

10
The Bostonian Hotel

North and Blackstone streets
Mintz Associates Architects/Planners,
Inc., 1980–82

The Bostonian Hotel is almost indistin-
guishable from its local ambiance.
Situated within the old seventeenth-century Blackstone Block, the hotel follows
the convex curve of North Street. Incorporating a six-story commercial structure
by Peabody & Stearns, built in 1889, it
conforms to the brick warehouses and
markets of that time.

In a high-media culture this low-profile
hotel constitutes an effective understate-
ment. To the north of Quincy Market, the
luxurious Bostonian is scarcely visible, so
completely in conformity is it with its red
brick surroundings. Its entry, too, is
unprepossessing – a circular driveway,
a central fountain, and a fleet of high-
fashion autos on view. Only the awnings
and wrought iron balconies distinguish
the hotel from neighboring buildings. If
old Boston conservatism is the keynote of
the exterior, a different note is struck on
the interior. Here we find the standard
lavish accoutrements of modern hotel design, a cacophony of fixtures, especially
evident in the public spaces, namely, the
lounge and The Seasons, for a time Boston's top four-star restaurant. In the
street-floor lobby, guests are seated within
a narrowly confined atrium where they
may turn a proprietary eye towards the
landscape of Maseratis, Mercedes, and
Bentleys in the courtyard, quite unaware
that the central fountain represents the
spirit of Boston rising from a granite map
of the eighteenth-century city.

Entrance court

11
The Devonshire

1 Devonshire Place
SBA/Steffian Bradley Associates, Inc.,
1980–83

A 43-story mixed-use building, largely residential, the Devonshire provides passage for pedestrians and vehicles from Washington to Devonshire streets, thus echoing the structure of an arcade. Its facade is dominated by horizontal window bands alternating with aluminum-clad panels. Modernist details are apparent in the asymmetrical placement of windows, the projections at the fifth and sixth stories, and the central position of the AT&T offices. On the Devonshire Street side the building rises in a flat mass, with a six-story unit at left, a design element repeated on the Washington Street facade. The service cores are distinctly articulated on both facades. Horizontally striped bands, wider at the ground and upper stories, create a somewhat disparate collusion of elements.

The interior lobby befits a luxury apartment building with its crystal octagonal chandelier, ficus tree, color-field painting, overstuffed furniture, and, not least, high security marked by a TV surveillance system. Another amenity is the rooftop health club, featuring an indoor swimming pool.

View from Washington Street

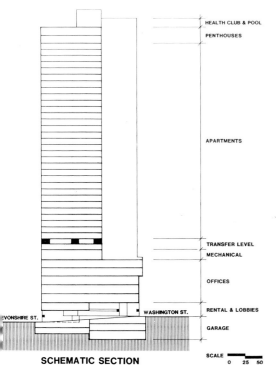

SCHEMATIC SECTION

SCALE
0   25   50

12
One Post Office Square / Meridien Hotel

Milk and Pearl streets/250 Franklin Street
Jung Brannen Associates, Inc., 1981

Rising next to the Beaux-Arts Meridien Hotel, formerly the Federal Reserve Bank, this 39-story office tower is marked by upper-story projections, forced asymmetrical patterns, and corners defined by windows. The coarse pebble aggregate interspersed with bands of finished concrete, the glass-grid canopy over the entry, and the supporting pier arcade at ground level do little to relieve the dull exterior. The structural system is composed of a tubular frame and a diagonally braced core. Color is concentrated in the lobby, dense with varying shades of Carrara marble in rectilinear patterns, travertine pavement, brass fixtures, and pseudo-classical piers. Access is provided to the adjoining Meridien Hotel through a three-story atrium, accessible by a bridge at mezzanine level. Designed by R. Clipston Sturgis in 1922, the landmark Federal Reserve Bank building retains its old Renaissance shell, whose high base of drafted masonry supports the grand lower story where paired pilasters frame arched windows. The three upper stories are quiet and reserved. Unfortunately, the cornice balustrade has been replaced by a three-story glass mansard roof, which is incongruous with the building's facade. Dining areas in the new interior atrium and in the former banking-room are overdesigned, as is the lobby with its crushingly low ceiling.

Exterior of One Post Office Square

Lobby of One Post Office Square

Opposite: Exterior of Meridien Hotel

13
Angell Memorial Park

Post Office Square
Earl R. Falnsburgh & Associates,
Inc.,1982

Forming a crucial downtown node, this small, 7500 square-foot park plaza was originally designed in 1912 by Peabody & Stearns. Dedicated to the memory of George Thorndike Angell, the founder of the Massachusetts Society for the Prevention of Cruelty to Animals, the park is built around a circular granite fountain, whose lion mascarons provided water for horses to drink. Later, the fountain became a more prominent landmark with the addition of a sixty-foot shaft that once served as the flagpole for the post office. The park surrounding the fountain, built in 1957 by landscape architects Shurcliff & Merrill, was in a deteriorated state when a team of architects and artists (City Life, Boston) joined forces to design an oasis within this downtown crossroads.

The resulting award-winning design owes almost as much to a privately established maintenance fund as to the intelligence of its plan. Plantings follow the contours of the triangle on the exterior, which are reinforced by benches with heavy-duty steel rods as seats and backrests. The three biomorphic forms that circumscribed the original fountain are now counterbalanced by the addition of a "creature" pond. Here the granite ring provides seating space for looking outwards toward the streets and buildings, or contemplating the species of pond life within-the salamanders and frogs cavorting among the lily-pads. Such an urban place in precious space revitalizes the entire area, which will be further enhanced by the adjacent Post Office Square Park, now under construction.

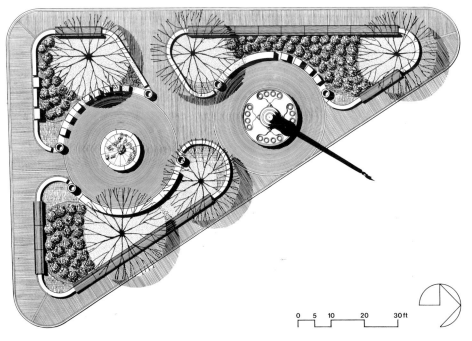

0 5 10   20   30 ft

14
Wellman Research Center, Massachusetts General Hospital

Payette Associates, Inc., 1981–84

The program for the Department of Molecular Biology required the unification of research laboratories scattered throughout the hospital. In collaboration with the hospital administration and city officials, the architects designed a building that serves as an entry to the courtyard, distinguished by the Bulfinch Pavilion of 1817. The two-story glass-enclosed lobby provides a physical link to the surroundings, echoing the arcade of the Ambulatory Care Center. On the street facade, the use of red brick and the articulation of windows and bays relate to the older Edwards Building. Overall, the proportions of windows and wall and the elegant but simple use of brickwork recall more seminal modern structures for medical facilities.

View from lobby towards Bulfinch Pavilion

15

Exchange Place

53 State Street
WZMH Group, 1981–84

There is a double presence to this 40-story office tower perched on a remnant of the Old Stock Exchange (1889–91, Peabody & Stearns), diagonally across from the Old State House. Patterned on its surface by a grid design, the tower is dynamically described by a series of subtle setbacks, its blue reflective glass providing a vivid contrast to the surrounding granite structures – but only at a distance. Close up, the black metal enframement hardly conceals the grimy windows. But surprises greet the visitor as he steps into the five story atrium. Here, as a backdrop to the chrome of the lobby and the standard potted palms and ficus trees is a white marble stairway, now serving as a misplaced setpiece. Once aligned with the building's entrance, the stairway has been moved from its original site, thereby losing not only its grandeur, but also its very purpose. The mirrored chrome ceiling heightens the glass-enclosed court, further accentuating the reflection of the colossal chrome columns in the adjacent hall. Such details as the circular granite fountain, the rich wood paneling of the elevator-bank, and the generously splayed rose granite contribute to the opulence of these interior spaces.

Exchange Place is a building born of compromise. The issues raised here are commonplace today: to preserve the Old Stock Exchange or to encourage economic development – thus was the Boston Landmarks Commission pitted against developers Olympia & York. After considerable debate, the State Street/Kilby Street facades were given landmark designation. Whereas the Landmarks Commission saw the maintenance of the fabric of old State Street as a healthy sign, others were less sanguine. Witness Robert Campbell, architecture critic of *The Boston Globe* (18 December 1984): "The seductiveness, in fact, is the problem with buildings like Exchange Place. They are spectacular enough to make you perceive them not in the way you should – as

pieces that ought to enrich and complete the jigsaw puzzle of cityscape around them – but rather as isolated objects, as if they weren't buildings at all but only huge sculptures at building scale... Tower and landmark come from different planets. They do nothing for each other... All authenticity is lost." The late nineteenth-century Romanesque Revival facade and the new office tower are hardly compatible. Questions concerning quality and the legitimacy of preservation are here brought to the fore. Where once stood the Bunch of Grapes Tavern, a meeting-place before the Revolution, there now exists a species of false history.

Opposite, top right: Lobby, model

16
One Lewis Wharf

Skidmore, Owings & Merrill, 1982

Site sensitivity was the motivation for this superior small structure. Commissioned by a law firm for their offices, the three-story building turns a blank brick and cast-stone face to Atlantic Avenue, but embraces the harbor. Somewhat like the coal-bunker that stood nearby until recently, the building appears as timber-frame cubicles from the water. Sunscreens collect and repel the winter and summer sun respectively and direct the views out to the harbor. The finest section is the third-level loggia across the rear, which provides the best waterfront view for the law firm's partners and their clients. Yet the low scale of the building allows the residents of the adjacent Lewis Wharf condominiums or of the apartment buildings across Atlantic Avenue to benefit from the revived harborfront.

17
Long Wharf Marriott

Long Wharf
Cossuta & Associates, 1982

Like much of Boston architecture along the waterfront since the mid-1970s, the Long Wharf Marriott was intended to be sympathetic with the surrounding environment by alluding to the city's maritime commercial life. A ten-story brick hotel, the Marriott vaguely assumes the guise of a Federal Period warehouse building or of the north and south warehouses of the Quincy Market complex. This conceit is complicated on the upper floors, where the architects used three double-level inset balconies within the general shape of a gabled roof. Simple massing, clean lines, and evenly spaced rectilinear and arcaded fenestration insure that the building remains as much a background object as its immense size permits.

Following the nautical theme, the harbor end of the hotel is treated as a series of projections that suggest the bow of a ship. Inside, the architects placed the lobby and public spaces — both uncomfortably narrow and vertical — at the second level to accommodate parking below and to afford a wider view over the adjacent Waterfront Park and the wharves.

When the Central Artery is eliminated, the building will become part of the long projected Walk to the Sea, a visual corridor from the Old State House to the harbor that will emphasize the historic importance of Boston's maritime life and of this particular wharf for the early commercial development of the city.

Opposite: View of hotel with Harbor Towers and Custom House Tower

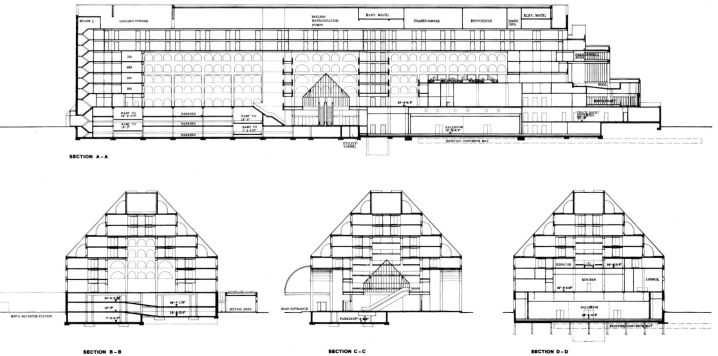

SECTION A - A

SECTION B - B   SECTION C - C   SECTION D - D

18

Boston Floating Hospital, Tufts New England Medical Center

755 Washington Street
Perry, Dean, Rogers & Partners, 1982

Bridging the street and forming a visual link for the group of buildings that form the Tufts New England Medical Center, the Floating Hospital resembles a stranded urban ship. This metaphor is especially appropriate for a hospital whose origins were a boat that toured the harbor from the 1890s onward, providing fresh air and sunshine for the families of the ghettos and medical services as well. For its modern landlocked descendant, the architects exploited issues of structure, mass, and materials in the intriguing (and confusing) eight-story building.

Steel framing and triple-level concrete piers allow the hospital to float as a diagonal slab across the street. A modular system embracing enameled aluminum panels and horizontal bands of windows defines the five-level northern facade, while the southern side is clad with vertically corrugated aluminum. All of the exterior aluminum is colored to match the concrete, except for a canted section on the eastern end of the entrance elevation where a note in magenta red proclaims the vertical circulation stack behind. The mechanical systems are confined to the top of the structure, producing a blank, heavy crown on the elevations. The architects slid the cylindrical entrance pavilion under the diagonal mass on the western side of Washington Street, and placed a constricted automobile entrance at its base. Within, nautical suggestions appropriate to the Floating Hospital can

be seen in details such as the tubular metal railings. Behind the entrance section but under the mass of the building, the MBTA Medical Center/South Cove station for the Orange Line emerges, emphasizing the importance of the New England Medical Center for this area.

19
Human Nutrition Research Center

711 Washington Street
Shepley Bulfinch Richardson & Abbott,
1982

This fourteen-story six-sided building
contains research laboratories devoted to
the study of human nutrition. Both housing and laboratory, the building is easily
zoned on the exterior. The first two stories,
liberally opened through a celebration of
the steel skeleton, comprise lobby,
auditorium, and other public functions.
Next come two floors for the mice and rats
used for experimentation, then laboratory
space for more than eighty researchers.
The ninth floor contains administrative
offices. The tenth level, as in the Tufts
Dental Building across Washington
Street, harbors the elaborate mechanical

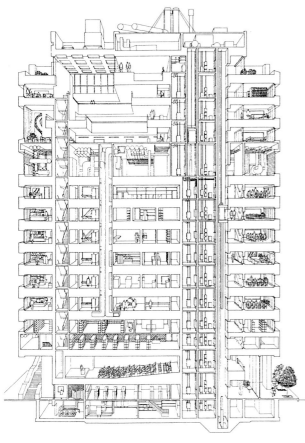

equipment required by the laboratories.
This floor also provides a visual and
organizational break in the facade, above
which rise the top four levels, devoted to
bedrooms, dining rooms, and other communal spaces, all organized around a
three-story atrium. The architects
reserved the best views for the human vol-
unteers.

By selecting a hexagonal plan, the
Shepley office provided continuity with
the line of buildings on Washington
Street, while opening a wider view into
the Tufts New England Medical Center
complex and securing a modest public
plaza at the intersection with Stuart
Street. They varied the reddish-brown
pebble aggregate facades of the tower by

patterns of fenestration, indicating the
uses for the different levels and emphasizing depth on the short ends and surface on
the wider sides.

20
Paine Webber Building

265 Franklin Street
Goody, Clancy & Associates, Inc., 1984

At first glance this building appears to be
symmetrical on all four sides. Conflating
the architecture of the twenties with that

of modernism, series of stepped setbacks rise from the building's entries. The pattern is reinforced by the use of such materials as rough-hewn rose granite on the lower stories and polished rose granite on the upper ones. A relatively ingenious rectilinearity dominates all. Subtle planar distinctions are evident, especially on the High Street facade, where setbacks constitute different wall planes and form quiet recessive elements. The structuring of the corners with stepped-back modules imparts an overall "Lego" quality to the surface. The lower six stories feature a glass-enclosed atrium, which forms a passage between Franklin and High streets. The whole bespeaks an eighties chic – the bar and lounge at one end, an information desk at the other. In between, the waters of a symmetrical pool of fountains trickle down into channels from above, forcing us to glance now up, now down, and predictably land on marble banks.

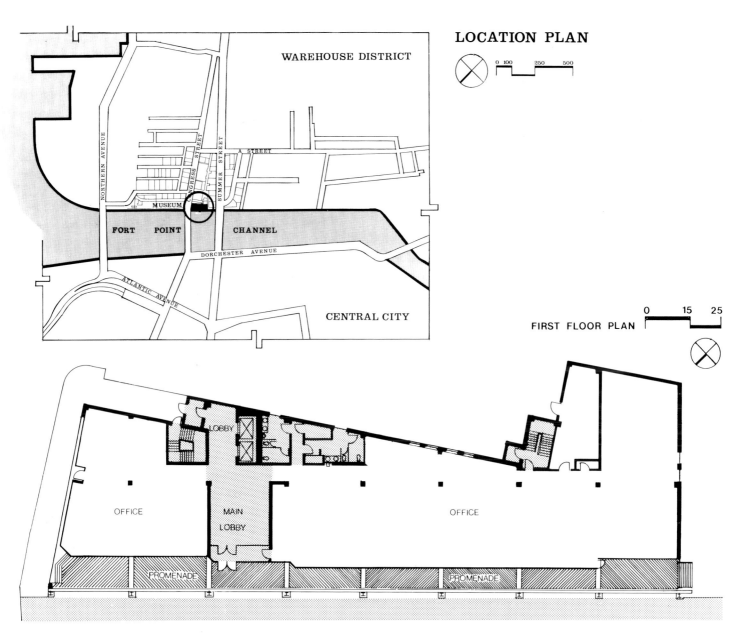

LOCATION PLAN

WAREHOUSE DISTRICT

0 100   250   500

NORTHERN AVENUE

CONGRESS STREET

SUMMER STREET

A STREET

MUSEUM

FORT   POINT   CHANNEL

DORCHESTER   AVENUE

ATLANTIC   AVENUE

CENTRAL CITY

FIRST FLOOR PLAN

0   15   25

OFFICE

LOBBY

MAIN LOBBY

OFFICE

PROMENADE

PROMENADE

21
303 Congress Street

Notter, Finegold + Alexander, 1984

The first new construction in the Leather District industrial area of South Boston in half a century, 303 Congress Street was an important stimulus for reinvestment in this neighborhood. The building is most successful in respecting the established scale and character of the district. The most prominent facade is a wall of glass and structural steel facing onto the Fort Point Channel. The diagonal steel bracing visually engages the adjacent Congress Street Bridge, while the two hues of swamp green in the glass curtain wall reflect the water's luminosity. A waterfront promenade along this facade continues the access to the channel that has been established with the development of surrounding buildings, including the Children's Museum and the Computer Museum across Congress Street. While the waterfront facade plays off issues of structure and color, the other elevations repeat the functional brick walls of the adjacent five- and six-story warehouse buildings. The interior plan allows a generous ratio of window to floor area, but the greatest success of this well proportioned building is its ability to complement the neighboorhood while retaining its unique integrity.

22
260 Franklin Street

The Stubbins Associates,Inc., 1985

This 23-story office building turns the corner of Franklin and Oliver streets. Its horizontal faceted window bands of reflective glass alternating with rose and light gray polished granite stripes follow modernist precepts, as does the matching articulation of the upper cornice and the lower arcade. Towers at the ends of the building differentiate the volume; a garage entry on Oliver Street is separated from the principal mass by a slightly receding bay. Square-set windows delineating the cornice line are balanced by a rectilinear portico that flows around the entry at ground level, creating an arcaded pedestrian passage. Space in the inner lobby is somewhat cramped, but completely straightforward.

23
One Financial Center

10 Dewey Square
Jung Brannen Associates, Inc., 1985

On a strategic site, opposite South Station and diagonally across from the Federal Reserve, this 45-story building lacks distinction. An oddly shaped six-sided structure with a glass-enclosed, six-story, 90-foot-high atrium on a granite base at ground level, One Financial Center is memorable only in its ordinariness. The steel-framed tower, clad with precast concrete and reflective glass, contains a rain-screen system to combat the effects of water penetration. Horizontal bands detract from the potential loftiness of the skyscraper, and its relative isolation adds to its awkwardness. The edges are weak, and the roofline is too constricted in view of the building's height.

If the building does nothing to define the confluence of streets at this crucial site, it does, perhaps incidentally, possess the means to become an active part of its ambiance. Wrought-iron tables and chairs, indoors and out, act as a wonderful vantage point from which to observe the panorama of downtown Boston at its southern boundary. But more, the plaza and lobby create a significant urban node – a natural and expedient meeting place, situated as it is next to local and inter- and intra-state transportation networks. The northern base fronts the new developments along Essex and Summer streets.

24
International Place

Fort Hill Square
Philip Johnson & John Burgee
Associates, 1985–

Of all recent projects none is more conspicuous, by dint of size or shape, than
International Place. Is it attempting to
create in Boston what the World Trade
Center has done in New York? Even the
name is indicative, for it is tied to the
same global economy. Further, its form
has as little to do with the shaping of space
as that of its twin counterpart. If the size
(2.6 acres, 1,800,000 square feet) does
not compete with the gargantuan
monoliths of Gotham, where commercial
and federal office buildings are
now contiguous to Battery Park, it is over-

whelming in the context of Boston.
When complete, International Place will
be billed as a high-rise, high-density
"urban village" composed of a cluster of
five buildings of varying heights and
shapes dominated by two cylindrical
towers, the tall 46 stories of phase I, now
occupied, and a smaller one of 35 stories;
three rectilinear office buildings of
different shapes will have 11, 19, and
27 stories. Reinforcing the theme
of a city within the city are diverse services – medical, health, retail, repair,
and dining, in addition to office-related
functions.

Built on an irregular pentagonal plot of
land at Fort Hill, International Place
occupies the site of a fortification that
served early settlers as protection against
sea invaders. Punctuated by a multitude
of arched Palladian windows on the

exterior and crowned by crenelated
parapets, the rose granite cylindrical
tower does retain vestiges of the area's earlier history.

At the center of this "urban village" is
the glass-covered court, the village
square; one is greeted by the sound of
steadily falling water midst a small
enclave of tall trees. As we approach the
55-foot fountain, we realize that "rain" is
falling from the skylight to the granite
floor, the sound overwhelming the sight.
Entering the atrium, one is almost surprised to find that much of the glistening
stone ground is not wet.

The highly reflective marble lobby
with its bold black, white and rust patterns flows into the interior of the court.
Perversely, the most wonderful part of the
vista may be the green-colored overpass of
the Fitzgerald Expressway (Central

Artery) with its gigantic trucks slowly navigating between Harbor Towers and the odd configuration of Rowes Wharf. Cafés are welcome amenities, and give one the chance to reflect on the logic of the Corbusier-like spiral stairs that lead to the main tower.

The details are amazing, none more so than the black wrought-iron sconces that adorn the arched entry. Metal castings made in France and assembled in Holland recall the turn-of-the-century lamps that adorn the McKim, Mead & White facade of the Boston Public Library. The semicircular space of the interior lobby with its pink marble Doric columns beneath a marble cornice almost makes the scale of Johnson's AT&T in New York seem intimate. Intricately-grained polychrome marbles in the elevators and throughout the lobby, including 24 columns tapering at the top, are from three quarries in Spain and Italy, finished in Carrara. Chiofaro Company, the developer, cites a local craftsman: "The lobby is the talk of Carrara. Nothing has been done like it in a long time."

Views are spectacular. In the words of a holding company executive who inhabits the top story, the master of all he surveys, "We don't have to look at the outside [of this building]." Even the Palladian windows appear as flat-topped on the interior due to the ceiling height. A roof garden at mid-level does relieve the aerial view. Still, outsiders may marvel at the medieval cylindrical keep in downtown Boston, with its relentless and frivolous window pattern. Even more bizarre is the projected tower, now under construction, dominated by a conical roof that echoes that of the nearby Flour and Grain Exchange (Shepley, Rutan & Coolidge, 1891–1893).

Philip Johnson may see this building as a type of deconstruction, namely six fragmentary components on a more or less triangular site, again recalling the earlier grain exchange. "I am serious, but playfulness is part of my art. Americans criticize pastiche, but architecture is a way of enjoying a city." Johnson proceeds as *homo ludens*, comparing the design of tall buildings to fashion, to clothing a skeleton. "Skyscrapers have nothing to do with functionalism. It's too expensive to build high."

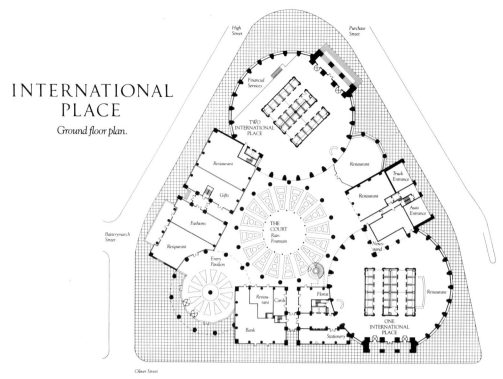

INTERNATIONAL PLACE

Ground floor plan.

25

Lafayette Place

1 Avenue de Lafayette
Mitchell/Giurgola Architects, 1985

Close to the big department stores and late nineteenth-century granite and brick buildings and on the edge of the theatre district, this multi-use project (hotel, retail mall, garage, restaurants) is dominated on the south (from Chauncy and Bedford streets) by an austere gray stone wall, relieved by a discreet pattern of red squares and lines – a minimalist logo with roots in the Bauhaus. Rising 22 stories, Lafayette Place distinctly walls off the combat zone, a tawdry entertainment district, and almost acts as a neutral backdrop to the late-eighties fantasies in the vicinity. Once within, the circular common area with restaurants and cafés – inner and outer – is the only clearly defined space of the labyrinthine network.

Disorientation mounts when we search for an exit, as priority appears to have been given to access through the three-level underground garage, Jordan Marsh, or Washington Street. Despite the location here of Le Marquis de Lafayette, a top dining establishment, the whole seems born of that concept of defensive space that came to the fore in the late sixties.

Details, such as the classical graphics denoting parking, are in good taste. The air vents are balanced with the pattern of square windows, and although the corner of Chauncy and the new Boulevard de Lafayette may be dull for pedestrians, it does provide a convenient entry to the hotel from the Central Artery (the expressway between the waterfront and the financial district/government center) – albeit an undistinguished doorway, marked by sets of traffic lights at each end. The shopping mall is visibly connected to the hotel by a glass gallery, open to pedestrians. Again, the linear brick motifs and red lamp-like projections where capitals once were are subtle, but the outside is remarkably unwelcoming, at times appearing like a cross between a warehouse and a parking garage.

If the exterior conveys a certain bland modernity, the interior is completely traditional, even repellent to modern eyes, with its overstuffed lounges and highboy-lined walls, its pseudo-early Americana and New England décor. Only the glass-enclosed anatomical mechanism of a watch advertising the Swiss Hotel is admirable.

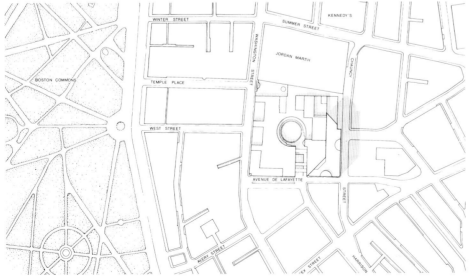

The main entry to the shopping mall is on Washington Street, and viewed from Temple Place it is indeed prominent – a large orthogonal marble frame with reflective glass contiguous with Jordan Marsh. Hence, the frontage along Washington Street continues the commercial activity of the thoroughfare, which is boosted by the covered passageways and pedestrian malls extending from the old department store.

Less immediately apparent factors are perhaps more successful: the integration with existing shopping sites, the renewal of Washington Street, the indoor all-weather environment, and the consolidation of parking. However, these assets cannot compensate for the problems inherent in the overall design – namely, the enclosed nature of the complex has too little relation to its immediate ambiance and the difficult circulation pattern within is exacerbated by the poor location of the street entries. Plans are already underway for early demolition, or at least partial rebuilding.

26
Marketplace Center

200 State Street
WZMH Group Inc., 1985

Situated below the contour of the Central Artery, this aggregate is an extension of Faneuil Hall Marketplace toward the harbor. Forming both a terminus and a beginning, the red iron- and glass-covered central passageway leads underneath the Artery to the waterfront. At the edges of this pedestrian walk are boutiques at every turn and every angle. The porticoed hemicycle curves back to embrace an area, whose pavement of patterned brick and granite reflects the texture of the structure; punctuated by circular stone seats, the whole constitutes a pseudo-amphitheater in which the show is continuous and ever changing. Flags contribute to the festive air, hanging from the rough granite piers that contrast with the smooth granite entablature; red iron stairways at each side form pavilions crowned by glass and iron pyramids, which repeat the central theme.

If the shopping arcade has some justification in terms of the Quincy Market area and as a gateway to the waterfront, the sixteen-story office tower rising on the State Street side of the complex is a travesty of contemporary building, both in its general form and especially in such details as the gabled roof, the red framing, and the choice of materials: it is flimsy, inauthentic, and weak. Still, as an urban space, the overall design has its virtues. Providing a welcome enclosure and a passageway to the waterfront, the "forecourt" has become an animated stage towards which pedestrians gravitate.

Site model with Custom House Tower

O'Neill Federal Building

Causeway and Nashua streets and Lomasney Way, at North Station
The Stubbins Associates, Inc., 1985–87

Extending over a considerable area on an irregular site, this building may be the nexus of the development around North Station. Materials appear shoddy; the atrium looks conventional; high security is evident. Despite certain design elaborations, this is not an atypical federal office building. Like so many government buildings, it is not entirely accessible to the public. All this may change when the area is further developed according to the master plan drawn up by Moshe Safdie in 1979, and now considerably revised. At present, however, even its entrance seems to be masked from the street. A clearer understanding of the irregular shape may be gleaned from the elevated Green Line train as it tracks past the massive structure. The plan is composed of two L-shaped masses, built around a central atrium and lobby, the lower housing public service agencies and the taller tower offices. A street-level arcade surrounds the building, with provisions for shops. Other spaces are occupied by an underground garage, courtrooms, and an auditorium.

On the facade, bands of horizontal reflective glass windows alternate with granite spandrels finished in dark red, revealing the floor levels. The granite panels (30 ft. × 7 ft.), prefabricated and set within a steel truss armature, look more like veneer than stone.

Viewed from the corner of Lomasney Way and Causeway Street, the building is almost a model of a two-point perspectival drawing. A sleek truncated corner terminates the tall eleven-story tower of warm gray stone, and the broad mass of the five-story rose granite block juts forth at the top and recedes until it reaches ground level; tall, slim piers form an arcade around the building's base. The entry, accessible by means of a flight of narrow steps, is not particularly welcoming.

Occupying the central space is an enormous five-story atrium, rather lifeless despite the sculpture by Mary Miss. Composed of a space frame with skylight above, the atrium functions as a passive solar collector. The proximity of the Federal Building to the commuter lines running into North Station contributes to its significance in the area.

27
Wang Laboratories

185 Kneeland Street
Anderson Nichols & Co., 1985

By virtue of its size, whiteness, and surroundings the arcuated structure is distinctive, if reminiscent of De Chirico's vision partially realized in the Palace of Italian Civilization, built in Rome in 1942. Visible at the end of a long axis, this white marble prism is composed of five bays on its long and three on its short sides, patterned equally throughout. Proportions are clearly written: the six intermediate stories form a grid with ten or six square windows on each level. The thermal windows below the roofline are balanced by the two-story glass-enclosed arcaded base. An off-center block on the roofline discreetly announces "Wang" on the two principal facades. On entering through the modest convex arch, one encounters offices on the ground floor, rather than the current more typical ceremonial, and often useless, grand lobby. Superficially, at least, this workplace is more concerned with the welfare of employees than with relations to the public at large. This is in keeping with the location near Chinatown; the labs were removed from corporate headquarters in Lowell in order to provide job opportunities for Chinese and other inner-city communities.

FEDERAL B...

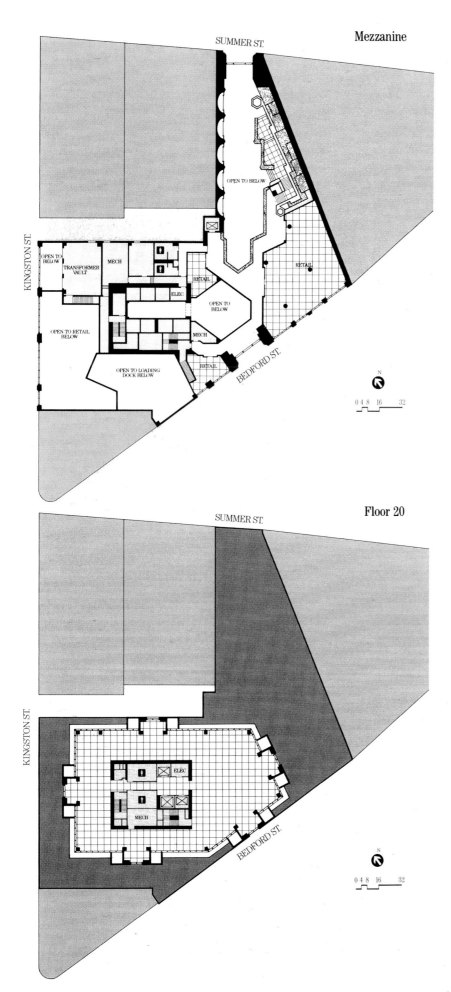

Mezzanine

SUMMER ST.

KINGSTON ST.

OPEN TO BELOW

OPEN TO BELOW

TRANSFORMER VAULT

MECH

RETAIL

RETAIL

ELEC

OPEN TO BELOW

OPEN TO RETAIL BELOW

MECH

RETAIL

OPEN TO LOADING DOCK BELOW

BEDFORD ST.

N

0 4 8 16   32

Floor 20

SUMMER ST.

KINGSTON ST.

ELEC

MECH

BEDFORD ST.

N

0 4 8 16   32

29
99 Summer Street

Goody, Clancy & Associates, Inc., 1986

One of the paradigms of postmodernism, this building is an embodiment of architecture in the eighties. Its statement is loud and lavish, inside and out. Adapted to an irregular site, and rising above a block of nineteenth-century commercial buildings, the gray granite-clad tower begins on the fifth floor; floor areas diminish from 20,000 to 10,000 square feet towards the crowning bright red attic roof. Intricate massing characterizes the tower, which aims to echo, in a brasher way, that of the nearby United Shoe Machinery Building. On all four sides narrow arched windows are interwoven with red enameled panels, creating an undeniable presence on the Boston skyline – that is, until 125 Summer Street diminished its impact, at least from the south.

Entering the building at ground level is no less astonishing, for here a rectilinear arcaded sequence is interrupted by a huge 70-foot arch on Summer Street. An indoor arcade leads from Summer to Bedford streets, animated by a five-story skylit marble atrium reminiscent of those found in Hyatt hotels. Here is the "Portmanization" of the office building, with its series of balconies, the grand stair, and the water channel descending from the mezzanine. The form of the hexagonal font just within the Summer Street entry is repeated in the polygonal floor pattern in the Bedford Street lobby. Long indigenous to hotel architecture, the plantings, the arcuated niches with potted palms, and the surfeit of marble extend the fantasy to the office building.

Some may commend the design for its conformity to the old street line at ground level, the surprise inherent in the shape of the impressive entry arch, and the distinct visual connections between the street and the skyline in the arcuated windows below and above.

Style? The building has been cited for its respect of, and relation to, the urban context. Only in an odd sense is this true, for above all 99 Summer calls attention to its old neighbors – the thirties garage, the Bedford Building, and that French Renaissance gem, the Proctor Building – and makes us grateful for their presence.

30
China Trade Building

2–20 Boylston Street
Original: Carl Fehmer, 1887;
Re-use: The Architectural Team, 1987

A century after construction as a rental commercial structure, one of Carl Fehmer's finest Boston buildings was renovated as a commercial center for retailers serving the nearby Chinese-American community. The light brownstone facade was cleaned and the ground floor restored, except that it was given poured concrete, pedimented entrances that are out of character with the older structure. The architects created a full-height atrium in the central section of the building, retaining some of the cast iron columns and inserting numerous stairways between the lower levels; large banners and brightly painted surfaces create in a microcosm the festival air of a Rouse development. The paved open space with trees in front of the building provides a convenient meeting area in this densely built, rapidly changing neighborhood.

31
Lincoln Wharf Condominiums

357 Commercial Street
The Architectural Team, 1987

Built in 1901, the former main power plant of the Massachusetts Bay Transportation Authority was in operation until 1972. From both an architectural and an economic point of view, the conversion of this massive structure to housing is extraordinary. The impressive brick facade with its triple grand arches beneath a diaper-patterned entablature and above a rusticated base on Commercial Street contrasts with the double-gabled facade of the harbor side, generously punctuated by unadorned windows, in harmony with warehouses along the docks.

Within, a ground-to-ceiling atrium was dictated by the once floorless space of the powerhouse and its extant steel columns supporting the skylight. However, the most commendable aspect of this water-front project is its designation for a low-to-moderate-income group in one of the most costly housing markets in the country. Both the City of Boston and the San Marco Housing Corporation are to be commended for this contribution to waterfront renewal, without displacement of long-time residents.

32

Rowes Wharf

Skidmore, Owings & Merrill, 1987

Approaching the Rowes Wharf gateway to Boston by water-taxi from Logan airport or by boat from the South Shore surely lifts the spirits of any commuter. To stroll along this newly rehabilitated wharf or dine on its terraces or sail from its slips adds a new-old dimension to city life. From an urbanistic point of view it is hard to cavil at the multi-use project of hotel, offices, health club, condominiums, six-story underground and undersea parking, shops, marina and ferry services, airport water-shuttle, and above all the waterfront plaza and its provisions for public use. As to the architecture itself, opinions vary widely. Heralded by some critics for its layout appropriate to the amalgam of different functions and for its mastery of complex surface details, it is seen by others as an unfortunate pastiche of local vernacular and high fashion. If we scan the skyline from the west, in the vicinity of South Station, it is less coherent than the older adjoining warehouses, but completely in context with buildings along the harbor. Viewed from the harbor, it is part of the landscape, a waterfront structure, while from Atlantic Avenue Rowes Wharf follows the street's building line. From the border of the Central Artery near International Place, the proportions seem weak and the massing odd, for the shallow dome of the entry sinks into the lower cen-

tral roofline. Only when we cross beneath the Artery is the six-story archway impressive, serving as a monumental frame for the maritime panorama. On the water's edge, a ferry pavilion with a copper dome overlooks the harbor like a transplanted gazebo or an eighteenth-century folly, for at present boats do not stop here!

The interiors of the luxury hotel and its observation tower are testimony to the décor of a bygone age. However, a dining table or a room with a view will surely compensate for the surfeit of all that comprises the complex. Public spaces are too enclosed; one must make an effort to enjoy the panorama.

The five-and-one-half-acre site between the waterfront and Atlantic Avenue is steeped in history. Built in the early 1760s, the Rowes and Fosters wharves housed a ferry terminal to East Boston from 1879 to about 1920, but the 1930s witnessed their decline. In our time, Rowes Wharf was due for a revival. Ready access to sea, land, and air transport have made it a natural focus for the Boston Redevelopment Authority, which stipulated (in a competition set for developers rather than architects) that height limits be respected so as not to block the views of buildings in the financial district.

The details of construction are intricate: to cut costs and time, a slurry wall was built to define the perimeter of the precast concrete and steel superstruc-

ture. Complexity is all too apparent in the rich array of materials, for steel beams are clad with panels of precast concrete, granite, and masonry, with fiberglass-reinforced gypsum panels underneath and inside the archways. In fact, it is often difficult to determine the material used as the reinforced concrete is framed with stone details. This textural density extends to all parts of the structure, including the ornamental patterns and the copper-clad dome. We may admire the fine craftsmanship and the grandeur of the six-story arched entry, 80 ft. by 80 ft., and the glass observatory beneath the copper-covered dome, but at the same time note the unrelieved texture of the windows; all are similar, constituting a monotonous pattern when applied to so broad an area and conveying no idea of the diverse functions of the aggregate.

In some ways this is another warehouse along the waterfront, where an attempt is being made to merge the domestic with the commercial. The arch is overbearing rather than monumental, for it never delivers what it promises, specifically an entry to the city. Hailed as a masterpiece of contrarieties, private and public, land and sea, playful and serious, Rowes Wharf converts the truly ceremonial to the commonplace.

Pavilion on waterfront near airport ferry

Opposite, top: Harbor view and marina with Harbor Towers in background

Opposite, bottom: Aerial view of Atlantic Avenue facade behind Central Artery

33
Boston Design Center

1 Design Center Place
Earl R. Falnsburgh and Associates, Inc.,
1988

In the future, this reconverted United States Army warehouse might serve as an exemplar of postmodernism. Almost every cliché of the movement is present in the eight-story west facade facing the city – the rigorous axial symmetry, the stepped entry with its drafted masonry granite base, the central colossal "Doric" pilasters enclosed between corner units (which continue similar design elements on the north and south sides), the separate entablature with polychrome "dormer" windows in dark blue adorned with a single red square (as on the "capitals" below), and the triangular pediment above the split cornice, whose crowning feature is a semicircular lunette framed by voussoirs, open to the sky! Several classical elements of the Beaux-Arts style are here, as too are the principles of the late nineteenth-century Sullivan skyscrapers with their tripartite divisions. Nighttime illumination heightens the spectacle, especially from a distance. Within, the two-story lobby serves as a transitional point between the main body of the structure and the facade and public plaza. Its décor partakes of all the glamor of Hollywood in the thirties – the curvilinear forms in rich marbles, granites, and wood against the rectilinear wall patterns with striking lighting features, and the opulent leather furniture arranged according to the best geometric conventions of modernism.

Notwithstanding the installation of new mechanical and electrical systems, the restoration of the exterior has been respectful to the original enormous warehouse, whose masonry forms a grid separating the glass panes.

Heralding the renewal of this particular segment of the waterfront as the first building in the Boston Marine Industrial Park, the Design Center gathers together a conglomerate of the design and furniture industry of New England and acts as a stimulus for the Economic and Industrial Development Commission's revitalization program.

34
75–101 Federal Street

Kohn Pedersen Fox Associates, P. C.,
1988

Bound to the State Street Trust Building at
75 Federal Street (Thomas James, 1929),
the new 75–101 Federal Street borders on
Federal, Franklin, and Devonshire streets
and on Winthrop Square, yet is often hard
to find, both at the street level and on the
skyline. The buff sandstone exterior of the
late twenties building, with its setbacks
and pyramidal crown, is adorned with
relief panels of terracotta and bronze, in
floral and figural patterns celebrating
industry and abundance. Details in the
old lobby are stunning – the warm marble
and bronze tones, the gilt and black elevator banks, the mailboxes of a bygone
era.

Kohn Pedersen Fox could hardly ignore
the richness and fine craftsmanship of the
earlier building. Thus, 101 Federal Street
is an attempt to coexist with this handsome neighbor both inside and out. On
the exterior, accommodation is effected
by the massing of the twin towers, the
alignment of windows and spandrels, and
the adjustment of the new fenestration to
the approximate size of the old. The
rectilinear framing, visible at the roofline
of the older building, is here repeated. At
ground level, the tripartite division has
three entries – two wide arched openings
(one serving the garage) framing a nar-
rower central doorway. The exterior
rhythm continues in the pedestrian
through-street corridor – a private space
completely accessible to the public.
Arched linear panels are drawn on the
ceiling, whereas silver and gilt panels
line the interior arcade. Aluminum-clad
elevators with their linear relief designs
are a match for their metallic predecessors. In the middle of this through-
fare, at right angles, we enter the passage
to the old building, where a warmer,
bronze tone replaces the cool silver.

Just beyond is the delightful, irregularly shaped island of Winthrop Square.
Here we can gaze upwards at the intricately wrought roofline, whose complete
frivolity is only revealed by its nocturnal
lighting.

Despite borrowed references, 75–101
Federal Street is one of the few recent
buildings to continue the true masonry
tradition of the early skyscraper. Its
details capture the opulence of a gilded
age – Art Deco revived, if not updated.

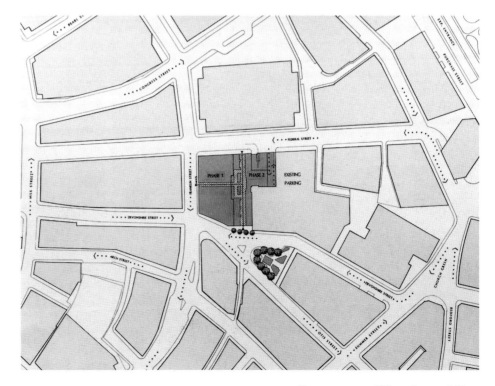

35
150 Federal Street

The Stubbins Associates, Inc., 1988

160 Federal Street
(United Shoe Machinery Building,
The Landmark)

Re-use: Jung Brannen Associates, Inc.,
1988

While owing something to the aesthetic of modernism, 150 Federal Street completely violates its canon. Both rectilinear and curved, a slab and a setback, all light-reflective glass with incongruously heavy pink granite lintels – in sum, this building seems to be trying desperately to be of its time, and yet to pay homage to the past, at least to its most immediate neighbor, the United Shoe Machinery Building (Parker, Thomas & Rice, 1928–30), with which it is connected. The new structure has many facades – the low-rise that follows the contour of Matthews Street is the site of the garage and secondary entrances. On High Street, the glass-covered curvilinear facade has an overall grid pattern. The lower level is marked by rose pebble aggregate with polished darker granite and "trimming" inset midway. Set back from the building line, the principal entry leads to a glass enclosed steel-frame atrium, with a grand clock acting as the single ornament. Within the lobby, even the color changes as we enter The Landmark, the new designation for the old United Shoe Building. Lighting fixtures are ravishing, as are the gilt elevators, the abstract carpets, and the carved details. An odd note is struck by Peter Haines's *Landmark Suite* (1988), a jade bronze sculpture that has been installed at the junction of the new building and the atrium leading to The Landmark. Despite its classical and modern references, this dismembered anatomical group bears little relationship to the architecture or to the prominent space that it occupies.

Both as modernist and high-style eighties, 150 Federal fails in its use of materials, but more in terms of proportion and scale. The grid pattern of thin white mullions creates an unrelieved monotony, hardly mitigated by disparate elements.

Opposite: 150 Federal Street in center; The Landmark at far left

160 Federal Street; The Landmark

Exterior, with Faneuil Hall (left) and Custom House Tower

36

One Faneuil Hall Square

Graham Gund Architects, 1988

On the site of the granite Sanborn Fish Market (destroyed by fire in 1979), between Merchants Row, Faneuil Hall Square, and high-rise offices, One Faneuil Hall Square is merely seven stories (70 ft.) high, topped by a hipped roof. Harmonious in context, the copper roof conceals mechanical systems. The building's foundations are on two levels – 60 State Street and at Merchants Row – a "skewed position" with pedestrian access throughout. A closer adherence to contextualism could hardly be imagined than in this simple cubic structure. Seen from City Hall, on line with Faneuil Hall, this branch of The Limited (a clothing chain based in Columbus, Ohio) stands before Quincy Market on one side and the Custom House Tower on the other. A bastion of trade in the heart of Boston's civic center is hardly unusual. The analogy may extend to its form, for example, the Renaissance palace harboring the textile industry in the midst of the civic center of fifteenth-century Florence.

Details are so consciously related to those on the facade of Faneuil Hall that one might feel a lack of invention in their distribution. The comparison with Faneuil Hall reveals variations on a theme – six bays in lieu of seven arched windows, the tondos, the lattice upper windows, the lunette in the pediment of Faneuil Hall repeated on the roof. Even the slightly curving projections between first and second and second and third stories echo the cornices of Faneuil Hall. The quadrilateral plaques surrounding the windows are part of the local vernacular. Squares and lintels are similar to those particulars in the nearby building on Chatham Street, while the blue-green tinted glass resounds with the vocabulary of neighboring skyscrapers. Withal, the building seems pale, weak, recessive, mannered. All that pink granite punctuated by gray, white, and dark rose appears to relate more to the color-coordinated contents of the shop within. While some may admire the building for its "contextuality," its deference to a public monument, its modest scale, and its fine craftsmanship, others have deemed it a "parody" of its immediate prototype. Once again, this sort of imitation diminishes the historic element, and if pushed to extremes may banish memory.

37
One Bowdoin Square

Graham Gund Architects, 1989

On a site where Cambridge Street turns into the Government Center complex, a new shell engulfs an earlier seven-story concrete and brick building. One Bowdoin Square is adjacent to the New England Telephone Building (one of Boston's few distinguished Art Deco skyscrapers) and Paul Rudolph's State Service Center, and fronted by a restored mini-park dedicated to Cardinal Cushing. Four stories have been added to the late nineteenth-century steel frame building. The principal design elements are reserved for the ground level and the cornice. There is a striped design in the "Tuscan" manner, punctuated by the outline of a "Renaissance chapel" and incorporating a Venturi type of ironic classical order, above which is a ring of circular fenestration. The facade is all surface, and it's as if this building doesn't know what to wear. Dark brown polished granite banderoles adorn the facade above the two-story entry and floor windows. Whereas the first three stories are in alternating dark- and light-striped pink/gray granite, the seven stories above are faced in red brick. Why the gilded chevrons, the slightly convex simulated burgundy aluminum balconies, the enormous circular windows on the third level surrounded by abstract geometric gilded patterns? An overbearing concave cornice with a row of semielliptical arches punctuated by flowing linear patterns drawn about the openings distantly recalls the exuberant floral designs that crowned Louis Sullivan's skyscrapers. This modern pastiche on a prominent site may become the paradigm of *fin-de-siècle* decadence – or delight.

38
75 State Street

Graham Gund Architects; Skidmore, Owings & Merrill, 1988

Even while under construction, the flamboyant elements of this 31-story tower became a landmark – to say nothing of its notoriety in local political and real estate annals for accused collusion between developers and politicians. From almost every direction the skyline suggests a bona fide Art Deco skyscraper, as does the entire building with its setbacks, its triple bays, its russet browns, its colored granites in rough and smooth finishes, some echoing the materials of older neighbors, and, not least, its abundance of gilded chevrons. Most distinctly, 75 State recalls those lavish New York towers of the Depression era, updated to conform to the aesthetic of the eighties. The lateral towers culminate in a hexagonal crown with ornamental cornices defined by gilded arcades.

Monumental pylons frame the State Street entry to the six-story skylit atrium, comprising offices and retail space and forming a pedestrian passage from Merchants Row to Kilby and Broad streets; parking for 700 cars lies below ground. The street facade summons up images of a thirties garage or a theatrical backdrop for a Hollywood film of that time. How else are we to explain the Egyptoid piers, the gilded balustrade above a granite balcony, the rustication, the appliqué, the excess of the whole? On the Broad Street side, the small open space at least provides a welcome place – a few café tables fronting a handsome three-story restaurant. Within, gaudiness gives way to lavishness. Polychrome marbles, rich dark cherry woods, bronze framing: expense has not been spared in this grand vaulted atrium lobby. Apsidal spaces frame the entry and the reception area at the juncture of the three aisles. Fine craftsmanship marks the wood boutique showcases, and the rectilinear designs of the thirties are incorporated in the brass lighting fixtures. Cold, private, ornate, and elegant in a postmodern way, this is a place of passage rather than of meeting.

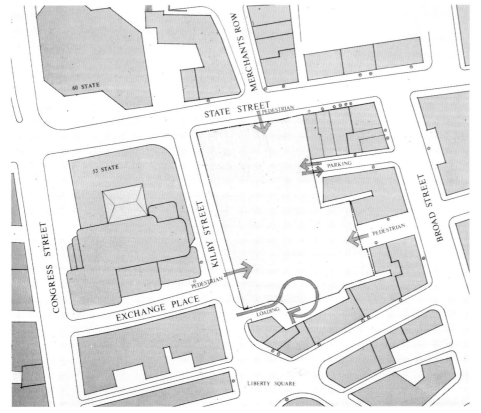

118 Downtown and Waterfront

39
20 and 21 Custom House Street

Bruner/Cott, 1989

In the midst of the Historic Custom House District, so designated in 1973, Bruner/ Cott in collaboration with developer Jaymont Properties have designed two buildings of ten and twelve stories that may be deemed exemplars of current contextualism.

In the area of the original Custom House, in view of the Grain and Flour Exchange, and with easy access to Rowes Wharf, the two buildings, relatively modest in height and scale, incorporate elements of their illustrious precinct – the granite skin, overall grid, fenestration, and general proportions. Echoes of the Custom House Tower appear in the articulation of the facade, while attention to the immediate surroundings within the block is made manifest by setbacks at intervals that indicate the irregular site. This is,

after all, Bulfinch territory, for not only did the Federal architect plan the Broad Street we see today to accommodate the increasing trade and the harbor expansion, but he built three adjacent warehouses there in 1806–07. These will be restored, with particular attention to the original brickwork, granite storefronts, and slate roofs.

Also included in the overall plan is an underground garage and, more significantly, the embellishment of Custom House Street (which runs between the two buildings) with brick pavement, provisions for seating, trees, and a kiosk display, including an engraved bronze inscription recounting the history of the site. In a sense, these buildings mark a turn to site-specific architecture in the downtown area.

40
745 Atlantic Avenue

The Stubbins Associates, Inc., 1989

Like many nineteenth-century downtown Boston buildings, 745 Atlantic Avenue follows the contour of the corner. Here, at Atlantic and Beach Street, the ten-story

central cylindrical tower stands between two quadrilateral masses with setbacks at the upper stories. Its most prominent feature is surely the conical roof, an echo of that of the Grain and Flour Exchange.

The facade is composed of pink granite and brick-faced concrete panels. Stone lintels frame the recessed windows and the rhythm of wider piers creates a seemingly tripartite division of bays. There are moments of modernity as the horizontal brick bands curve around the corner, but these are soon dispelled by the multiplicity of extraneous elements, designed to be in context with the materials and massing of the nearby brick structures. However, a glance at the late nineteenth-century neighbors reveals corbeled brickwork and cast-iron frames, as exemplified in the pseudo-Romanesque facade at 717 Atlantic Avenue with its biform windows and projecting crenelated corner. One may reflect on the plainness of the new when comparing 745 Atlantic with the well adorned older generation down the street in Boston's former leather district.

Refurbished with planters and seating along the tree-lined brick sidewalk, the building imparts a measure of urbanity to the streetscape of the South Station area.

41
South Station Redevelopment

Summer Street and Atlantic Avenue
Project architects: Stull and Lee, Inc.,
1989–

Among the great railroad terminals built
around the turn of the century, that of
South Station (Shepley, Rutan &
Coolidge, 1899) is one of the least distinguished. The same may be said for the
group of office buildings and bus terminals that have risen at the side of the terminal.

Still, the turn of the corner on Dewey
Square, marking the once grander and
busier station, lends a monumental air to
the whole. The central portion of the
curved granite facade is dominated by a
three-story free-standing Ionic colonnade
above a triple-arched entry. Attached
"wings" on the lateral facades are sym-
metrically disposed with generous fenestration in a grid pattern, perched on a two-
story base of rough masonry. Above the
balustrade rises the central clock tower
with its crowning eagle. If discordant, the
general configuration is nonetheless
assertive.

Newly rehabilitated, the main entry is
once again through the three portals on
Dewey Square. Since the interior of the
station has been in shambles for so long,
its restoration to full use, in almost any
workable condition, is particularly welcome. Passing through a low-ceiling vestibule, one suddenly emerges into the vast
hall that constitutes the new waiting-
room, with its sparse seating of light wood
elliptical benches. The trusses supporting
the roof recall earlier train stations, as
does the impressive height of the interior.
From the short side of a grand trapezoid
the space expands outwards in full view of
the glass grid wall overlooking the tracks,

which run parallel to Atlantic Avenue.
The walls are pierced on both sides by
arches faced with fine granite: the left portico leads to the ticket hall, where we are
surprised to find an intricately carved
polychrome coffered ceiling, and the right
to restaurants and cafés. Increasing
amenities and attractions (a large-scale
model of an old-time electric train with all
appropriate accoutrements) in the great
hall accommodate the growing traffic and
lend a positive prognosis for the future of
Amtrak and commuter rail in the Northeast.

The present renovation is part of the
MBTA transportation center — the chief
interchange for Amtrak, intercity buses,
and commuter rails. Garages, hotel and
office buildings, and assembly space for
high-tech industries are projected for the
total complex.

42
Parkside West

170 Tremont Street
Cannon Associates, 1989

First in a series of apartment buildings
planned to help revitalize the "hinge"
between the Downtown Crossing commercial district and the theater district,
Parkside West is better as a planning concept than as an architectural solution.
Perhaps the speed with which the building was constructed accounts for the mea-
gerness of the design. The blocky massing
of the eighteen-story building is topped by
peaked pavilions at the roof. The abrasive
newness of the light buff cast stone panels

at the lower levels and in the central and
corner pavilions contrasts abruptly with
the red brick body. The rustication of the
first three floors is veneer-like and
unsatisfying.

Because this district of Tremont Street
has been an underdeveloped section of
Boston in recent decades, any new build-

ing can establish its own context. Indeed,
the structure is guaranteed maximum visibility by its site facing the Boston Common. While the continued growth of housing in this neighborhood is clearly desirable, one hopes that future structures will
prove more enriching as additions to the
Boston streetscape.

43
101 Arch Street

Hoskins Scott Taylor & Partners, Inc., 1989

In the heart of the Central Business District, 101 Arch Street may serve as the archetype of late-eighties architecture and preservation. This is a building designed to provoke controversy, both in the form of the new 21-story tower, set back from Summer and Arch streets, and in the old red-brick Kennedy Department Store (1873) that wraps around it above street level. Little redeems the combination of disparate elements of the rose granite-clad tower, its piers interspersed with green cast stone spandrels, and its obligatory crowning pediments, enlivened by two illuminated clocks on the north and south fronts. Most enigmatic, perhaps, is the convex balcony (a seemingly direct reference to Michael Graves's Humana Building in Louisville) on line with the principal setback, although the copper roof is hardly less so. Still, a fragment of Boston Victoriana, the top three floors of the Kennedy store, has been preserved!

Entering the building through Bussey Place, we are confronted by a five-story glass-enclosed atrium. This time, however, it seems as if we had stepped onto a stage, the side-wings being the nineteenth-century buildings, one of which includes a wrought iron spiral stairway. Escalators lead up to the office lobby, where we glide across a highly polished marble floor beneath a coffered wood ceiling, while trying to dismiss the stone and mahogany details. All sense of proportion is missing in the mammoth polychrome columns resting on heavily polished granite bases. Escalators lead to concourse shops, underground passages, and to the MBTA Downtown Crossing, the whole resulting in a useful public indoor thoroughfare.

Despite, or because of, compromises between the developers, the Boston Landmarks Commission, the Boston Redevelopment Authority, and preservation consultants, the result appears to be a paradigm of postmodernism – pure kitsch.

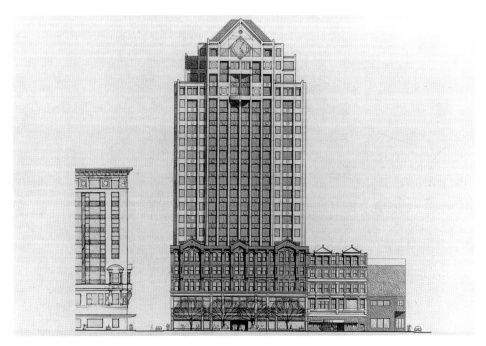

44
125 Summer Street

Kohn Pedersen Fox Associates, P. C.,
1989–90

For a prominent but awkward site Kohn
Pedersen Fox have designed a 22-story
commercial building that incorporates
several late nineteenth-century commercial buildings on Summer Street and a six-
story ventilator shaft for the Central
Artery to the south. The tower takes its
design cues from the granite Victorian
buildings at its base and others in the so-
called Commercial Palace Historic District to the north and west. Using a rose-
gray granite, glass, and cast architectural
stone, 125 Summer Street, when viewed
from South Station, resembles a colossal
column with accretions at its base and
top. This allusion to overscale classical
forms recalls recent postmodern architecture, particularly that of Ricardo Bofill
and the Taller de Arquitectura or the "late
entries" for the Chicago Tribune competition.

In plan the building is L-shaped, with
major entrances from South and Summer
streets and a parking entrance on Lincoln
Street. The ventilator shaft, which the
architects wanted to incorporate in the
design, remained an obstacle for the site,
forcing the L-plan configuration for the
building. A five-story lower register wraps
around the building, with new construction taking its scale and, to a certain
extent, its character from the nineteenth-
century facades incorporated. Entrances
from Summer, South, and Lincoln streets
give access to a T-shaped lobby and commercial galleria, intended to encourage
internal circulation through the building.
The tower is crowned with a grouping of
peaked and segmentally arched pavilions
reminiscent of the fantasy designs of Leon
Krier or a parodic comment on the crowning elements of New York City skyscrapers from the 1920s. The building continues a pattern of architecture and
development in the Summer Street corridor that includes 99 Summer Street and
101 Arch Street. In all three examples,
new historicist towers overwhelm surviving street-level fragments, reduced to
only veneer facades at 125 Summer
Street. The consistency of the nineteenth-
century survivors is not repeated in the
highly individualistic designs of the new
towers.

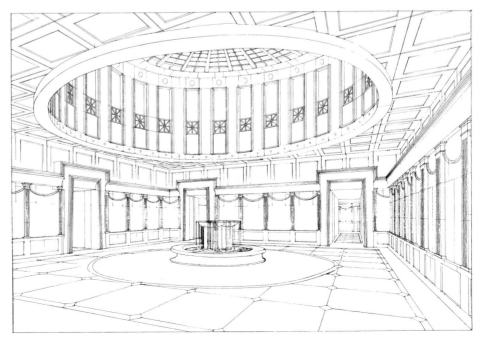

45
Burroughs Wharf

Notter, Finegold + Alexander, Inc.,
1989–

Between Union and Battery wharves and directly behind the recently renovated Lincoln Wharf, the firm has designed two seven-story luxury condominium buildings named for Francis Burroughs, who conducted maritime trade from this wharf in the early eighteenth century. The south-ern building, 40 Battery Square, will somewhat resemble the wooden MBTA coal-bunker that stood on the site. The heavy timber framework of the bunker and pier have been reinterpreted in steel, mahogany, and glass. To the north 50 Battery Square, will be built on a new pier and will repeat the massing and exposed structure of the other building in masonry.

Accommodating 86 units, the complex will also contain parking for 96 cars below grade, a park with fountain between the two buildings, and a landscaped public promenade around both piers. Berths for private boats, a yacht for the residents' use, and a water-taxi to the airport, as well as new headquarters for the two Boston Harbor fireboats, will insure picturesque and animated views from the apartments and townhouses. Although the coal-bunker image may not be the most appro-priate inducement for purchasers of these top-of-the-market residences, the archi-tects and developers should be compli-mented for producing a design that retains a sense of the historic use of the pier.

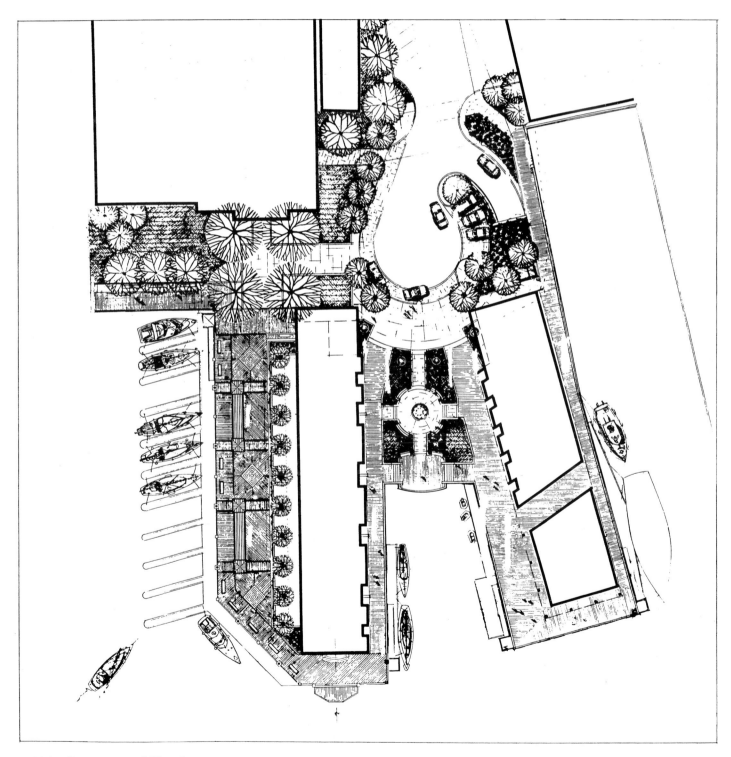

Implosion of Travelers Building, March 1988

46
125 High Street

Jung Brannen Associates, Inc.,
1989–[92]

Ground-breaking for this full block complex with two high-rise buildings occurred with amazing speed on the site of the Travelers Building, imploded on a Sunday morning in March 1988. Even the project renderings make one nostalgic for the blue and white bands which encircled this fine example of the International Style, built in the 1950s.

The new block will include two office towers of 30 and 21 stories, three restored nineteenth-century buildings at the corner of Purchase and Oliver streets, a

new fire station for the City of Boston, and a museum dedicated to Alexander Graham Bell (appropriate for a development where New England Telephone will be the prime tenant and partner). The fact that this immense project attracted virtually no opposition may be partly because of the care the developers took in meeting community demands and partly because of its site, overlooking the Central Artery and adjacent to the gargantuan International Place development. The towers will be set at right angles and joined by an eight-story marble-incrusted atrium, providing a public focus for the complex and substantial retail space. The exteriors will be clad in two shades of light rose granite, glass, and ornamental metal panels. The pyramidal Inca roof forms of the taller tower play off the crowns of 1920s/30s skyscrapers, such as the New England Telephone and Telegraph Building (Cram & Ferguson, 1943) diagonally adjacent to the site.

47

Inpatient Towers, Massachusetts General Hospital

55 Fruit Street
Hoskins Scott Taylor & Partners, Inc.,
1989–[93]

The first of two patient-care towers planned for Massachusetts General Hospital
by Hoskins Scott Taylor & Partners rises
25 stories adjacent to the White Pavilion
(Coolidge, Shepley, Bulfinch & Abbott,
1939). When a second, sixteen-story
tower and a five-story base connecting the
two shafts are completed in 1993 more
than half of the existing MGH beds will
have been replaced and restructured in
flexible specialized units. Changes in
health-care delivery and the role of
technology have required substantial reorganization of the MGH complex.

Nevertheless, the proposed new structures have aroused strong opposition from
historical, neighborhood, and architectural organizations. The towers will definitely interrupt the view of the river from
Beacon Hill and add to the chaotic
melange of the MGH complex. The
faceted, reflective gray glass box of the
first tower is anonymous, unrevealing,
and unrelated to any of the existing buildings. Perhaps the architects thought the
reflective glass would diminish the
impact of the buildings on the Boston
skyline. The image of the modern hospital
as a bureaucratic machine is definitely
reinforced by the emphasis on efficiency
and technology that underlies the design.
Requiring the demolition of four MGH
buildings, the inpatient towers are the
most visible evidence of a long-term reorganization of the hospital to make it a
safer, more economical, and more
technologically sophisticated medical
plant. Above all, the scale and prominence of these towers are an icon for the
strength of hospitals and medical
research institutions as a growth area for
Boston architects well into the 1990s.

48

Post Office Square Park

Ellenzweig Associates, Inc., 1989–
Landscape architects: The Halvorson
Company, Inc., 1990–

A desire to enhance the surroundings of
this downtown area led to the creation of
the Friends of Post Office Square in 1983.
Backed by the City of Boston and financed
by the Bank of New England, this group of
business and civic leaders initiated a
design competition for the new park to be
built above an underground garage, on the
site partly occupied by the old four-story
garage.

Situated at the very heart of the financial district, this 1.7-acre parcel bordered
by Congress, Franklin, Pearl, and Milk
streets will create a dramatic open space
in a densely built area. Complementing
the oasis of Angell Park, the irregular
triangular space is framed by distinguished older buildings – the Art Deco
fronts of the Post Office and the New England Telephone, and that of the Beaux-
Arts Hotel Meridien. Further, its distinct
space will help to orient people in a district of anomalous and confusing street
networks. Like all well-planned outdoor
spaces, Post Office Square Park should
provide respite and relaxation and serve
as an ideal meeting-place. Whereas
architectural and landscape features –
seating, lighting, paving, plantings, water
elements, public art – constitute the visible attractions of the park, Ellenzweig
Associates and Le Messurier Consultants,
architects and structural engineers, have
worked with Parsons, Brinckerhoff,
Quade & Douglas, engineers and planners, to build a garage on seven levels
below-grade. As well as facing up to the
problems of deep excavation and circulation, the architects tried to integrate garage facilities into the park structures.
Hence, café, escalator, ventilation shaft,
and elevator are disguised as garden
pavilions with trellis columns, lattice
work, and copper-clad pitched roofs.

While one may question the wisdom of
the Friends of Post Office Square in
encouraging the flow of downtown traffic,
they are to be commended for sponsoring
this city-owned, non-profit enterprise,
which will bring a breath of fresh air to a
crowded neighborhood.

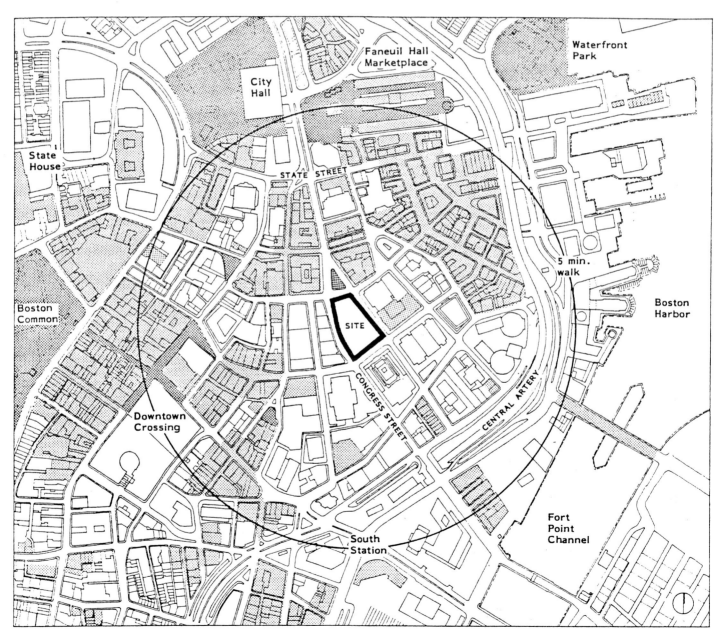

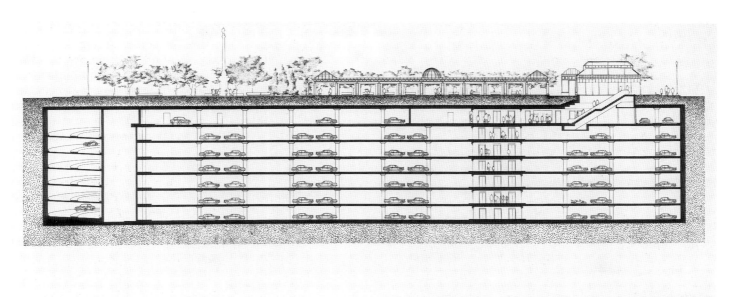

Post Office Square Park and Garage
Friends of Post Office Square, Inc.
Post Office Square Redevelopment Corp.

Longitudinal Section

Ellenzweig Associates, Inc.
Architects

Back Bay and Beacon Hill

I glow with the warmth of these soiled red bricks,
their unalikeness in similarity,
a senseless originality for fact,
"Rome was," we told the Irish, "Boston is."

Robert Lowell, *History*, 1973

Few townscapes in any American city are as distinctive and delightful as Boston's Back Bay. Built on old tidal flats, the land-fill district, legally born in 1856, extends from the Public Garden in the east to the Fenway in the west, from the Charles River in the north to the railroad tracks in the south.

Broad tree-lined streets based on a gridiron plan are remarkable in a city where development generally followed topographical conditions or cumulative patterns of growth. Much of the late nineteenth-century fabric is still extant in this area of fashionable brick and brownstone bow-front townhouses, with mansard roofs, and gardens behind wrought ironwork. Restrictions on height and building lines contributed to the cohesiveness of the townscape and the general airiness of the district. Cultural institutions rose on the less expensive land around Copley Square, and church towers became landmarks. Commercial development on a grand scale did not occur until the building of the Prudential Center in the 1960s and the opening of the Hynes Auditorium. Compared with other parts of the city, growth has been relatively restrained, especially in terms of height, and, as a glance at the map will reveal, limited to the southern edge of the Back Bay, more specifically along Boylston Street.

Looming above all is the 60-story Hancock Tower. Ingeniously poised on a visually strong yet physically delicate site, its reflective skin mirrors the city as well as its immediate surroundings. All the problems of late modern architecture can be studied here; ecological and economic questions hitherto underplayed are now dominant. Observing the daily transformations from glass sheathing to plywood to glass again, as falling windows were temporarily replaced, even the public became acutely aware of the problems inherent in skyscrapers. Still, it seems fitting that John Hancock, so prominent in old Boston—author of that grandiloquent first signature on the Declaration of Independence two hundred years ago, and occupant of the site marked by a classical stele in the Old Granary Burying Ground—should become the most visible symbol of the new Boston. The passing clouds transfigure the face of the structure, testifying to its ephemeral and ultimately poetic nature—the mirage of the city as it was and is, proclaiming the inevitability of future change.

For a short while after the Hancock debacle – although one has to admit it was the right building on a questionable site – there was only a sporadic growth in real estate, but a monumental increase in the urban conscience of the public. As a result, two major projects of the sixties have since been rebuilt, namely, Copley Square and the Hynes Convention Center.

The vast Christian Science complex, designed by I. M. Pei, began the development towards the south, and this was followed by the aggregate of hotels, apartment houses, and department stores revolving around Copley Place—a suburban type shopping center in the heart of Boston. Recent growth has been relatively circumspect, as there is now more of an effort to maintain the distinctive character of the area. This is immediately apparent in the addition to the Ritz and, to some degree, in the red brick bay-windowed apartment houses opposite the Public Garden, as also in the clamor which greeted the proposals of Philip Johnson and John Burgee for 500 Boylston Street.

Probably the most vital sign of new life is the opening of Back Bay Station, together with its connections to the subway and commuter lines. Its grand arch is reminiscent of the great days of railway transportation, and the renewed emphasis on mass transit, though sporadic, lends a positive prognosis to Boston's urbanity. This public aspect of the Back Bay becomes more evident day by day. A case in point is Newbury Street. Just two decades ago, the elegant street was decidedly dowdy; now, it is a lively thoroughfare extending from the Arlington Street Church to the Tower Records landmark on Massachusetts Avenue. Cafés line the sidewalks as strollers cruise its length on summer nights. Cross streets reveal the massive Hynes Auditorium, and when a convention is in session lights from its upper stories cast a glow over the entire Back Bay.

Development up until 1990 proceeded at an accelerated pace; buildings were erected in all sizes and for all purposes, particularly residential and commercial. Some projects are still underway. None is more ambitious than the projected reconstruction of the Prudential Center; what failed to become a monumental multipurpose complex in the sixties will perhaps be given another chance.

Opposite: View from Charles River towards the New England and Hancock

49
John Hancock Tower

John Hancock Place, Copley Square
I. M. Pei & Partners (Henry N. Cobb,
design partner), 1968–75

Back in 1975, the 60-story slab seemed to
be the perfect swan song to the American
skyscraper. Who would have thought that
it was only the beginning? What once
appeared to be the fulfillment of the 1920s
vision of the glass tower was beset by
structural problems largely caused by its
shape, its site, and the barely perceptible
mullions that supported the glass panes.
Legal battles were in progress before the
building's completion, and these were
soon succeeded by agreements to "refrain
'in perpetuity' from any public discussion
of the building's problems." Recently,
lapses in engineering technology have
been revealed by William Le Messurier
("Learning from the Hancock", *Architecture*, March 1988): in the first place, the
wind-testing was insufficient, risking
total collapse, and effects of gravity were
not adequately reckoned with. However,
the "vulnerable narrow side" was
strengthened and faulty windows

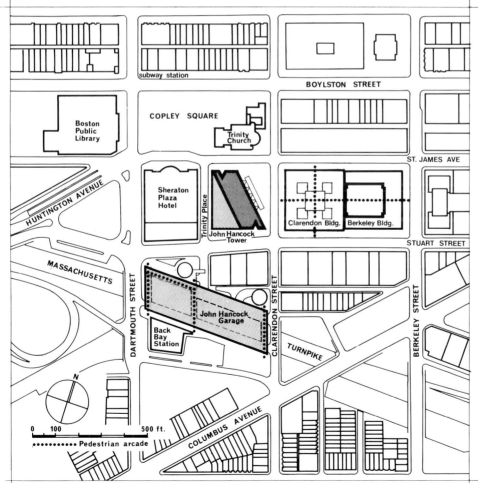

replaced by double-layered ones with reflective glass, framed with anodized aluminum. With hindsight, we now realize that the architect's vision went beyond available technology, and could not benefit from the testing methods and building codes so commonplace today.

At present, the entry plaza on Clarendon Street seems too large, the canopy too heavy and insufficiently integrated with the mass of the building. However, the lobby is beyond expectations. One cannot but respond with delight to its subtle grandeur, made manifest by the impressive chrome columns, the shades of gray with red details, the supergraphics announcing the elevator floors, the luxurious leather banquettes, and the most conspicuous décor of all, Old Glory with fifteen stars at one end and a banner "By the name of Hancock" at the other. The mirrored wall rising above quasi-futuristic domed entries (now replaced by glass pyramids) set on a granite plaza proclaims the poetry of the modern city. A resolution of opposites is at play – the illusion of the past, the relatively immutable presence of Trinity Church, and the ever mutable atmospheric conditions. The knife-like edge of the parallelogram is set at an angle to Copley Square, with its reflective skin paying homage to the entire city and to the forces of nature. Its apparent weightlessness sometimes yields to the clarity of its form, which overshadows that of the rival Prudential tower as a beacon in the Boston townscape. From its observation deck the visitor enjoys a panoramic view of the city, whose development can be followed by studying the 1775 model and listening to the narration of Walter Whitehill.

No one speaks more persuasively about the Hancock than its architect Henry Cobb: "The strength of the building as well as its limitation is the fact that it is so simple-minded. It is impoverished because of its simple-mindedness, but that gives it its drama. It dramatizes the predicament of this enormous thing hovering in that place. And I find that, for me, dramatizing the predicament is perhaps as legitimate a role for architecture as solving the problem."

View towards Copley Square from New Old South Church (Trinity Church and New England Life in background, Boston Public Library in foreground)

Opposite, top: Wide angle roundel of Copley Square, view east

Opposite, bottom right: Structural problems

50
Institute of Contemporary Art

955 Boylston Street
Graham Gund Architects, 1975

"Once a police and fire station shared space at No. 941–955 Boylston Street. The fire station is still there, but when the police station moved to new quarters next door, the Institute of Contemporary Art renovated the empty half of the building. Inside the Romanesque shell are art galleries and meeting rooms. The ornate tower on Hereford Street around the corner is still used for drying fire hoses." (Inscription on historic plaque)

The ICA is a pioneer among institutional conversions, and one which has been followed in domestic architecture as well. In 1885 Arthur Vinal built a police station and engine house for the city of Boston; the latter remains in use, but the police station was converted to the ICA. Its exterior retains the old "Romanesque" round-arched windows and entry, the rough-hewn brownstone at lower and smooth stone at upper levels, dark and massive but clearly articulated.

The Richardsonian facade of the old police station masks the highly modern interior of the ICA. The design itself, in color and form, involves the shaping of space characteristic of warehouse loft conversions of the seventies. Hence, the galleries with their flowing spaces, hardwood floors, exposed beam shafts, and expanses of wall are particularly suited to the display of contemporary art. Space at ground level and directly below, originally designed as a restaurant, is separated by a dynamically intricate staircase. The lower area now serves both as an additional gallery and as a gathering place, related to, but distinct from, the space above.

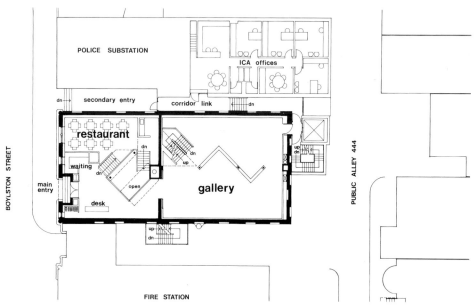

51
37 Newbury Street
(formerly Knoll International)

Gwathmey Siegel & Associates, Architects, 1980

A Bauhaus-inspired gem in the Back Bay, the former branch of Knoll International furniture design conforms to the building line of neighboring mixed commercial and residential structures, but is somewhat out of context in terms of form and fabric. Whereas the facade obeys the orig-

Stairway and gallery

inal street line, the curved display window elegantly complements the projection of the adjacent buildings.

In a play of asymmetrically ordered shapes, a harmony is achieved between the convex curve of the street-level storefront and the strong horizontal lintel of the first story. Balancing the vertical stairwell of glass blocks rising the height of the building at right are the horizontal window strips of the three upper office stories. This crisp, taut design bespeaks the architectural vocabulary of the twenties as exemplified by the International Style, and revived in the seventies by a group of architects, including Charles Gwathmey, who sought to counteract the encroaching pluralism. In recent times, the white stucco so gleaming in the photos has become buff-colored in reality, with the jointings now frayed at the edges. Once, the aluminum bands and Knoll letters conveyed the power of modernism – and gave proof, if needed, that good design contributes to the complex harmony of this particular street. Any doubts concerning the success of 37 Newbury may vanish if comparison is evoked with 399 Boylston – a paradigm (and parody) of contemporary contextualism.

52
Back Bay Hilton

40 Dalton Street
Irving Salsberg & Associates, Inc., 1982

Dalton Street is a chronological and architectural dividing line between two major developments in the Back Bay. On the east side lies the area developed from the mid-1950s onwards, known as the Prudential Center complex. To the west and south is the rehabilitation project undertaken in the late 1960s for the Christian Science Mother Church. On Dalton Street, these two major developments are reflected in the Sheraton and Hilton hotels. Just as the Sheraton reiterates the scale, massing, materials, and detailing of the Prudential Center complex, the Hilton is one of the last repetitions of the concrete formula of the nearby Christian Science Church development. Both hotels are pale reflections of their prototypes.

The Hilton is a 25-story cast concrete tower of a triangular plan with an attached parking garage on Belvedere Street. A three-story trapezoidal-plan wing on Dalton Street contains the lobby, restaurant, and other facilities. The sculptural potential of the three-sided mass is blunted by the small openings, containing minimal mass-produced windows. Both the Hilton and Sheraton hotels assume subsidiary service relationships to the adjacent Hynes Auditorium; as such, they quickly become background buildings in this mid-rise district of the city.

53
Ritz-Carlton Addition

Arlington Street and Commonwealth
Avenue
Skidmore, Owings & Merrill, 1981

An addition to the Back Bay Historic District as large as the Ritz-Carlton expansion naturally aroused the interest and fears of preservationists and neighborhood advocates. Therefore, this structure received the scrutiny and frequent alterations that committees always produce. The result is a caricatured rendition of the elegant 1927 Ritz-Carlton Hotel by Strickland, Blodget & Law. SOM repeated the

View from Public Garden; Equestrian statue of Georg
Washington (Thomas Ball, 1869)

basic envelope – a thirteen-story tower with penthouse, and the color of materials – red brick for the mass with two-story granite base and granite corner pavilions. The building contains a basement-level garage, the hotel ballroom at the second level, new hotel rooms on the fourth through seventh floors and condominium apartments above, called Carlton House and reached through a Commonwealth Avenue entrance.

The building expresses a tension between old and new. The fine detailing of the old Ritz has been reduced to flat surfaces; the new tower is a modernist box with a veneer of brick, angular, projecting window bays of aluminum and glass, and recessions for bandcourses in place of projecting cornices. Least successful are the bay windows of the second level, which project on the Commonwealth Avenue facade to relate to the neighboring

houses but are suppressed within the wall-plane on Arlington Street to suggest the richly detailed windows of the old building's main dining room. Nevertheless, for its date the new Ritz was attempting to confront its physical and functional context in an honest and direct manner. Viewing it from any angle, we recognize the homage it pays to its more distinguished neighbor.

54

399 Boylston Street

CBT/Childs Bertman Tseckares &
Casendino, Inc., 1982–84

Within the context of a traditional Back Bay street, this office building is generally considered noteworthy for the manner in which its bulk is minimized. Still, there seems to be little relationship between the new structure and the adjacent eight-story Warren Chambers Building (1896), which was once occupied by medical offices and was rehabilitated as part of this project. Here is your prototypical postmodern building of limestone veneer and brick, with a glut of bay windows and a crowning "penthouse" of round arches fronting a heavy glass curtain wall box, set back and rising to thirteen stories. However, this upper glass wall is far too prominent, especially when viewed as a backdrop for the handsome spire of the Arlington Street Church. Designed to echo the brick vernacular of the Back Bay townhouses, a glance at its turn-of-the-century neighbor will put its "contextual taste" into question. While bringing the Back Bay into the competitive office market, 399 Boylston manages to maintain the vitality of the area by the generous glass shopfronts at street level. The interior lobby is sustained by brick walls and a convex aluminum-faced balcony. This convexity is the main feature of 425 Boylston Street, a nine-story building now under construction by the same architects. On a narrow plot, six stories are composed of single elliptical bays, with due emphasis given to the entry. In its present state, it seems perfectly suitable to accommodate a discreet parking garage.

View along Boylston Street towards Arlington Street Church

55
One Exeter Plaza

Jung Brannen Associates, Inc., 1984

Someone dubbed this fourteen-story office tower the Darth Vader Building, giving it perhaps an undeserved notoriety. Unfortunately, its site directly across from the Philip Johnson addition to the Boston Public Library is strategic. So much is objectionable, and pretentiously so, from a design point of view that it is difficult to know where to begin. Decidedly awkward is the green-tinted glass-enclosed attic roof, especially as it reaches obtrusive heights when turning the corner. Almost as disturbing is the rhythm produced by the projecting bays, seemingly tacked on, that extend the entire length of the building. And, in the three-story lobby, we are overwhelmed by the superabundance of marble panels in monochromatic brown tones arrayed in rectilinear patterns, the expensive but dull void created by the too grand space, and the indeterminate below ground level area, where a ficus tree now serves as the lone adornment.

Here is a building that completely violates the fabric of the Back Bay, and, more specifically, of Boylston Street. In terms of its height, mass, and materials, this bully overpowers the entire block. Seen against the picturesque New Old South Church on the Dartmouth Street corner, which gently joins the narrow four- and five-story commercial structures, the east brick facade with its opaque glass attic is too dominant. Nothing can redeem the gross articulation of this building, especially in an area graced by the late nineteenth-century masterpieces bordering on Copley Square.

Boylston Street facade

Lobby

56
Church Court Condominiums

490 Beacon Street
Graham Gund Architects, 1983

Ruins are often romantic, but here the remains of the Mount Vernon Church, largely destroyed by fire in 1978, are uncomfortably juxtaposed with a cluster of condominium towers. At a major intersection, Beacon Street and Massachusetts Avenue, the stone tower, gabled openings, and triple-arched entry of the neo-Romanesque church front the Church Court development. In order to evoke the rich past of the Back Bay, the architect-developer created 43 units in an odd melange of quadrilateral turrets and convex window bays, which supposedly echo the fenestration, brick patterns, and polychromatic details of neighboring structures. However, it is all rendered in a higher key: the bricks are too red, the balustrades too green, the skyline too complex, the contrast between the stone

Opposite: Courtyard

View along Massachusetts Avenue

lintels and general surfaces too strong. Glass pyramidal forms on the roofline as well as the open-framed skyline give hints of modernity. Set around a verdant court, whose landscape was designed by Carol Johnson Associates, the whole retains the aspect of a church close. Perhaps with time, its patina will be in harmony with its surroundings.

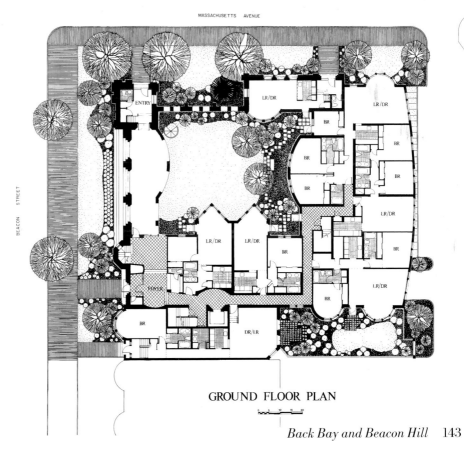

GROUND FLOOR PLAN

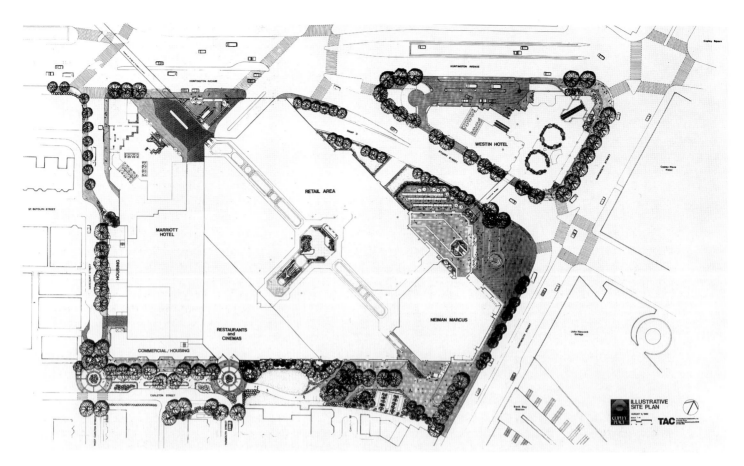

View from Huntington Avenue towards Prudential Tower

57
Copley Place

Copley Square
The Architects Collaborative, 1980–84

On the site once occupied by S. S. Pierce, in the heart of the Back Bay, this luxury designed suburban-type mall comprises 9.5 acres, and the air rights above the Massachusetts Turnpike, Copley Square exit, and the railroad tracks. Bordered by Huntington, Dartmouth, and Stuart streets, the 3.7-million-square-foot complex is "the largest single-phase private development in New England history" – the whole bounded by the Westin Hotel and the Marriott Hotel at east and west ends respectively. Neiman-Marcus with its frontage on three sides sets the appropriate tone for the high-style aspect of the place. Within, passages connect the hotels and the multi-use complex associated with the Prudential Tower. Sculptor Dimitri Hadzi's glistening waterfall, composed of a variety of granite, travertine, and rare stones, acts as a lively setpiece at the core of the complex, no less a natural meeting place. Branching off from this center are cinema compounds, elegant shops, restaurants and cafés, banks, and all manner of boutiques and services, including underground parking, and offices above the two main levels, extending to limited housing in a low-rise building. Glass-enclosed skywalks span the streets, resulting in an enormous climate-controlled area.

A two-story glass grid facade marks the entry to Copley Place at the Westin Hotel. Situated at a precarious traffic junction (Dartmouth and St. James streets, the gateway of the "Mass Turnpike Points West"), a six-story lower volume envelops the high-rise irregular tower. Bands of striped dark and light pebble aggregate separate the rows of windows, creating a travesty of modernism. The turnpike wall of the hotel is marked by wide bay windows with lateral recessions, a slight improvement on the flat facades visible from Copley Square. Access to the Westin is hardly usual: escalators and stairs ascend to the main floor, while roaring waterworks pour forth from jets set into the overhanging marble-veneered balconies, adorned with the predictable plantings; a star hexagonal ceiling introduces us to the general glitter of the hotel, which does provide a free, sheltered, and often welcome passageway to the shopping area. The main entry to the latter is on Stuart and Dartmouth streets, a glass-enclosed atrium-like stairwell alongside Neiman-Marcus. On the exterior, uncomfortable iron spring benches are set within the wide brick plaza, whose center is dominated by two bronze horses on a circular stepped podium, a type of public art that does encourage a fair amount of activity, especially for children.

Although the architecture, dominated by precast concrete facades, is undistinguished, Copley Place is the product of long and careful deliberation. Tunney Lee, professor of architecture at MIT, headed a Citizens Review Committee composed of different groups representing different interests – lawyers from the Back Bay, activists from the South End, city-wide architects and planners, and scores of concerned local residents. They considered questions of circulation, height, density, and housing, as well as land use and design criteria. Thus, the developers, the Urban Investment and Development Company, were legally committed to take account of guidelines suggested by the community before putting their grand scheme into operation. *Architectural Record* (August 1986) praised the democratic process enacted here, as also the "urban quality" of the complex. However, a mall is essentially a non-urban mode and Copley Place is no exception. In a typical Boston cold wave, convention goers staying in contingent hotels are content to promenade on the rich stone pavement of the galleries, without ever venturing forth into the city.

Atrium with fountain by Dimitri Hadzi

58
Four Seasons Hotel and Condominiums

200 Boylston Street
WZMH Group, 1985

The Four Seasons and the State Transportation Building, both completed in 1985, share the honor in leading the revitalization of the Park Square district of the city. Capitalizing upon the views over the Public Garden, the Four Seasons comprises a twelve-story hotel with its entrance on Boylston Street and a fifteen-story condominium tower with a smaller entrance from Hadassah Way. An unassuming structure in red brick and glass, the building provides a bridge between the simple, sculptural masses of the State Transportation Building to the east and the more detailed Heritage on the Garden to the west. In other ways, however, the building is determinedly antiurban: the entrance is designed for cars, not people; and to reach the main doors one must cross the traffic of the entrance driveway that is pulled into the mass of the building along Boylston Street. While the generous lobby and circulation areas create successful public spaces, the historicist interiors of the Four Seasons Hotel seem out of character with the stark appearance of the exterior.

A landscaped plaza behind the hotel forms a new public place opposite the statue of Lincoln emancipating the slaves (Thomas Bell, 1874), the historical focus for Park Square. The ultimate character of the revived area will be determined by the construction of The Pavilion, an office and condominium structure designed by Childs, Bertman, Tseckares & Casendino, to be built on the south side of Park Square.

59
State Transportation Building

Stuart Street between Tremont and Charles streets
Goody, Clancy & Associates, Inc., 1985

In 1975 the Commonwealth of Massachusetts decided to combine all of the state divisions and agencies dealing with transportation into one building. The result has been greater efficiency in this immense governmental entity. The block-long complex designed to house these activities has sparked the revitalization of the Park Square and theater districts and

has spurred the demise of the Combat Zone.

The Transportation Building succeeds more in urban than in architectural terms. Goody and Clancy fit the building into the heterogeneous character of the surrounding blocks through frequent breaks in plan and elevation. The street-like corridors through the center of this very large building furnish important links between the theater district, Park Square, and the Common, by way of Tremont Place. Similarly, the ground-floor shops along Stuart Street and the multi-level interior atrium provide life for the occupants of the building and the surrounding neighborhood. Called Cityplace, the commercial and service facilities of the Transportation Building were orchestrated by a private development firm in partnership with the state. The day and night vitality of this structure is reinforced by the performance space at the center of the atrium, the Artists Foundation Gallery, the day-care center for the transportation workers' children, and the Transportation Library. Below grade, the building contains parking for 275 cars and an innovative heating and cooling system fueled solely by the excess heat generated in the building. Here, the infrastructure and mechanical support systems are logically distributed in a color-coded design.

Aerial view with Transportion Building in center foreground

60
855 Boylston Street

The Architects Collaborative, 1986

From the architectural firm that was the original standard-bearer of international modernism in Boston, 855 Boylston is a building that speaks in the language of the Victorian revival. The twelve-story structure echoes the mid-nineteenth-century architecture of the Back Bay through its brick-red mansard roof, its semicircular bay windows, and its panel brickwork. Yet

this overscale townhouse manages effectively to triple the height of its four-story models. The domestic features and the proliferation of balconies, however, make one believe that this office building must certainly be an apartment structure. The monumental postmodern central balcony and competing horizontal breaks that announce multiple "tops" to the building complicate the street facade.

Like most recent Boston commercial architecture, 855 Boylston gives special emphasis to the lobby. The black and white marble floor and the black, white

and silver wall treatment bear no relationship to the exterior of the building. Nevertheless, the lobby remains one of the most pleasant and restrained of these recent commercial setpieces, especially when contrasted with the gaudy marble lobbies designed by Jung Brannen.

61
Newbury Street Housing
(Prince School)

201 Newbury Street
Sharky/Grassi, 1986

Built in 1875 by George Clough, this building has been recycled for condominiums and shops. The original roof had long since been decapitated when the third story was added. Attempting to follow the existing street pattern of set-back houses, the renovation is mindful of the once occupied stoops, with the planted areas between sidewalks and storefronts. Considering the severity of the whole, the projecting two-story bay windows are a bit too prominent. Details are self-conscious: the brownstone lintels, the buff and gray wood framing, and, above all, the arched attic windows on Exeter and Newbury streets, as also the projecting shop fronts. Tasteful graphics are wanting; one would have hoped for a higher level of artistic display than is now in evidence. Even though the old street layout has been retained, there is too great a distance between the pedestrian preserve and the building line. More astute attention to landscaping could mitigate these defects.

Exterior in the nineteenth century

62

Back Bay Station

Dartmouth and Clarendon streets
Kallmann, McKinnell & Wood
Architects, Inc., 1987

Boston's Back Bay Station, originally built in 1897 as part of the old New York, New Haven and Hartford line, was destroyed by fire in 1928. Rebuilt a year later, it had reached a sufficiently decrepit state by the time it closed in 1979. Few would have envisioned, a decade ago, its present resurrection as a symbolic gateway to the city. Grand arches of rust-colored laminated wood reach to a height of forty feet to span an entry to the station and its main concourse between Dartmouth and Clarendon streets. Recalling late nineteenth-century railroad sheds, the concourse receives an abundance of natural light, which pours in from the glass block clerestory windows. The side passages bordering on the great hall have been likened to the aisles of a Roman basilica. Changes in scale and variations in materials (the double glass block windows between the spanning arches) add to the excitement of the interior.

On each side of the entrance extend porticos articulated by heavy red and black brick piers, with blind arches expressed in concrete; fine linear patterns separate the bays. Perhaps the most prominent feature is the striated brick tower in the parking lot behind the station. Its monumentality belies the function of this ventilation stack, crowned with a trussed

pediment and standing on a granite base that doubles as a seating area. Details in the waiting-room and ticket lobby are also intricate, even redundant; here massive granite seats repeat the circular shapes of lighting domes above steel-beamed lights, the whole interspersed between concrete mushroom columns. Dominating this area is a bronze seated statue of A. Philip Randolph (1889–1979), labor leader and fighter for civil rights.

Less apparent immediately is the engineering feat accomplished in the construction: the depression of the railroad bed below the water table called for a slurry wall technique ("reinforced steel is

lowered into slurry-filled trenches; concrete is then poured in replacing the mud-like slurry"), by now in common use in the renovation of the MBTA system.

New perspectives are discovered at every angle, such as the dull facade of Neiman-Marcus upon emerging at the Dartmouth Street main exit, the lively three-quarter-mile park behind Copley Place, built above the transit tunnel, or the housing complex of Tent City. Back Bay Station succeeds in integrating modernism with context to create an appropriately monumental structure.

How did this enormous transformation come about? Conceived at a time when

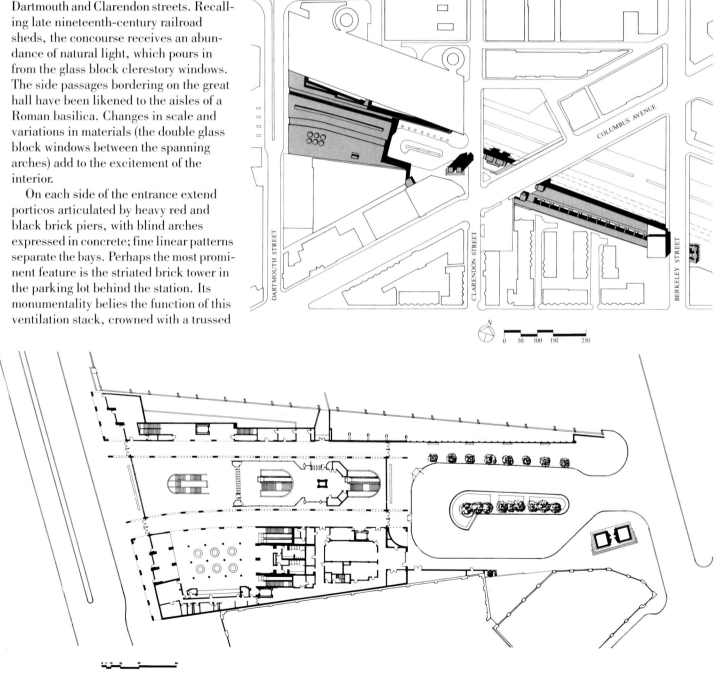

the tide was turning away from the building of expressways, Boston received a welcome federal grant for a public transit project along the Southwest Corridor. Included in the station project were such connective links as an arcade to the Hancock garage and an underpass to Copley Place, whose glass block windows enable us to see the trains whiz by in cinematic-like frames. The station now functions as an "intermodal" transportation center, comprising interstate (Amtrak), intrastate (commuter lines), and local (subway) transportation, the latter being a terminus on the newly refurbished Orange Line.

63
The New England

Phase I, 500 Boylston Street
John Burgee Architects with Philip
Johnson, 1989

Phase II, 222 Berkeley Street
Robert A. M. Stern Architects, 1989–

No structure in the Back Bay since the
Hancock has aroused a greater outcry
among public, press, and local landmarks
commissions than these two 20- and
25-story towers – a major project of Gerald
D. Hines Interests and New England Life.
Concerns initially focused on environmental problems, such as the shadows the
buildings would cast on their surroundings. Recently, criticism has shifted to
questions of style.

Why the protest? As part of the expanding commercial development of the Back
Bay, the projected towers occupying a full
block were to be in harmony with the red
brick facades characteristic of neighboring streets. Few people were prepared for
the flamboyance of Johnson's building, its
conspicuous arched skyline, its copper
barrel vault, its monumental forecourt, its
overwhelming street entries, and its undeniable presence alongside Trinity Church.
Dramatic elements are striking, not least
the high entry-arch on St. James Street, a
weak pastiche of the same architect's
postmodern manifesto in the AT & T building in New York. Aesthetically, this high
profile building is wanting. The surface
seems to be all veneer – flat slabs of
marble granite and factory sash windows, in such abundance that we may well
say more window than wall. The windows
are over defined by steel grid frames,
while blind panels conceal the floor
levels. Rose and gray granite form a pavement pattern that is transformed to black
and white marble on the interior, which,
not surprisingly, abounds in glistening
stones. The double-columned arcade
defining the grand theatre-like hemicycle
may achieve closure, but the composition
is weak. Little uncertainty, however, mars
the clear identification on the lintel
announcing FIVE HUNDRED, the corporate affiliation assumed. At ground level
the ample exedra, replete with café setting backed by fountains and flora, has
already proven its success as a vibrant
public space. Only an ingrate could cavil
at a mid-day repast accompanied by a
brass band and lavishly flowing fountains
under sunlit skies.

Quite in keeping with Johnson's recent
works, there are too many historical references, as also a surfeit of variations on
local themes: arcades, window articulation, and decorative details such as balustrades, urns, lanterns, and diaper brickwork pattern are all around in the Old
New England, the Berkeley Building, the
Boston Public Library, and Trinity
Church. Where is the principle of selec-
tion that might justify contextualism?

Dissatisfaction with Johnson's building
was so rampant that for the second tower
at 222 Berkeley, a revised design was
commissioned from Robert Stern with
Jung Brannen. Far less daring, Stern's
proposal is more in line with traditional
Georgian Revival, with the red brick and
white stone embellishment characteristic
of the nearby Ritz. A skylit winter-garden
on the second story will host public
events, while a pedestrian arcade at

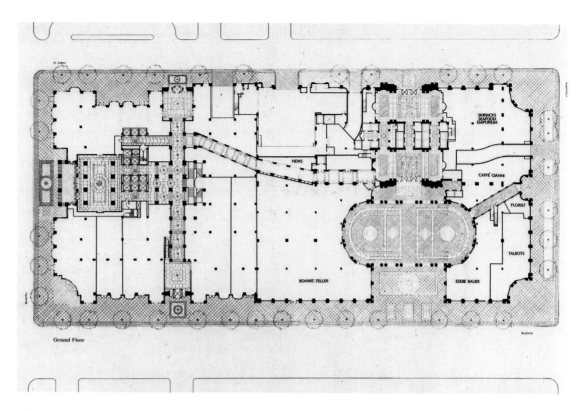

Ground Floor

ground level provides access from Boylston to St. James.

For reasons not completely obvious, Johnson's building has been damned and Stern's praised for its relative discretion and its harmony with the fabric of the old Back Bay, specifically its recesses and bay windows (in lieu of its neighbor's block-like larger mass). Essentially a pastiche of the classic early skyscraper, it has a six-story base surmounted by a block of wide-windowed offices. Above, a setback two-story colonnade beneath a row of oculi supports a mansard roof, in some ways echoing the trapezoidal form of the old New England Life. The entry on 222 Berkeley Street and the tripartite division of the facade will, it is claimed, strengthen the urban quality of the design. Both buildings have looked more to the language of the past than to the exigencies of the present.

Opposite: New England Life: 222 Berkeley Street and 500 Boylston Street. In foreground, Louis; in background, Hancock (Rendering by Frank Costantino)

500 Boylston Street, plaza at night

64
Berkeley Building

420 Boylston Street
Original: Codman & Despradelle, 1909
Re-use: Notter, Finegold + Alexander,
1988

With the departure of Boston's interior
designers to the Design Center in South
Boston, the Berkeley Building became
available for rehabilitation. In 1905, Codman & Despradelle had created here a
terra cotta and glass confection totally out
of line with the conservative local taste in
public architecture. Désiré Despradelle,
design professor from 1893 to 1912 at MIT
(then located diagonally across Boylston

Street), had provided his adopted city
with a new model for commercial architecture worthy of his native Paris.

Notter, Finegold & Alexander have
restored the fanciful terra cotta ornamentation to a seductive brilliance and have
used the surviving metal and wood storefronts as inspiration for a reworking of the
ground-floor facades along Boylston
Street. The main entrance on this street
has been elaborately opened with its Art
Nouveau-type frontispiece. Within, the
original corridor and modified stairwell
lead to an atrium where office windows
and hallways surround a glass-roofed
court with new white glazed tile walls.
When first constructed, the building's
ephemeral and flamboyant exterior

created a startling impact on Boston's
business world: glittering white commercial palaces began to rise along Washington Street, Boylston Street, and elsewhere. Now, the successful restoration of
the exterior of the Berkeley Building is
being matched by the rehabilitation and
expansion of 745 Boylston Street. Both
projects should inspire greater appreciation for the rich Boston heritage of early
twentieth-century glazed terra cotta commercial architecture.

65
Heritage on the Garden

300 Boylston Street
The Architects Collaborative, 1988

Overlooking the Public Garden on
Boylston Street from the corner of
Arlington Street, the Heritage is a
paradigm of the recent retro mode. Part of
the development of the Park Plaza area,
this twelve-story mixed use building
contains luxury condominiums, offices,
restaurants, shops, and a health club.
A promotional brochure cites "custom-
made European . . . with gadgets, jacuzzis
and bidets, a style usually only encoun-
tered in great homes of an earlier era." At

first, we might see an exterior whose materials relate to the type of apartment house
that comprised the main stock of the twenties and thirties, in harmony with an elegant Back Bay vernacular. On closer
inspection, however, the general massing
of the building reveals a complexity
characteristic of the eighties. The bisymmetrical composition is masked by an
intricate series of setbacks in the upper
stories. Hanging gardens would enhance
the facade, and it is indeed likely that
plantings will soon emerge behind the
grilled iron railings of the terraces; greenery would soften the overwhelming brick,
limestone, and granite veneers, as well as
the overly complex fenestration patterns —
curved and angled, whole and fractured,

grouped and isolated, plain and bordered. From this plethora of details we
turn to the earlier buildings with renewed
admiration for their relative candor and
clarity.

The Providence Street facade with its
window frames of white wood is more modest, its entry more accessible. Like the
nearby Ritz, the Heritage on the Garden,
as its name implies, is designed to
acknowledge the presence of Boston's
past.

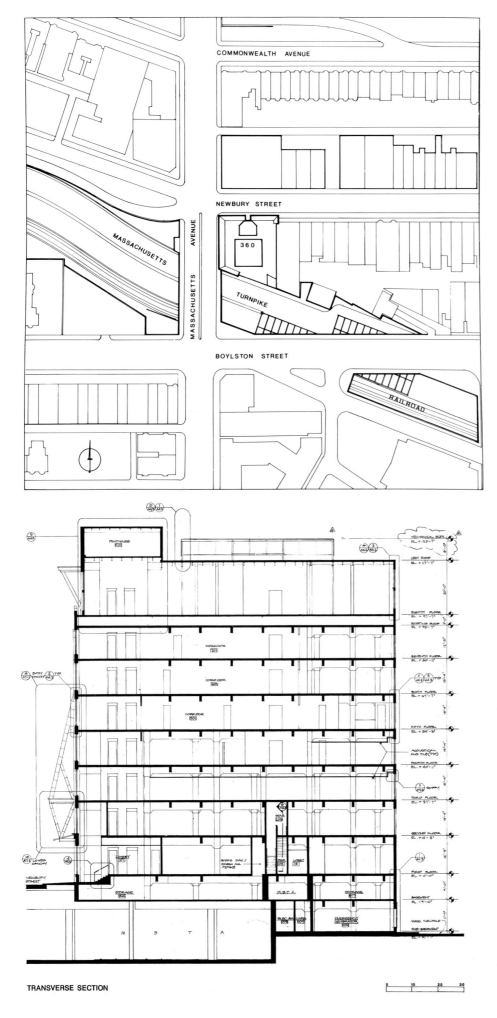

TRANSVERSE SECTION

0   10   20   30

66

Tower Records

360 Newbury Street
Original: Arthur Bowditch, 1918
Conversion: Frank O. Gehry Associates
with Schwartz/Silver Architects Inc.,
1987

This once ordinary seven-story commercial structure on Massachusetts Avenue spanning the Turnpike was formerly occupied by the MBTA. Frank Gehry marks his debut in Boston with a variation on his most popular theme – a building within a building. An old concrete-frame and buff brick warehouse with bas-relief patterns on the lintels has been restructured with an additional story formed by diagonal metal struts projecting upwards from the original roofline. As a counterbalance to the upper profile, similar struts protrude from the second story to form a canopy over the ground floor. This steel-frame marquise also spans the entry to the Massachusetts Avenue subway, and forms a protective area for a major bus stop. Pink granite is the keynote of the ground floor, the whole forming an odd cacophony in the true Gehry manner. Unexpected elements continue on the Boylston Street side, where two bays of brick suddenly metamorphose into a gray lead-coated copper facade, its planes joining to form a disparate whole with green framed windows – the upper right corner to be enhanced by a Claes Oldenburg teabag, a pop reminder of the Boston Tea Party. The whole is offbeat, but conveys an undeniable strength, and with its dramatic night lighting the building has become both a town and a turnpike landmark.

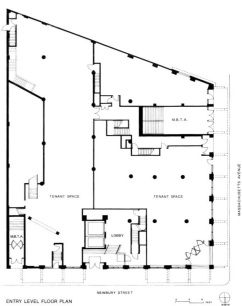

ENTRY LEVEL FLOOR PLAN

Defining the corner of Newbury Street and Massachusetts Avenue, the entry to Tower Records is separate from that to the building's offices, which are reached through the small but opulent lobby on Newbury Street: the receptionist sits against the birchwood-paneled wall behind an angular configuration of finely grained marble – a Gehry desk, poised on a matching blue granite floor. The store interior is pure warehouse, boasting the largest record collection in New England. Each floor is characterized by the rhythm and décor appropriate for the particular music it features. Art galleries and related enterprises will occupy the upper stories.

The true power of the structure, with its weighty steel brackets and metal cladding, is perhaps most apparent in the view from the southeast. It is a perfect Gehry site, for the building looms above the Turnpike and seems to coexist harmoniously alongside the latter's chain link fence and the mechanical equipment of the adjoining subway station, with its open grilled roof. At a distance we cannot but admire the articulation of the rectilinear fenestration, the fine balance between the projecting struts and the indentations of the roofline, the force of the gray lead panels, all of which evoke historical elements in the most subtle manner. Tower Records succeeds as an extraordinary modern composition, being of our time, yet perpetuating the memory of older times.

Tower Records prior to conversion
Background: Richard Haas mural at left; Prudential Tower at right

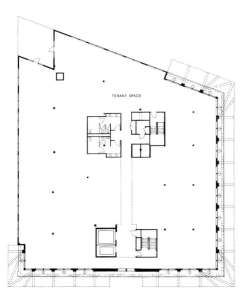

8th FLOOR PLAN

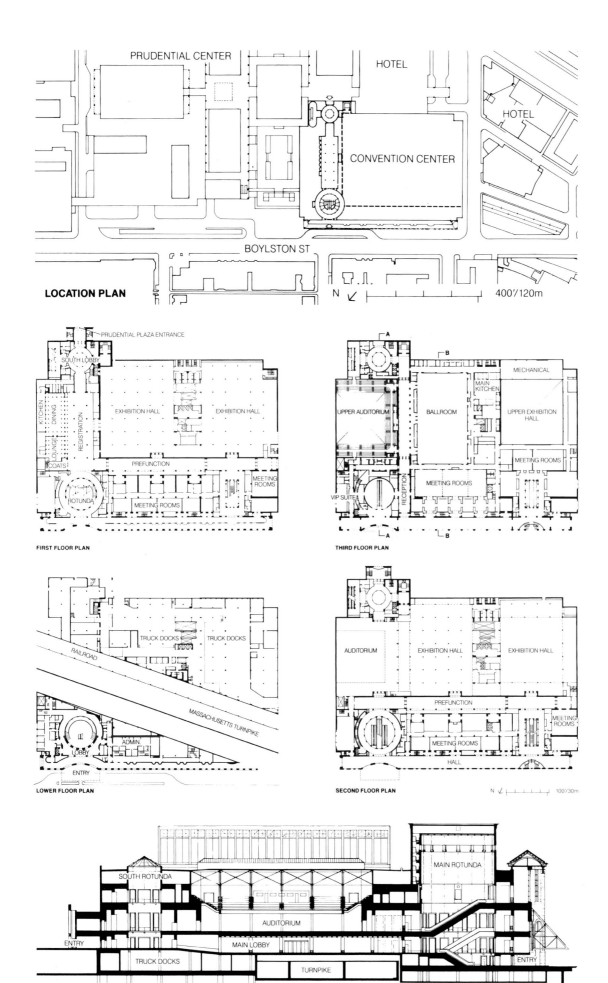

LOCATION PLAN

PRUDENTIAL CENTER

HOTEL

HOTEL

CONVENTION CENTER

BOYLSTON ST

N

400'/120m

FIRST FLOOR PLAN

PRUDENTIAL PLAZA ENTRANCE

SOUTH LOBBY

KITCHEN

DINING

LOUNGE

COATS

REGISTRATION

ROTUNDA

EXHIBITION HALL

EXHIBITION HALL

PREFUNCTION

MEETING ROOMS

MEETING ROOMS

THIRD FLOOR PLAN

A

B

MECHANICAL

MAIN KITCHEN

UPPER AUDITORIUM

BALLROOM

UPPER EXHIBITION HALL

MEETING ROOMS

VIP SUITE

RECEPTION

MEETING ROOMS

A

B

LOWER FLOOR PLAN

RAILROAD

TRUCK DOCKS

TRUCK DOCKS

MASSACHUSETTS TURNPIKE

ADMIN.

LOBBY

ENTRY

SECOND FLOOR PLAN

AUDITORIUM

EXHIBITION HALL

EXHIBITION HALL

PREFUNCTION

MEETING ROOMS

MEETING ROOMS

MEETING ROOMS

HALL

N

100'/30m

SOUTH ROTUNDA

MAIN ROTUNDA

AUDITORIUM

ENTRY

MAIN LOBBY

ENTRY

TRUCK DOCKS

TURNPIKE

SECTION AA THROUGH AUDITORIUM AND ROTUNDAS

67
John B. Hynes Veterans Memorial Convention Center

900 Boylston Street
Original: Charles Luckman and
Associates and Hoyle, Dovan and Berry,
begun 1959
Expansion: Kallmann, McKinnell &
Wood Architects, Inc., 1985–89

In 1982 the Massachusetts Convention
Center Authority decreed the enlarge-
ment of the Hynes Auditorium, that massive faceless structure completed in 1965.
The motivation was strictly economic,
namely, to make Boston one of the leading
convention centers in the country, and
thus add to the general financial prosperity of the city. Since the original Hynes
was built the area has accumulated an
enormous support system for this activity:
three major hotels; the Prudential shopping, commercial and residential center;
Copley Place; and, not least, the reopen-
ing of the Back Bay station, with the restoration of commuter lines and ancillary
transportation facilities.

Twice as large as the old Hynes
Auditorium, the new center can accommodate 22,000; it features five exhibition
halls, 38 meeting rooms, an auditorium,
an escalator bank under a cylindrical
saucer-topped dome, and a four-story
rotunda with links to the Prudential plaza.
Unlike in most concrete-clad convention
centers, interior meeting rooms are wood
paneled, a ballroom has a barrel vaulted
ceiling, a corridor is a tour-de-force of
illusionistic perspective. Its principal
space, the upper-story loggia, commands
an impressive vista of the Back Bay.

Architecturally, the main transformation has been effected by the erection of a
longitudinal pavilion extending along the
entire axis of Boylston Street from the Prudential to Dalton Street. The rationale is
clearly stated on the presentation drawing, which reveals an addition attached to
the main complex, almost like a Renaissance shell encapsulating an older building. Its principal facade is composed of
gray granite-veneer slabs, separated by
quasi-rusticated rose lintels that continue
around the building. The buff-colored
walls on the east and west facades are
marked by an overall grid, terminating in
rustic quoins and punctuated by stone
stringcourses. This simple but intricate
pattern conceals the windowless exhibition spaces of the building and retains

traces of the old structure's original bays.
In effect, the predominant traditional granite gives way to recessed large glass windows and steel plate girders at the upper
story – reminiscent on the exterior of the
arcuated fenestration of the Boston Public
Library's main reading-room, creating a
space that forms an ideal meeting corridor
and is cognizant of the city at the same
time. The glass-enclosed hall on Boylston
Street occupies the upper two stories of
the pavilion, beneath the roof cornice.

Some of the design decisions are
subtle, almost puzzling. Whereas the
long covered stepped arcade along Boylston provides a rare and welcome urban
amenity, considering the extremes of local climate, it hardly responds to the exigencies of the site or the general fabric of
the city, nor is there any provision for con-

comitant activity provided by shops or
stalls. The pier articulation is delicate,
fraught with historical references; is it related to the structure behind, or is it
merely a detail to create a subtle tension
between line and mass, a kind of linear
ornament in the Renaissance mode on
a basically severe wall? Fine granite
bollards and a sophisticated series of lanterns complete the street facade.

The overhanging iron-ribbed glass marquise, the principal feature of the pavilion
facade, sounds a discordant note at first.
However, this bold canopy has been
praised as an entry "sign," as too the entrance hall within the cylindrical drum
where escalators mount towards the skylit
dome. Thus, a service element becomes a
primary formal detail. Or is this the late
twentieth-century transformation of the

celebratory all-encompassing staircase of the Paris Opera, a building distantly evoked in the complex section drawings of the Hynes? From Gloucester and Hereford streets we may be conscious of the entry's lack of symmetrical alignment, but it does mark the principal axis of the building, in line with the domed spaces behind. The functions of the building are determined by the plan, which is far more coherent than is suggested by the exterior. Clear divisions into rectilinear spaces, large and small, lavish and simple, all serve the usual activities of the modern convention.

Emphasis on the Boylston Street facade responds to the Tennis Club opposite at ground level and to Pei's geophysics tower at MIT, visible across the Charles River from the top of the main escalator. It is in this upper hall extending the length of Boylston Street that we may understand the rationale of the building – the white walls, the stone courses, the funereal oversized mahogany benches in mid-line, the floor-to-ceiling windows with white mesh draw-curtains, the surprising vistas and chambers glimpsed from near and far, the palette limited to black and white, with a dash of burgundy. A Hollywood set? Total theatre? Surely, a clue to our culture is here at hand. Looking outwards, however, there is little mystification, for the Hynes attempts to uncode the city. But does it succeed? Can a tight-security building, where admission is restricted to conventioneers, be discussed in terms of civic architecture, even if the Boylston Street facade enhances the city, especially when ablaze with lights?

Despite the questions here raised, this is without doubt a seminal structure, and an ingenious solution to a problematic assignment. In fact, the Hynes Auditorium may be considered a breakthrough in the design of a modern building type whose program actually advocates a kind of anti urbanism in the heart of cities. Rejecting the prescriptive enclosed structures of the megalopolitan convention centers, the architects have activated the facade by integrating it with the street. Since the Boston complex has become a vital part of the townscape, the visitor has a chance to "participate," however remotely, in the life of the city.

Top: View from Hereford Street

Bottom: Reception hall

68
Louis

234 Berkeley Street
Original: William Gibbons Preston, 1862
Re-use: CBT/Childs Bertman
Tseckares & Casendino, Inc., 1988–89

While the exterior of Louis's new home is a faithful restoration of William Gibbons Preston's original 1862 building for the Museum of Natural History – including a stabilization and brown-painting of the brownstone trim – the interior has been substantially recast as a supreme example of designers' architecture (interior architecture by Lea Group; interior decoration by Stedila Design). The most significant modification in the building, which from 1947 housed Bonwit Teller, has been the construction of a monumental black iron, brass and glass staircase as the focal point for the first two stories. The shop incorporates a café at the rear of the first story and a barber shop on the third level.

To appreciate the original and altered character of this building, one must ascend to the fourth floor to view the quality of Preston's stucco decoration and its rehabilitation. The interiors, here and elsewhere, have been lavishly painted with faux marble in earth tones to create the appropriate understated elegance for top-of-the-market men's and women's clothing. An outdoor oasis for the tired consumer, the re-landscaped grounds make this significant Back Bay survivor more accessible to shoppers and pedestrians. Louis's former building (Samuel Rosenberg, 1982) at 470 Boylston Street, now demolished for the second phase of the New England Life complex, was one of the first self-conscious Boston examples of postmodern classicism.

69
Grant-Hoffman Building

745 Boylston Street
CBT/Childs Bertman Tseckares & Casendino, Inc., 1987–89

CBT have here rehabilitated and expanded two early twentieth-century commercial buildings as an internally consistent office development. The restoration of the facades of these fine buildings is marred, however, by new elements, especially the clumsy functional columns that support the upper floors of the elegant 1903 structure by Clinton J. Warren, probably the first glazed terra cotta cladding in Boston. Behind and above these facades the buildings have been substantially changed. The most prominent addition is the bulbous multistory copper mansard roof on the terra cotta building, which is clearly visible from many points in the Back Bay. This

copper extravaganza is totally incongruous with the design and fabric of the structure. The smaller building has also been raised two stories, the top one set back behind a new balustraded parapet; new cast decoration has been added to this building, recognizable by the abrupt manner in which the rolled-out ornament is sliced off as needed. Access to the complex is through the central door of the terra cotta building. Chrome, wood, glazed tile and pink neon lighting give the elevator lobby a bewildering and funky appearance. At every turn one misses the level of quality inherent in the original structure.

Exterior with Copley Place

70
116 Huntington Avenue

CBT/Childs Bertman Tseckares & Casendino, Inc., 1990

For CBT, 116 Huntington Avenue marks an important turning point in their practice. As the firm's largest building in Boston to date, this office structure represents the metamorphosis of CBT from a small scale rehabilitation practice into a firm entrusted with large scale new construction, in Boston and elsewhere.

Nevertheless, 116 Huntington Avenue clearly betrays the firm's roots in preservation projects. The bulbous copper roof relates the building to CBT's renovated Grant-Hoffman Building at 745 Boylston nearby. In a neighborhood of poured con-crete and latter-day modernist boxes, their fifteen-story Huntington Avenue office building attempts to create a new richness in plasticity and materials. The polychromatic granite, enriched by carved panels, plays against the inset promenade at the base of the building and the arched and circular forms at the skyline. Whether the firm has successfully made the jump to larger projects will be evident in the near future, if a series of projects now on the boards is actually brought to completion.

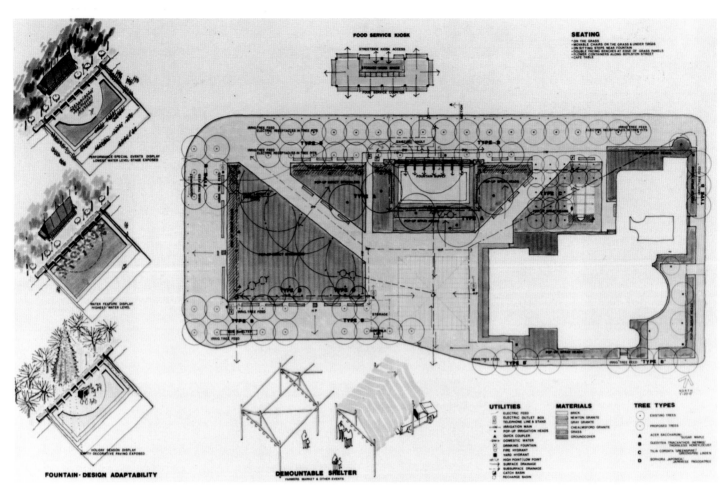

FOOD SERVICE KIOSK

SEATING
• ON THE GRASS
• MOVABLE CHAIRS ON THE GRASS & UNDER TREES
• ON SITTING STEPS NEAR FOUNTAIN
• DOUBLE FACING BENCHES AT EDGE OF GRASS PANELS
• FLOWER CONTAINERS ALONG BOYLSTON STREET
• CAFE TABLE

PERFORMANCE SPECIAL EVENTS DISPLAY
LOWEST WATER LEVEL-STAGE EXPOSED

WATER FEATURE DISPLAY
HIGHEST WATER LEVEL

HOLIDAY SEASON DISPLAY
EMPTY-DECORATIVE PAVING EXPOSED

FOUNTAIN · DESIGN ADAPTABILITY

DEMOUNTABLE SHELTER
FARMERS MARKET & OTHER EVENTS

UTILITIES
ELECTRIC FEED
ELECTRIC OUTLET BOX
TELEPHONE LINE & STAND
IRRIGATION MAIN
POP-UP IRRIGATION HEADS
QUICK COUPLER
DOMESTIC WATER
DRINKING FOUNTAIN
FIRE HYDRANT
YARD HYDRANT
HIGH POINT/LOW POINT
SURFACE DRAINAGE
SUBSURFACE DRAINAGE
CATCH BASIN
RECHARGE BASIN

MATERIALS
BRICK
NEWTON GRANITE
GRAY GRANITE
CHELMSFORD GRANITE
GRASS
GROUNDCOVER

TREE TYPES
EXISTING TREES
PROPOSED TREES
A ACER SACCHARUM
   SUGAR MAPLE
B GLEDITSIA TRIACANTHOS INERMIS
   THORNLESS HONEYLOCUST
C TILIA CORDATA GREENSPIRE
   GREENSPIRE LINDEN
D SOPHORA JAPONICA
   JAPANESE PAGODATREE

71
Copley Square

Renovation: Dean Abbott with Clarke
& Rapuano Inc., 1989

A significant node in the grid of Back Bay,
Copley Square is an admittedly difficult
site, once bordering on the railroad and
now with the turnpike at its southern and
western ends. It was cheaper land that
originally created Copley Square, and
prompted the building of its surrounding
cultural institutions. Enhanced by the
confluence of noteworthy architecture –
the remarkable quartet of the Boston Public Library, Trinity Church, the Hancock
Building, and the newly refurbished New
Old South Church – the site has been the
object of several competitions and proposals since 1893, but because of the diversity of building types, heights, materials,
and styles, a unified enclosed plaza has
been difficult to achieve. It remained a
traffic center for years, lacking sufficient
density in the immediate surroundings to
become a viable urban plaza.

Almost from its inception, the first-
place competition design of Sasaki, Dawson & DeMay (1966) was criticized for the
concrete wall that formed the north edge,

thereby clearly separating the plaza from
the surrounding streets. Yet the truncated
pyramidal form of the fountain, echoing
that atop the old New England Life, did
form a focal point. In 1983, on the occasion of the hundredth anniversary of the
2.4-acre public park, the Copley Square
Centennial Committee was formed, its
main goal being to remedy the errors of
the sixties design. This public/private collaboration representing a broad citizens'
consensus sponsored a competition for
the park's renovation. Guidelines called
for a more flexible space and such specific requirements as provisions for greenery, food, and seating, the whole to create
a "people-oriented green urban space."
Most prescriptive was the mandate to
relate the plaza to the street, taking
advantage of the block front of Boylston
Street, a true urban thoroughfare, warts
and all.

Winners among the 309 entries for the
most recent competition, architects Dean
Abbott with Clarke & Rapuano have
designed a street-level plaza that endows
the area with a more park-like aspect.
Where once concrete was dominant and
plantings were few, grass has now taken
over. Where once the sunken area posed

problems regarding security, clientele,
and maintenance, the open plan contributes to a protective feeling and, it is
hoped, to the increased usage of the
square. Provisions for seating (fixed
benches and movable chairs), a café and a
food kiosk, and diagonal paths with
ornate stone and brick patterning across
the plaza are designed to encourage natural movement, adding to the vitality of the
area.

Rows of sycamore trees planted in lat-
ticed iron grills interrupt the intricate
pavement on Boylston Street, which is
enhanced by patterns of variously colored
stones, granite, and brickwork. As seen
from either street or park, a fountain constitutes the principal ornament, its elements derived from nearby buildings.
Forming an edge on Boylston Street, with
its obelisks, niches, and wall-jets, the
austere cast stone and granite fountain
has the aspect of a memorial, though its
inscription only pays homage to local officials. Children are hardly intimidated as
they romp over its stepped retaining wall
or wade in its basin. On the park side, the
arcuated backdrop wall recalls Renaissance town fountains, which served as
troughs for horses and a public water sup-

ply. The semicircular pool appears to have been designed to incorporate both a performance space and a water theatre.

The new Copley Square is an open plaza rather than an enclosed space, an area that is linked physically and visually to the surrounding streets. A green space, the square is designed as a comfortable and congenial place with ample provision for a host of functions – for respite and relaxation, for picnic and play, for activity and contemplation. Even if it is a defensive space, Copley Square is now an urban park, as well as a welcome place of passage. Its success can only be measured by its use.

Built into the guidelines were provisions for operation and maintenance. To this end, a Copley Square Trust has been proposed, to be managed by the Boston City Parks Department in partnership with the CSCC, thus continuing the exemplary civic participation instrumental for the rebirth of the plaza.

Opposite: Site plan (original competition drawing)

Top: View towards Boylston Street and Trinity Church

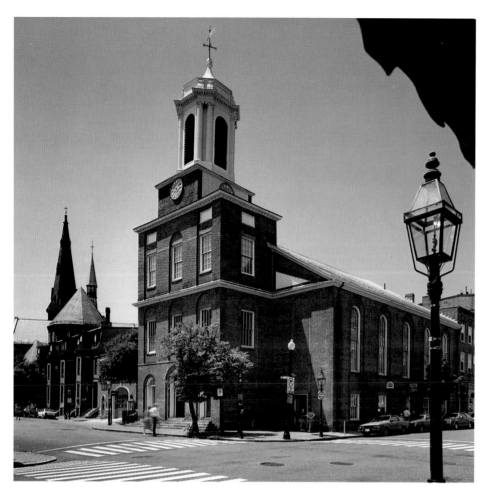

72

Charles Street Meeting House

70 Charles Street
Original: Asher Benjamin, 1804
Re-use: John Sharratt Associates, Inc.,
1982

Through the intervention of the Society for
the Preservation of New England Antiquities, the erstwhile Universalist Meeting House was converted from a redundant church into an office and retail building. The exterior was restored but not
altered, with the exception of the transformation of a basement window into a door
on Charles Street. Within, the building
was essentially gutted. Entered through
the original doors on Mount Vernon Street,
offices on the first and second levels
replace the original sanctuary. Four shops
fill the depth of the basement, with a common entrance hallway from Charles
Street. Above the office floors John Sharratt adapted the interior spaces in order to
accommodate his firm's office, creating
dramatic, beautifully lit working areas.
Residential quarters occupy a top story.

Interior (offices)

SECOND FLOOR

LOFT

73
Deutsch House

Beaver Street at Beaver Place
Graham Gund Architects, 1983

Exceptional as a new single family residence in the Beacon Hill area, the Deutsch House rises casually from the back garden of a Beacon Street townhouse. Graham Gund used existing garden walls and a one-story carriage house as the base for this two-and-one-half-story structure. The lower floor still contains a garage and service areas. The second story is distinguished by gables on four sides and a more decorative treatment. A layer of rough cast buff stucco is wrapped by widely spaced, gray-blue treillage, from which the burgundy windows and balcony door project. A module established by the scale of the window mullions

FIRST FLOOR

DEUTSCH HOUSE

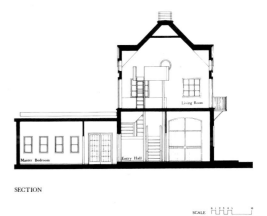

SECTION

SCALE

and latticework is counterbalanced by the circles and diamonds of the windows.

The high hipped slate roof is cropped by a skylight. A popular building with many Bostonians, the Deutsch House

quietly conceals the designation of interior space and creates a whimsical sense of character somewhat akin to the Sunflower House (Clarence Luce, 1878) nearby on Mount Vernon Street.

South End

"Thunderation," Father said, "there is a man in his shirt sleeves on those steps." The next day he sold his house for what he had paid for it and we moved to Beacon Street. Your grandfather had sensed the approach of change; a man in his shirt sleeves had told him that the days of the South End were numbered.

John P. Marquand, *The Late George Apley*, 1937

More heterogeneous demographically than architecturally, the South End has remained a distinct area of the city since its rapid development in the mid-nineteenth century.

The Washington Street corridor in the center of the South End represents the narrow neck of land that connected the Shawmut Peninsula, on which Boston was founded, to the mainland at Dorchester. Scattered development, primarily on filled land to the north and south of this spine, coalesced into a new middle-class residential district in the 1850s–70s. Already extant railroad lines formed the northern boundary of the district and created an important barrier between the South End and its slightly younger neighbor, the Back Bay, also constructed on man-made land.

Within the first two decades, it became apparent that the South End would be eclipsed as a middle-class neighborhood by the Back Bay. As the bourgeoisie moved out, the South End became the home of Boston's immigrants and a district of boarding houses converted from private family residences. Here new Americans found inexpensive lodging in deteriorated dwellings, and at the same time a sense of community with other recent immigrants. By the turn of the century, the South End was one of the most intensively inhabited urban areas in the country. Today, the South End remains ethnically mixed, with a 46% black, 34% white, 11% Asian, and 8% Hispanic population.

A new influence began to occur in the 1960s. The quality of the housing stock and the character of the loosely organized squares throughout the district were magnets for young middle class would-be homeowners who saw the depressed prices of real estate and the proximity to the Back Bay as distinct advantages. This upwardly mobile element helped to stabilize the neighborhood, but also confronted the indigenous population with the new pressure of gentrification. Since 1965, millions of federal dollars have been devoted to improvements in public facilities and streets and to new or rehabilitated housing in the district. The creation of the South End National Register Historic District (one of the largest such urban districts in the country) in 1973 and the establishment of the Boston Landmarks District in 1983 have spurred the preservation of older buildings.

Unlike the Back Bay or areas closer to the downtown district, the South End has not been the target of intensive development. In fact, new projects such as Tent City or Villa Victoria have come from "the community." The most ambitious of these community-generated initiatives has been the South End Neighborhood Housing Initiative (SENHI) to promote the development of affordable housing throughout the area. Inaugurated by the Boston Redevelopment Authority in 1986, SENHI is proposing to acquire approximately seventy South End parcels, beginning with large sites along Washington Street. Other public/private ventures have emerged, including the recent redevelopment along Massachusetts Avenue and the Douglas Plaza apartment complex along the Southwest Corridor improvement at the northern edge of the South End.

New or rehabilitated market-rate housing projects include 2 Clarendon Square, the St. Cloud rehabilitation in the Boston Center for the Arts district, and the proposals for the St. Botolph neighborhood. Non-residential development has continued along the southern edge of the district, with the slow expansion of the Boston City Hospital and University Hospital complexes.

Plans for the future focus on the Washington Street corridor, where the dismantling of the elevated Orange Line has dramatically changed the physical appearance of the heart of the district. Also, the Linkage Program, requiring developers of major downtown projects in the central city to provide funding for housing and social services throughout the city, should have a bearing on specific South End sites. The relatively slow pace of renewal may provide sufficient time for neighborhood organizations to insure that the South End of the future will maintain the variety and vitality for which it has long been known.

Opposite: View past the St. Cloud towards Union Park

74
Villa Victoria

Tremont Street at Shawmut Avenue, West Dedham and West Newton streets
John Sharratt Associates, Inc., 1972–82

Villa Victoria is a rare example of true participatory architecture, where the residents of a Puerto Rican neighborhood collaborated with urban planners and architects in the building process. Backed by local church officials, the dedicated community leaders challenged the Boston Redevelopment Authority's renewal plan.

The entire complex of about six hundred units is accessible to the urban grid, yet apart from it. Immediately noticeable on West Newton Street is the modernity of the town house at a corner; its sharply pitched roof leads to tree-lined streets with a variety of house types. A monochromatic color scheme dominated by yellow, russet, and ochre is applied to the stucco, and is pleasantly offset by the brick work, the gardens, and the greenery, all set against massive apartment blocks – six-story buildings and a high-rise for the elderly. Still, the three- and four-story row houses constitute the principal design scheme. But the aggregate on the whole is so distinct – in part due to the alterations initiated by users – that it forms an entity that strikes a discordant note in the fabric of the South End. Whereas some critics praise the development as an urban village, the row houses more nearly approach suburban tracts.

Perhaps the most successful part of the complex is the square bounded by the high-rise and the apartment blocks. The arcaded sidewalks with shops fronting the plaza suggest a southern clime, whereas the plaza itself forms an appropriate area for enacting rituals and festivities, and for formal and informal meetings. Part open and paved, part shaded and treed, with ample retaining walls and benches serving as seating areas, the plaza may double as a town center. Some details are less fortunate, such as a fountain pool filled with debris where water should be, thus calling attention to problems of maintenance.

Pressures mount to preserve this low-to-moderate housing market in an area of rapidly rising real estate values. Further, shifting social attitudes intrude: the visual separation of the architecture from the overall patterns of the South End, and the psychological distinctness fostered by the Hispanic street names. These factors may be desirable in an age stressing ethnicity, but will inevitably be less so in a succeeding generation that fosters complete integration.

Court and Houses
Arcade and high-rise apartments

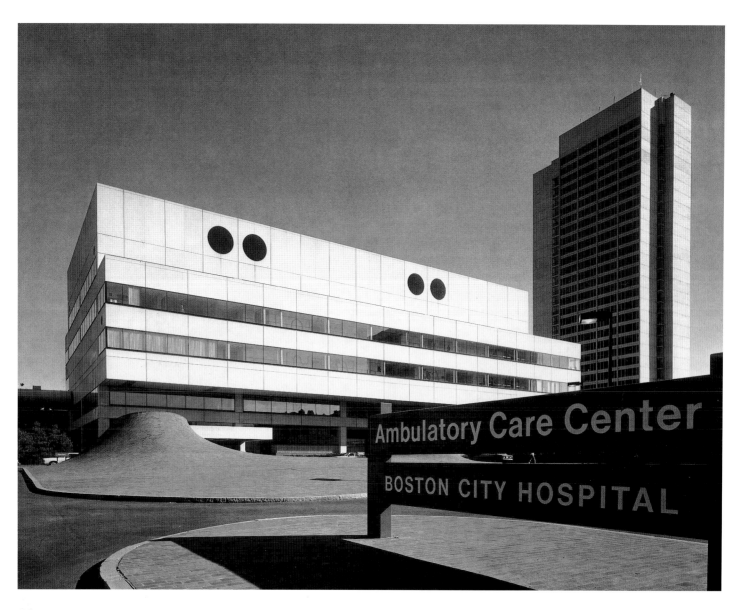

75
Outpatient Facility,
Boston City Hospital

Massachusetts and Harrison avenues
Hugh Stubbins and Rex Allen Partnership, 1977

Here is the standard large institutional
building of the sixties and seventies – concrete with glass-enclosed lobbies and
waiting rooms. Various departments are
indicated by murals relating to specific
parts of the body, visible through the glass
walls. This Bauhaus-derived structure
spans Massachusetts Avenue, with links
to medical staff housing. Two pairs of tondos, which also serve as ventilation ducts,
enliven the pre-cast concrete building
with its metal panels and broad horizontal
fenestration. Two additional air-shafts disguised as mounds rise from the brick
plaza, resulting in a rather forbidding
driveway.

76
Mechanical Plant,
Boston City Hospital

Albany Street between Springfield and
Concord streets
Hugh Stubbins and Rex Allen Partner-
ship, 1976

The Modern Movement is alive and exciting in this exemplary work. In an excellent composition the white-faced
aluminium panels are enhanced by the
large gridded-glass triangular pyramid,
which adds a lightness to the massive
structure. Beneath the cylindrical funnels
on the roofline the orange shutters form
striking complements to the long yellow
service duct that snakes through the hospital buildings above ground level, creating a not unlikely metaphor for the
technology of modern medicine. The
whole is designed to accommodate future
additions and changes.

77
Atrium Pavilion, University Hospital

88 East Newton Street
Hoskins Scott Taylor & Partners, Inc.,
1987

The Atrium Pavilion serves as the organizing element for and public entrance to the University Hospital complex. An eight-story structure of dark red pebble aggregate, the pavilion contains a three-story lobby resembling a modern hotel, leading to nursing-care units, kitchen and dining facilities for the hospital, and emergency and surgery departments. Through elevated walkways the building connects to the Evans Research Building, the doctors' office building and parking garage, and to most of the University Hospital and Medical School divisions. The Atrium Pavilion is L-shaped in plan with a canted interior angle containing the entrance. A full height glass cylinder slides down behind the entrance wall. The courtyard formed by this angle provides the pedest-

rian and vehicular entrance to the complex. Paved with red and gray cast stone blocks, the courtyard is littered with scores of poured concrete bollards that confuse, more than direct, access to the building. Once inside, an ample multi-story lobby provides a tranquil waiting area, anchored by islands of seating and plantings and surrounded by balconies, mezzanine walkways and escalators to animate the space. The soothing colors of the interior public spaces and tasteful graphics welcome the arriving patient or visitor and facilitate use of the entire hospital compound.

78
St. Cloud Building

567 Tremont Street
Original: Nathaniel J. Bradlee, 1869–70

Mystic River Bridge Building

557 Tremont Street
1879
Re-use: Arrowstreet Inc., 1987

The St. Cloud Hotel is one of the finest surviving examples of the "French flat" residential hotel type constructed in Bos-ton from the late 1850s onwards, and deemed the ancestor of the modern apart-ment building. Even the name betrays the Parisian origin of this form, in which dwellings are organized horizontally, unlike the vertical townhouses that characterize much of the South End. The St. Cloud and its adjacent brick loft struc-ture, the so-called Mystic River Bridge Building, have been rehabilitated as housing to benefit the nearby Boston Center for the Arts. Both buildings were partially restored and additional stories added – a penthouse level between the two towers of the St. Cloud and three stories to the top of its brick neighbor. Retail and gallery space in the base of both buildings has served as an important magnet for activity in the area dominated by the Boston Center for the Arts. The developers did not use historic preserva-tion investment tax credits for the rehabilitation of these structures, as the substantial changes at the top of the two buildings illustrate. Fortunately, the St. Cloud Hotel, the better designed of the two structures, was less damaged visually by these additions.

Section through early scheme

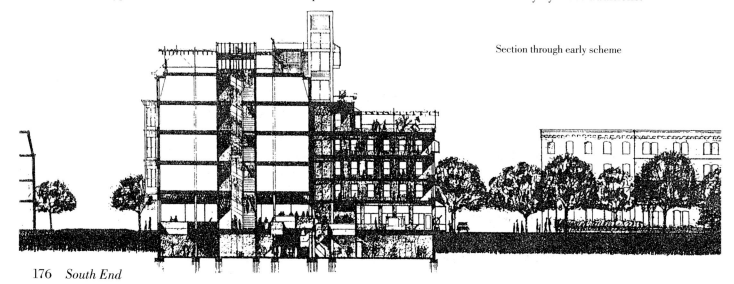

79
2 Clarendon Square

Notter, Finegold + Alexander Inc., 1988

A key anchor in the revitalization of the Boston Center for the Arts district, 2 Clarendon Square has a checkered history that reflects recent activity in this area of the South End. As a type, the project clearly relates to the Church Court Condominium reclamation done in 1983 by Graham Gund for the Mount Vernon Church in the Back Bay. Of several disastrous fires, the one in 1982 left four precariously standing walls of the Clarendon Street Baptist Church (S. J. F. Thayer, 1861) and a pile of historic rubble; neither the original building nor its surviving walls equaled the Mount Vernon Church in quality. However, the conversion of the Clarendon Street church to condominiums represents an attempt to resurrect this particular building.

Not surprisingly, therefore, the crucial problems at Clarendon Square lie in massing and materials. The combination of the damaged shell with matching, but new, bricks and cast stone makes the overall building appear chaotic. And the program for this building may really have been beyond the possibilities of the structure, such as the incorporation of a garage for 32 cars in the basement. At the top of the building, new gables in brick and imitation slate and copper are overwhelming. The original steeple was replaced by a clock tower, similar in silhouette to the clipped-off tower of the Cathedral of the Holy Cross (visible in the background when looking down Clarendon Street), and a lower flanking tower in brick, copper, and glass. An indication of the developers' concern for the history and significance of the church is, however, shown in the new stained-glass rose window, commissioned from Burnham Studios of Rowley, Massachusetts. As with all development projects in historic districts, the architects had to accommodate the visual and financial requirements of the neighborhood activists, the South End Landmarks Commission, and, not least, the developers.

The Clarendon Square project also included the rehabilitation of The Townhouse, the adjacent four-story 1880s apartment building on Clarendon Street, and of The Fire House, a turn-of-the-century fire station around the corner on Warren Avenue, both to designs of Bialosky & Manders. Renaissance Properties, who tackled this risky project, are among the most active developers in the South End. Two blocks away, they have also developed Dartmouth Square (designed by Arrowstreet, Inc.), two late nineteenth-century public school buildings converted to condominiums in 1985. And 75 Clarendon Street, a new apartment building designed in a late nineteenth-century image by Notter, Finegold & Alexander was completed in 1990, three blocks north of 2 Clarendon Square.

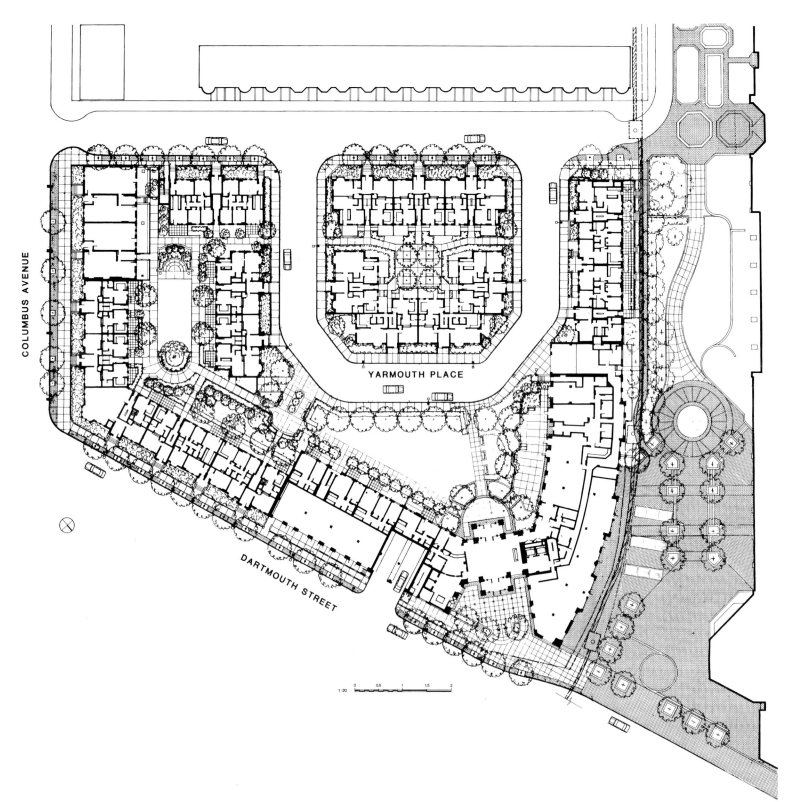

COLUMBUS AVENUE

YARMOUTH PLACE

DARTMOUTH STREET

1:20

80
Tent City Leighton Park

130 Dartmouth Street
Goody, Clancy & Associates, Inc.
Architects, 1986–88

Tent City, an apartment and town house complex for predominantly low- and moderate-income renters, represents the positive result of a two-decade-long struggle. The land on which it stands was proposed

in the late 1960s as the location for a parking garage to service the planned adjacent commercial development of Copley Place. When South End residents and housing advocates opposed this proposal and proceeded to occupy the site, the parcel became the focus of a citywide effort to secure more affordable housing in the South End and elsewhere. Through a consortium of neighborhood organizations and private institutions, the Tent City Corporation was formed and the parking

garage site dedicated to a mixed-income housing development with the needed parking buried below the structure.

Goody and Clancy have been involved with other recent schemes for affordable housing, including the Harbor Point redevelopment of the 1950s housing project at Columbia Point. Tent City is clearly the finer product of the office in mixed-income housing efforts. The complex

View from Yarmouth Place

announces the residential zone of the South End above the blank strips of commercial indifference in the adjacent Copley Place development. It fills several blocks, bounded by Dartmouth Street, Columbus Avenue, and the new Southwest Corridor Park, which separates the complex from Copley Place. The architects constructed an eight-story apartment building on Dartmouth Street, across from Copley Place, and then changed the scale to lower units along Columbus Avenue and townhouses on Yarmouth Place, the U-shaped street that was created behind the main building. The combined apartment structure and townhouses are grouped around an interior landscaped space that provides communal privacy for residents. The massing and materials of all the buildings emphasize variety, especially through boxy projecting bays and the use of orange-red, purple-gray, and buff bricks with highly-colored glazed bricks for accents. Retail spaces along Dartmouth Street provide for some of the basic needs of the occupants. Tent City is an important addition to the South End. Seen from the Back Bay, its presence helps visually to join these historically disparate neighborhoods.

Charlestown

Leaving the Boston penninsula, I came to the historic penninsula of Charlestown with its United States Government Navy Yard. Order and peace reigned in this vast establishment, for, since the Peace of 1814, most warships had returned to their home ports and the enormous machines that were here lay idle.

Jacques Gerard Milbert, *Picturesque Itinerary of the Hudson River and Peripheral Parts of North Amerika* (translated from the French), 1828–29

The founding of Charlestown actually predates that of Boston. John Winthrop, the first governor of the Massachusetts Bay Colony, and his colonists settled here in 1629, but moved to Boston in the following year because of the sources of fresh water on the Shawmut peninsula. While always second to Boston in size, colonial Charlestown enjoyed an active maritime trade. During the revolution, General Washington chose Breed's Farm in Charlestown as one of the sites from which to bombard the British, then occupying Boston. The British counterattacked in the Battle of Bunker Hill (1775), burning most of the town to the ground. Thus, the Bunker Hill monument (completed in 1840) marks one of the sadder moments of the revolution. Peace secured, the first bridge between Boston and the mainland provided direct access to Charlestown in 1786, making it the initial stop on the land route to Cambridge.

More significant for the local economy was the establishment of the Boston Navy Yard at Charlestown in 1800. Here the frigate *Constitution* (Old Ironsides, 1797), the oldest commissioned ship in the U.S. Navy, is still berthed, a magnet for tourists and a popular stop on the Freedom Trail. The character and importance of the Navy Yard was enhanced by the functional but elegant granite structures built by Loammi Baldwin and Alexander Parris from the 1820s through the 1840s. In 1974, the Navy Yard was declared surplus and the property was transferred to the National Park Service and the Boston Redevelopment Authority. The former maintains a naval museum, and the latter has supervised the conversion of historic structures and the construction of sympathetic new

buildings to create a residential quarter with panoramic views of the harbor and city.

Beyond the walls of the Navy Yard, Charlestown has experienced parallel redevelopment of its historic neighborhoods, especially in the area of Monument Square. The city is now under attack with the first phase of the Central Artery depression project creating a vast construction zone between the city center and the Navy Yard.

North End

At the time of publication, Jane Jacobs' view of the North End as a vibrant neighborhood, an essential component of a great city, challenged the conventional wisdom of contemporary urban planners. Almost an island when it was founded by the Massachusetts Bay Company in 1630, the North End remains so today, brutally severed from downtown Boston by the Central Artery. In pre-revolutionary times, the North End was lined with wharfs and its residents prospered. However, this thriving economy waned in the nineteenth century as the area became host to successive waves of immigration – Irish, Jews, Portuguese, and, more recently, Italians. The population remained dense and the housing stock decayed.

Testimony to the North End's continued prominence as part of "Old Boston" is the Freedom Trail winding past its historic monuments – Paul Revere's House, the Old North Church, Copps' Hill Burying Ground – before crossing the bridge over Boston Harbor to Charlestown. Yet, since the 1950s the district has been transformed, but, almost miraculously, the scale has remained the same. Buildings have been restored within and exteriors have been repainted to an earlier pristine state, while the main streets are alive with shops and traffic. Young professionals, office workers, and students are gradually replacing the Italian population as the older families are moving to northern and western towns and suburbs. With the depression of the Central Artery, and the proposed rebuilding of North Station and the Boston Garden, the North End is bound to become a more integral part of downtown Boston.

81
Constitution Quarters

Charleston Navy Yard
Anderson, Notter, Finegold, 1978–81

The initial adaptive reuse project in the
Charlestown Navy Yard, Constitution
Quarters established a solution for subsequent rehabilitation and conversion
projects in the Navy Yard and elsewhere.
Immense brick and granite machine-
sheds were here remodeled for market-
rate condominiums and apartments. The
architects created floor-to-ceiling atria
within these buildings, using a restrained
modernist vocabulary of stark white with
blond wood trim for the lines of balconies
overlooking the open interior spaces. The
scheme is similar to the earlier remodel-
ing of Mercantile Wharf by John Sharratt
in 1976, but the Constitution Quarters
atria are bland, vapid spaces that no
quantity of banners or sails hung as
sculpture will ever fully rectify. The complex incorporates a swimming-pool for the
tenants and landscaping that retains walls
and metal skeletons from the industrial
buildings previously on the site. The general organization of interior spaces around
a daylight court-area, as seen here, continues to be copied for industrial-to-resi-
dential rehabilitations.

82
Shipyard Park

Charlestown Navy Yard
CBT/Childs Bertman Tseckares
& Casendino, 1981

No better documentation for the idea that parks are magnets for development can be found than this marvelously landscaped water-playground and the buildings that have been rehabilitated to frame the site.

As with most of the redevelopment of the Navy Yard, Shipyard Park incorporates an historic fabric as the centerpiece of the park design. CBT "deconstructed" a small two-story brick industrial building by removing the east wall, the windows and much of the interior framing. Now, the upper level serves as a loggia from which to admire the panorama of the Boston skyline or to overlook the water garden behind the structure. Here, the architects

have organized an elaborate multi-level fountain with large faucets or giant candy-cane-shaped pipes spewing water into pools and slides of granite.

The remainder of the park is crossed by walks that are sheltered by locust trees and flanked by fruit trees and pines. Banked lawn areas mount to the water garden from three sides. A large wooden climbing structure in the shape of a galleon sails across a sea of sand, and a smaller granite pool is ideal for those tots too small for the main fountain.

Shipyard Park is adjacent to Constitution Quarters, the earliest of the rehabilitated structures in the Navy Yard. Now nearing completion on the water side of the park is The Shipyard, an eleven-story conversion of an industrial building to market-rate housing, designed by The Architects Collaborative. The children (and adults) who inhabit these buildings will benefit from one of the most extraordinary parks and playgrounds in the Boston area.

83
Building 34 (Parris Building)

Charlestown Navy Yard
Original: Alexander Parris, 1837
Rehabilitation and expansion:
The Architectural Team, 1987

Building 34 is one of the finest surviving structures designed by Alexander Parris for the Charlestown Navy Yard. As completed in 1837, the building was only one side of a proposed complex to contain a square courtyard. Recognizing the significance of Parris's building and the potential for an historically appropriate extension, the Boston Redevelopment Authority issued specific guidelines for Building 34. These included a careful restoration of the original structure and a partial extension through two wings that could suggest the intentions of Alexander Parris. The BRA and the Boston Landmarks Commission stipulated that the additions must be clearly derived, but obviously separate, from the Parris building. The Architectural Team's solution includes recessed brick reveals at the meeting points of the original building and the additions and the use of a pinkish cast concrete for the new wings. As the only building in this section of the Navy Yard where they permitted additions, the city authorities were determined to make these evident but sympathetic. Unfortunately, the power of Parris's design is lacking in the detailing of the brick ends of the extensions. Still, the historic building retains its original integrity, especially the low segmental passageway that marks the entrance to the proposed courtyard.

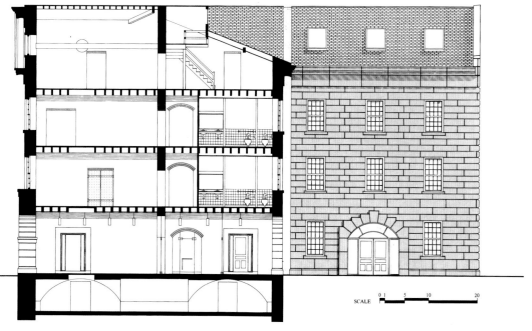

SCALE

SECTION A-A

84
Pier 7 (Constellation Wharf)

Charlestown Navy Yard
Notter, Finegold & Alexander, 1988

Breaking with the materials and massing of the industrial survivals at the Navy Yard, Constellation Wharf suggests a more modern and domestic waterfront image. The pier becomes a street flanked and crossed by town house units. Parking is intelligently incorporated into the lowest level, while small open spaces and exterior walkways provide loci for public interchange. The horizontal lines of the gray clapboarding are broken by the vertical divisions of the town houses and their inset or projecting balconies and terraces. All units assume a trapezoidal format in plan to capitalize on the view towards Boston and the harbor. The marinas on both sides of the pier provide extensions and enhance the nautical flavor of the complex, seen in stretched-canvas railings, bollards, and flagpoles. The choice of materials and the quality of construction are especially noteworthy in this project.

View from waterfront

85
Navy Yard Rowhouses

First Avenue and 13th Street
Harbor Edge
William Rawn Associates, Architects,
1988–89

Considered among the "best designs of 1988," the 50-unit Charlestown Navy Yard Rowhouses are that rarest of all contemporary architectural species – well-built, affordable housing. Located at Harbor Edge, the series of rowhouses along Thirteenth Street is bounded on the town side by a taller gabled structure and on the water's edge by a cylindrical tower. If the latter is reminiscent of a lighthouse on shore, the former pays homage to the old industrial structures nearby, and at the same time provides views of the sea through its grand arches.

Aligned along the street, the very design of these rowhouses imparts a sense of urbanity to the site. Composed of brick and granite with a copper roof, they recall – with the stone checkerboard pattern and the crisp white window frames – both the typology of late Victorian working-class housing and the specific local townscape of the nineteenth century, when the navy site was the nation's largest shipyard.

86

Paul Revere Housing Cooperative

59 Prince Street
Comunitas, 1988

The institution that gave us our first taste of community life, the elementary school, often served the entire neighborhood for recreational and civic purposes. In recent years, these buildings occupying prime locations have frequently been abandoned in many inner-city areas.

Built by Peabody & Stearns in 1897, the Paul Revere School in the heart of the North End was subsequently used as a parochial school under the Archdiocese of Boston for thirty years before it closed in 1982. Together with the Planning Office for Urban Affairs, the archdiocese opted to convert the school to mixed-use housing. Of the 24 units, half were sold as condominiums at market rates and half as low-to-middle-income cooperatives for local residents. No distinctions in layout or accommodations were made between the two categories, and the profits from the condominium units were used to subsidize the lower-cost housing, whose inhabitants were determined by lottery. No public subsidies were involved.

From an urbanistic standpoint, the Prince Street restoration is exemplary. Not only does it pay tribute to the fine qualities of the old structure – its massing, ample fenestration, fine drafted masonry, brickwork and ornamental stonework, and interior skylights – but the architects have succeeded in modernizing the building. They have accomplished this by adding double-glazed windows that reduce heat loss and gain, and by adapting the large areas of an educational institution to the variety of spaces demanded by residential units, including provisions for a garden at the rear. Located at the center, the entrance on Prince Street is perhaps too imposing, as is the location of the central canopy and walkway, replacing the lateral flights of steps which once led to the school lobby. The dramatic integration of old and new is most apparent in this hallway, where a circular brick opening overlooks walls animated by mosaic tiles; what is more, the vaulted brick ceiling, though part of the original building, exemplifies the best of the Modern Movement.

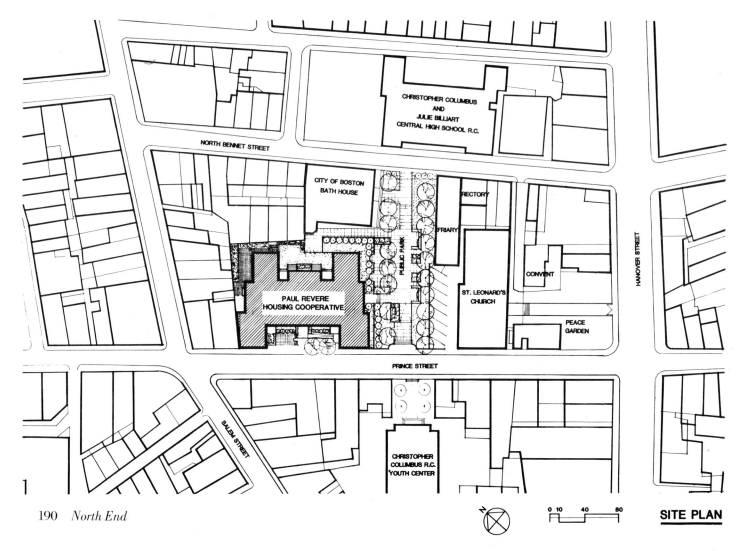

SITE PLAN

192   *Columbia Point (Dorchester)*

Columbia Point (Dorchester)

Why the mudflats and mosquitoes of the Back Bay should have seemed more attractive to the rich Bostonian of the 1860s than the breezy hills of South Boston with their splendid marine views is one of the unsolved questions in Boston's history.
Walter Kilham, *Boston after Bulfinch*, Cambridge, MA, 1946.

Like South Boston, adjacent Columbia Point provides spectacular views of sea and skyline for visitors to the Kennedy Library, readers in the Archives, students at the University of Massachusetts, inhabitants of Harbor Point Housing, and workers of the Bayside Exposition Center. Situated in Dorchester, a rural town settled by Puritans in 1630 and annexed to Boston in 1804, Columbia Point juts into the harbor on landfill. Modern development began in the late 1950s with the Columbia Point housing project, now being resurrected as a mixed-income waterfront community. In 1974, the University of Massachusetts moved its Boston operation to the massive red-brick campus on the peninsula. But access to the University as also to the residential sector, largely via the Southeast expressway, remains difficult, so that both complexes appear as isolated compounds. So too the Kennedy Library. Here, however, the isolation heigthens the drama, creating a monument on the waterfront that pays tribute to a native son, and more, celebrates the omnipresent sea.

Aerial view of Boston harbor and
Columbia Point

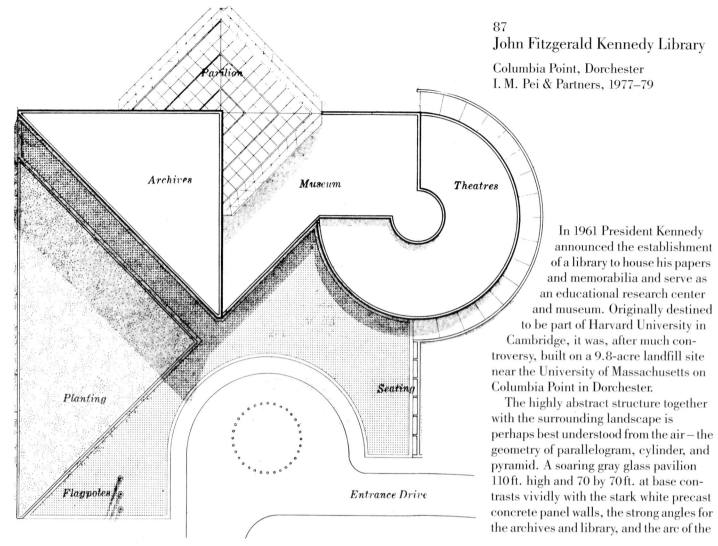

87

John Fitzgerald Kennedy Library

Columbia Point, Dorchester
I. M. Pei & Partners, 1977–79

In 1961 President Kennedy announced the establishment of a library to house his papers and memorabilia and serve as an educational research center and museum. Originally destined to be part of Harvard University in Cambridge, it was, after much controversy, built on a 9.8-acre landfill site near the University of Massachusetts on Columbia Point in Dorchester.

The highly abstract structure together with the surrounding landscape is perhaps best understood from the air – the geometry of parallelogram, cylinder, and pyramid. A soaring gray glass pavilion 110 ft. high and 70 by 70 ft. at base contrasts vividly with the stark white precast concrete panel walls, the strong angles for the archives and library, and the arc of the

194   *Columbia Point (Dorchester)*

auditorium. The imposing ten-story glass enclosed space-frame is the heart of the building, its only décor a stone bench and an immense American flag. Like other skylit space-frames used by Pei, it is composed of heat-strengthened gray-tinted solar double glazing, and exemplifies the architect's fondness for incorporating daylight into grand public spaces, to reflect the constantly changing atmospheric conditions. Sunlight, cloud formations, and water impart a magic to this "empty" realm, causing us to focus on the magnificent views of the harbor, where JFK's sailboat is moored.

To the right of the building's entry, the vegetation is reminiscent of Kennedy's beloved Cape Cod—pines, bayberries, and rugosa roses rise midst evocations of island dunes; here there are provisions for picnics and observation. A curved stairway following the contours of the auditorium descends to the sea. The element of surprise is uppermost as a view of the city unfolds across the harbor. Little wonder that this geometric nautical composition – the symbol of a man and an era – has been deemed a lighthouse on the sea.

196　*Columbia Point (Dorchester)*

88
Massachusetts Archives

220 Morrissey Boulevard, Dorchester
Arrowstreet Inc., 1986

Opposite: Reading room

A pleasant, well-lit research room lies at the heart of this building, which includes the Museum of the Commonwealth with exhibits focusing on government, legislation, and politics, and artifacts and documents of the state's history. The Massachusetts Archives are the repository for records of state agencies, such as charters, maps, and genealogical, historical and military sources.

Between the University of Massachusetts and the Kennedy Library, this rough-stone bastion overlooks the bay. The profusion of materials on the exterior is extended to the interior – the same rough and smooth granite, the same concrete pavement. There is an effort to counter with stone the surfeit of brick in the university buildings and to limit

height accordingly. The abundance of details and materials such as cherry wood and variously textured stones may act to the building's detriment. Design elements appear overblown, and the overall shape is unclear and illogical. Before the entry, a low stone slab marks a Vietnam memorial. While the memorial is integrated with the landscape, one wishes that it assumed greater prominence.

Generally, details are harsh, whether in the vestibule seating or in the stairway leading to upper levels. Perhaps, as befits its function, the orientation turns inwards (where the working conditions are deemed to be excellent), with far less attention given to the potential of a stunning site.

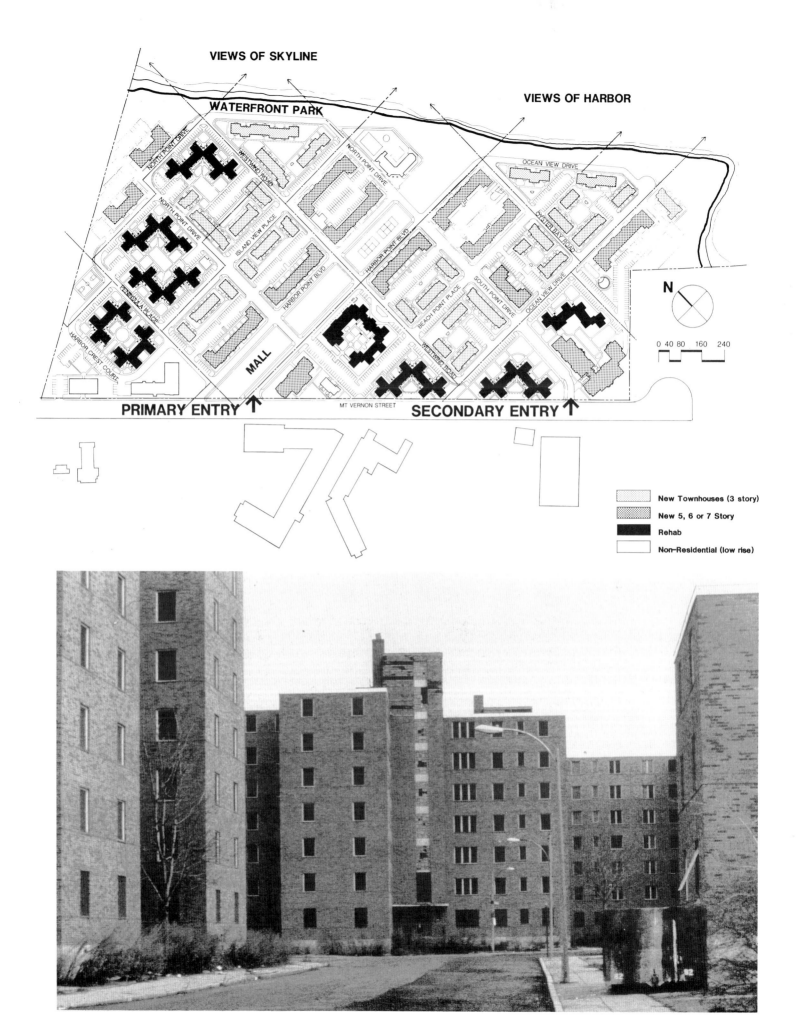

VIEWS OF SKYLINE

WATERFRONT PARK

VIEWS OF HARBOR

OCEAN VIEW DRIVE

NORTH POINT DRIVE

WESTWIND ROAD

ISLAND VIEW PLACE

NORTH POINT DRIVE

NORTH POINT DRIVE

HARBOR POINT BLVD

HARBOR POINT BLVD

OYSTER BAY ROAD

PENINSULA PLACE

HARBOR CREST COURT

BEACH POINT PLACE

SOUTH POINT DRIVE

OCEAN VIEW DRIVE

MALL

WESTWIND ROAD

PRIMARY ENTRY

MT VERNON STREET

SECONDARY ENTRY

N

0 40 80   160   240

New Townhouses (3 story)

New 5, 6 or 7 Story

Rehab

Non-Residential (low rise)

198   *Columbia Point (Dorchester)*

89
Harbor Point Apartments

1 Harbor Point Boulevard, Dorchester
Goody, Clancy & Associates, Inc.,
1988–

Opposite: Project before renovations

Below: Project after renovations

The goal of Harbor Point, formulated in 1986, is commendable – namely to transform a troubled public housing project into an experiment in interracial living covering different economic strata. Earlier proposals for renovating the site, dating from 1978, have been shelved.

Built in the 1950s on undeveloped land, isolated from the city and far from convenient public transportation, the Columbia Point project became crime-ridden and physically deteriorated. The current attempt at gentrification and diversification is supported by a vast array of public and private investments, including state loans, federal housing subsidies, and HUD grants. The goal is to provide 883 market-rate apartments alongside subsidized units, thereby creating a mixed-income population.

Architectural details are shoddy: unattractive brick facing is trimmed with cast-stone lintels; pediments, bay windows, and stucco décor are characteristic of late 1980s renovations, especially the addition of such features as birdbaths and gazebos in the courtyards. Though new, the furnishings in the lobbies are dowdy.

The new design aims to banish memory of the old, but in the building process a false memory has been created. Viewed from Kennedy Library, the gray-clad wooden Cape Cod houses on the shore seem about as authentic as a trompe-l'oeil painting by Richard Haas.

200 *Cambridge*

Cambridge

*Technology plays its part in the architectural boom at Cambridge. . . .
[Here] you are in the mainstream of innovation. . . . The world's foremost
expert on the use of plastics in building . . ., studies on the modular aspect
of building . . ., Techbuilt houses, . . . acoustical research . . .: Cambridge
really is the center now for the spawning of new techniques.*

Christopher Rand, *Cambridge, U.S.A.; Hub of a New World*, 1964

Late twentieth-century Cambridge has two faces: on the one
hand, Harvard and the Massachusetts Institute of Technology,
the Wall Street of academe, high-tech, culture-bound, international – with a decreasing residue of old New England gen-
try; and the other Cambridge, blue collar, immigrant, down-
to-earth. It is a problematic mix, the base of a constituency
where global priorities overshadow local concerns.

Although Boston has stolen its fire, the transformations in
the urban fabric of Cambridge are hardly less spectacular.
Recall that in the mid-sixties a survey of cities with about
100,000 inhabitants by *Time* magazine could allude to Cambridge as "low income, stagnant." Times have changed.
Research and development corporations that once held sway
along Route 128 and in California's Silicon Valley are now
moving into East Cambridge – from Kendall Square to
Lechmere Canal and the Charles River. Software capital of the
world – so proclaims the new breed of technological entrepreneurs, who find the proximity to the Massachusetts Institute of Technology crucial. As scientists seek new horizons in
the spheres of artificial intelligence, genetic engineering, and
advanced computers, developers are following on course. Pre-
dicting an expanding market, they are working on the
periphery, stacking these research compounds with structures
for housing and offices, commerce and retail, shopping and
entertainment.

Harvard Square remains the hub of the area and, compared
with the rest of the city, superficial changes have been minimal here. Still the most important urban node, the remodeled
and expanded Harvard Square Station of the Massachusetts
Bay Transportation Authority has made the district more
accessible to all, none more conspicuous than the youth of the
Greater Boston area. Independent retailers and services can
hardly survive in this prosperous clime, where stores turn into
banks almost overnight. Building in the immediate area has
been relatively cautious. On the site of the proposed Kennedy
Library (now located in Columbia Point) is the Kennedy
School of Government, comprising the Littauer Center for
Public Administration (1979) and the Belfer Center for Public
Management (Architectural Resources, 1985), whose red
brick and general scale are not entirely out of keeping with the
neighboring Harvard dormitories. Nearby Charles Square has
all the accoutrements of a luxury development; its center is
the Charles Hotel, which shares a public square with shops
and costly condominiums. Towards the Charles River, the
John F. Kennedy Park (Carol Johnson, 1988) provides a welcome and appropriate tribute to Boston's native son.

In Cambridge, Massachusetts Avenue extends from the
Arlington border through Porter Square and Harvard Square
to the massive complex of MIT along the Charles River.
Deteriorating facades are being refurbished and signs of
mixed use appear throughout, as exemplified by the renovation of the old Sears building in north Cambridge – thus far a
failed commercial venture, proving that location remains a
decisive factor. Nevertheless, the disorderly eclecticism of
Massachusetts Avenue may well belie Venturi's dictum that
"Main Street is almost all right." General chaos in the form of
high-rise apartment houses and commercial offices has
replaced the variety of small scale businesses that recently
lined the avenue, testifying to a free-wheeling type of zoning.
Central Square, the node between Harvard and MIT, is a bastion unto itself, managing thus far to resist the "upgrading"
that is transforming the area. That the respite is temporary
may be posited by the rise of University Park, now taking
shape on land owned by the Massachusetts Institute of
Technology. The 1.5-million-square-foot development promises to be the western counterpart to what has been done in
East Cambridge.

If sheer quantity is the yardstick, the American Institute of
Architects award to Cambridge in 1988 for "excellence in
urban design" seems well deserved; in terms of quality and
social relevance of architecture, however, Cambridge today is
sadly wanting.

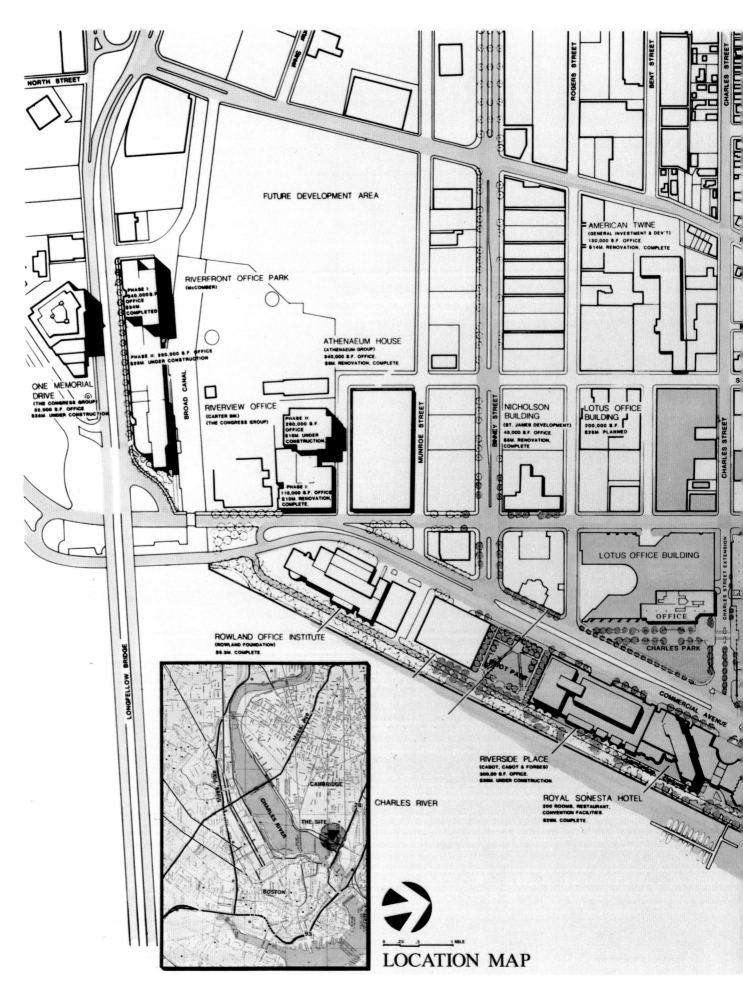

NORTH STREET

FUTURE DEVELOPMENT AREA

AMERICAN TWINE
(GENERAL INVESTMENT & DEV'T)
130,000 S.F. OFFICE
$14M. RENOVATION, COMPLETE

RIVERFRONT OFFICE PARK
(McCOMBER)

PHASE I:
340,000 S.F.
OFFICE
$94M.
COMPLETED

PHASE II: 280,000 S.F. OFFICE
$26M. UNDER CONSTRUCTION

ATHENAEUM HOUSE
(ATHENAEUM GROUP)
340,000 S.F. OFFICE.
$8M. RENOVATION, COMPLETE.

ONE MEMORIAL
DRIVE
(THE CONGRESS GROUP)
32,000 S.F. OFFICE
$38M. UNDER CONSTRUCTION

BROAD CANAL

RIVERVIEW OFFICE
(CARTER BK)
(THE CONGRESS GROUP)

PHASE II:
280,000 S.F.
OFFICE
$16M. UNDER
CONSTRUCTION

PHASE I:
116,000 S.F. OFFICE
$10M. RENOVATION,
COMPLETE.

MUNROE STREET

BINNEY STREET

NICHOLSON
BUILDING
(ST. JAMES DEVELOPMENT)
45,000 S.F. OFFICE.
$5M. RENOVATION,
COMPLETE.

LOTUS OFFICE
BUILDING
200,000 S.F.
$25M. PLANNED

ROGERS STREET

BENT STREET

CHARLES STREET

CHARLES STREET

LOTUS OFFICE BUILDING

OFFICE

CHARLES STREET EXTENSION

CHARLES PARK

LONGFELLOW BRIDGE

ROWLAND OFFICE INSTITUTE
(ROWLAND FOUNDATION)
$6.3M. COMPLETE.

COMMERCIAL AVENUE

RIVERSIDE PLACE
(CABOT, CABOT & FORBES)
300,00 S.F. OFFICE
$30M. UNDER CONSTRUCTION.

CHARLES RIVER

ROYAL SONESTA HOTEL
200 ROOMS, RESTAURANT,
CONVENTION FACILITIES.
$25M. COMPLETE.

MASS. PIKE

CAMBRIDGE

CHARLES RIVER

THE SITE

BOSTON

93

28

0   .25   .5   1 MILE

LOCATION MAP

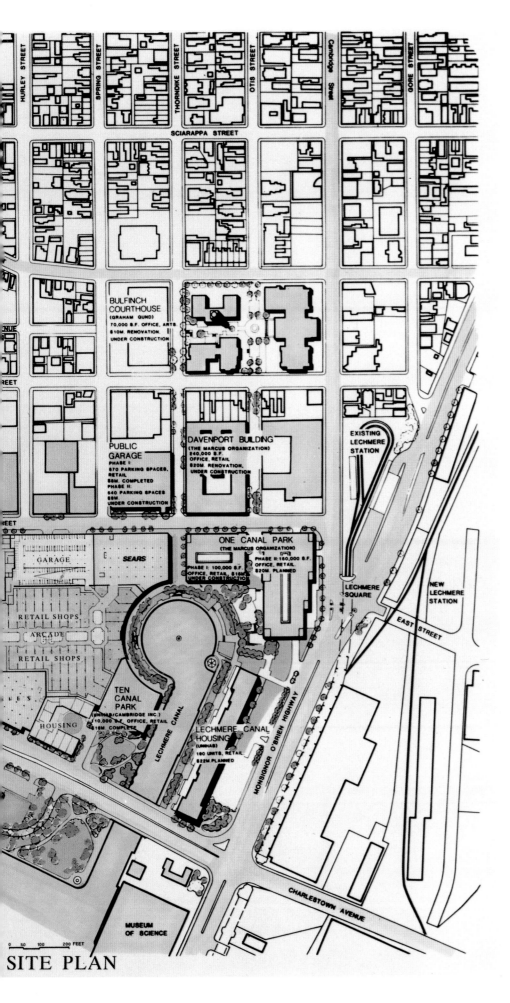

SITE PLAN

90

East Cambridge Riverfront

Master plan: New England Development, 1978

"Lotus Land" is now in East Cambridge – literally. The 84-acre right-angled triangle bounded by Monsignor O'Brien Highway, the Charles River, and First Street, which from Memorial Drive to Cambridge Street forms the hypotenuse, is dominated by Lotus Development Corporation, the computer software firm. Unlike Technology Square, however, the overall master plan calls for a round-the-clock operation – condominiums, stores, restaurants, and the requisite shopping mall. A once down-and-out industrial area of warehouses and factories was until recently notable only for the presence of Lechmere, a discount appliance store. Times have changed, and valet parking is now available. The following are representative works now in progress.

Lotus Development Corporation

1 Rogers Street
Tsoi/Kobus & Associates, 1989

Founded less than a decade ago in a Kendall Square basement, Lotus has expanded with amazing speed. The company's latest building is a six-story compound containing offices for research and development, an auditorium, and such amenities as an employees' store and provisions for day care. Space is also made accessible for public use in Eliot Park, which links the area to the river and waterfront. Stipulations for maintenance are built into the program.

Lechmere Canal Park

Carol Johnson, 1988

Thomas Graves Landing

Unihab, 1989

One of the first areas to be developed was the five acres around the reclaimed Lechmere Canal, with its powerful sixty-foot-jet fountain giving instant life to the complex and creating a place. Here is the first residential building, named after Thomas Graves, the first settler in Cambridge on this very site in 1628. Pedimented pavilions break the dominant horizontal mass of the eight-story condominium structure, whose brick walls are lined with white-trimmed balconies. All units have southwest exposure, river views, and the usual amenities; the presence of the concierge says all. Thomas Graves Landing stands opposite Ten Canal Park offices, across the artificial canal. Both buildings were designed by Unihab, who pioneered rehabilitation of old Cambridge structures in the seventies.

CambridgeSide Galleria

160 CambridgeSide Place
Arrowstreet Inc., 1990

Only the shopping mall is missing in this grand scheme, and, of course, a three-tiered galleria forms the nexus of the next phase of development. Its grand crescent faces the canal basin and extends over an enormous area. New England Develop-

ment sets the tone for the entire complex: "The setting is picturesque... CambridgeSide's 150 select retailers reflect the discriminating tastes of an upwardly mobile consumer market with discretionary dollars; ... the first mixed-use development in the country to fuse the cosmopolitan flair of a festival marketplace with the drawing power of a super-regional shopping mall."

Esplanade

75 Cambridge Parkway
Moshe Safdie, 1989

Memories of Safdie's brilliant Habitat at Expo '67 in Montreal quickly fade as we gaze at the complex massing of the brick facade, its multiple windows, and concrete surface. No doubt the terrace views will be enjoyed by the luckier inhabitants, especially those occupying the tower facing the Charles River upstream.

River Court

10 Rogers Street
SBA/Steffian Bradley Associates, 1989

Viewed from the banks of the Charles River across the newly landscaped Eliot Park, three leaning open-arched "pediments" announce this apartment house with its prominent courtyard. Only fourteen stories tall, the massive red brick building extending from First Street to Commercial Avenue is a weak imitation of a pre-World War II apartment building.

Royal Sonesta Hotel

5 Cambridge Parkway
John Olson, 1984

Still dominating the skyline of East Cambridge, the green towered addition is only rivaled by the Embassy Suites Hotel downstream. The Royal Sonesta logo mounted on the original building is a

further sign of ostentation. Whereas the boxed grid facade of the old wing was typical of the fifties, the new addition is a model of 1980s postmodernism. Pediments are ubiquitous and they come in all shapes, sizes and colors – in green tile and in copper; they are open, closed, painted and etched. Within, Art Deco is one of many decorative modes, as tones of pink and gray bring the color scheme up to date. Theatrical aspirations in public spaces compete with artworks, hardly surprising as the owner is an art collector. Further, in the concourse leading to the Lotus Development building on the riverside, the hotel does boast one of the longest corridors since the demise of the transatlantic liners.

Complexity and artifice abound: senseless piers, stumps as columns, copper pediments, useless grilles, fiberboard facing, ponderous porticos. Logic and the basic elements of design and proportion are completely absent in massing and detail. This building bespeaks the complete trivialization of architecture.

All these new buildings enhance the few old ones in the area, especially Con Electric. Standing nearby, the Carters Ink Co. is a typical shoddy restoration, especially in comparison with The Athenaeum (the old printing company), at least until we enter the latter and become conscious of such details as the sprayed vaulted ceiling; however, the design at least seems to be functional. In sum, the new development comprises a group of undistinguished buildings in the luxury housing category alongside a huge shopping galleria for the low-to-middle-income market. That the combination runs counter to true urbanistic qualities is evident. Even from the developers' perspective, the forecast is cloudy.

East Cambridge Riverfront
Aerial view towards Downtown and Back Bay

River Court

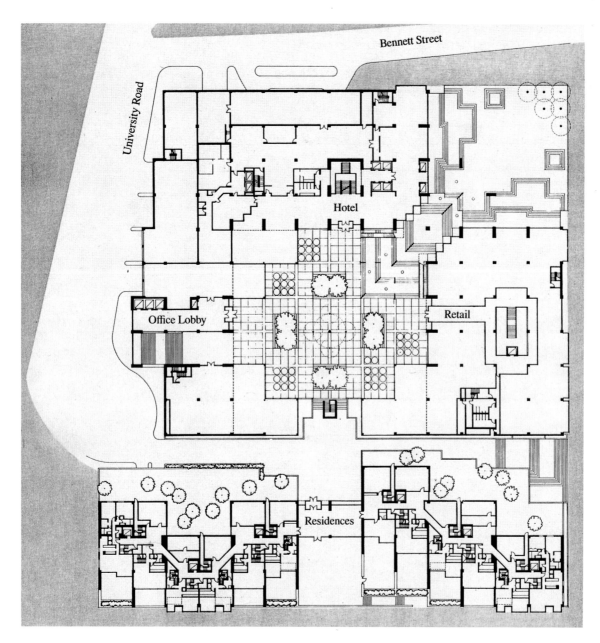

Bennett Street

University Road

Hotel

Office Lobby

Retail

Residences

91
Charles Square

University Park, Bennett Street,
Memorial Drive
Cambridge Seven Associates, Inc., 1984

Occupying a prime location near Harvard Square, a stone's throw from Brattle Street, Harvard University, and the Charles River, this multi-use development could not but succeed. The Charles Hotel fills a void in an area where demand always exceeds supply. Generating certain amenities, the hotel shares these with the adjacent office building and the condominiums opposite.

The proximity to Harvard Square, with memories of student demonstrations and offbeat activism, makes one wince at the luxury of this complex, with its general air

of pretension in the classy boutiques, expensive restaurants, health spa and pool, and parking garages. Approaching the open plaza from the street, one is greeted by flagpoles flying colored banners, striking a festive note. Trees and benches casually arranged make this an attractive public space. Broad terraced steps lead to the square at the heart of the development, the open court distantly recalling the disposition of the entry to Aalto's town hall in Säynatsälo, Finland.

Long horizontal slabs of glass framed with bands of white and trimmed with slim red mullions contribute to a lively but well proportioned pattern of fenestration. On the river facade, however, restraint succumbs to profusion, as closed and open projecting glass balconies seem to deny the integrity of the wall. Brick is veneer

and there's a lot of it, relieved by white spandrel panels.

Although privately operated, the square is occasionally open for public events such as concerts on summer nights. Hotel, shops, and apartments all overlook the courtyard, but their shared materials and scale contribute a unifying aspect to the whole. Groups of trees rise from beds whose granite enclosures double as seats. Like the tables of the corner cafés, they are geometrically ordered on a checkerboard brick pavement. A two-story skylit atrium marks the retail area, where a café is built around an open stairway. Thus, street plaza, enclosed atrium, and open courtyard adjacent to the hotel are linked on the street side, while offices and residences are most distant from public access – a totally logical and well-designed arrangement.

92
Sackler Museum, Harvard University

Broadway and Quincy Street
James Stirling, Michael Wilford and
Associates (and Perry Dean and Stuart),
1985

Few buildings in the Harvard Square area
have aroused the passions of the general
population as much as this bichromatic
brick building on the corner of Broadway
and Quincy Street. Why? First, it fails to
heed the urban context, which in reality is
quite attuned to the neighboring prima
donnas and supporting casts. Just look at
the adjacent corner of Quincy and Kirk-
land streets, where Memorial Hall, the
Busch-Reisinger Museum, the Social

Relations Center (better known to students as the Soc-Rel Hilton), the Sweden-
borg Church, and Gund Hall have
coexisted for more than twenty years. To
complete this battle of styles, recall too
that on the site of the new Sackler once
stood Burr Hall, a small model of modern
architecture, built shortly after World
War II as a lecture hall for the physics
department.

The second critique concerns materials. Brick is beautiful, but the brick
used here is decidedly not of the best vintage, and its bands of orange and gray
strike a discordant note alongside the
dominant old brick of Harvard Yard and
even its Victorian immediate neighbors.
Dubious tonalities are hardly mitigated by
the bright green rails encircling the building at ground level.

Thirdly, the entire design has been
questioned. The monumental entry with
its stucco simulated stone quoins bears
resemblance to a Mycenean tomb in its
massiveness. Even more controversial are
its two concrete pylons, their anchor bolts
still waiting to receive the bridge that
would serve as a gallery-skywalk over
Broadway, thereby joining the Sackler to
the Fogg Art Museum. Standing alone,
these broad columns are used as air
shafts, and have been compared to the
plug-in architecture created by Archi-
gram. Local boards objected to the span
over Broadway, and so Stirling's original
intentions have not been fulfilled. But if
the entry is overwhelming, the lobby is
cramped despite its height, forming an
awkward reception area. It is a mean
introduction to a great art collection.

The way in which the building rounds the corner says less of its function as a museum than does the neo-Georgian fire station directly opposite. If the exterior design seems disturbing a greater shock will occur on entering: a steep, narrow stairway rises the height of the building, towards no particular climax at its summit. If the materials and colors are objectionable on the exterior, they are far more idiosyncratic on the interior; the highly chromatic schema composed of lavender and ochre applied to rough stucco surfaces is oddly adorned with fragments of Coptic sculpture.

Criticism of the Sackler must be tempered by a consideration of the circumstances attendant on its building. The L-shaped site was severely constricted, the budget more so, and, conversely, the program was overloaded with a host of functions – galleries for classical and Asian collections and temporary exhibits, offices for faculty, spaces for conservation laboratories, rooms for seminars, an auditorium for lectures, museum shop and lobby reception area. In view of these restrictions, Stirling's solutions may be deemed brilliant. By now some of the polemic has abated, and visitors to the museum may admire the series of intimate gallery rooms. The faculty members housed in the Sackler are content with their new up-to-date quarters and their views over the college campus. And, rather than carp at the sparse modernity, "outsiders" too have begun to appreciate the irregular placement of windows on the exterior, reflecting the spaces on the interior. And, not least, even the staircase has become an object of wonder: separating the six stories of offices from the three floors of galleries, and poised beneath a glass roof, it is seen as an ingenious tour-de-force, an animated street whose neon-light installed handrail provides warmth on winter days. The staircase effectively separates the private from the public sphere, the business of the university from the public world of the museum.

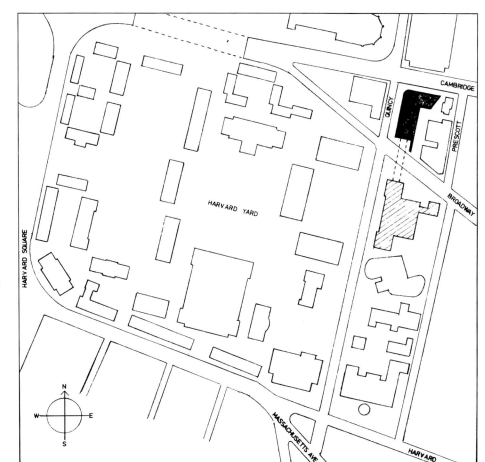

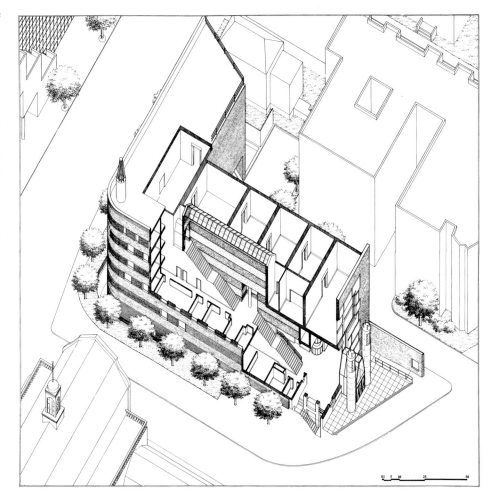

93
Wiesner Center for the Arts &
Media Technology, Massachusetts
Institute of Technology

20 Ames Street
I. M. Pei & Partners, 1985
The white aluminum-clad structure on the
MIT landscape is designed to express the
function stated in its name. Radically
conceived as a collaborative undertaking
between I. M. Pei and a trio of artists, the
building provides a model for future works
where borders between art and architecture will be eliminated. Not all occurred
as originally planned, for the artists began
their work only after the building was
completed.

Sited at the junction with the east-west
pedestrian axis of the old and new cam-
puses, the high-tech four-story Wiesner
Building (named after a former MIT president and chairman of its Arts Council)
stands among a group of structures of
varied styles and materials. To unite these
disparate buildings and open spaces,
Richard Fleischer designed an irregularly
shaped outdoor area, based on a complex
but lively modular pattern following circulation routes. The slatted wooden benches
(a modern version of designs by Charles
Rennie Mackintosh) and the granite
"cubes" provide seating and viewing.

The monumental gateway on Ames
Street forms a principal entry to the building. Our introduction to Kenneth

View with Health Sciences Building in background

Noland's work on the exterior is subtle: three colored panels with blue bands are but a prelude to the five-story mural on the interior skylit atrium lobby. A cool, predominantly gray glazed space, it is enlivened by the odd curves of Scott Burton's concrete seating and open stairwell descending to the below-ground level, and by the convex balconies overlooking the area. By far the most dramatic space is the four-story windowless cube, which functions as the center's workshop laboratory and experimental media theatre. During performances, midst the catwalks and scaffolding, programs of electronic music, New Wave dance, and science fiction opera may be taped on a battery of advanced computer hardware or played on synthesizers. Composers are challenged to experiment with "hyperinstruments" and to manipulate acoustical patterns, while designers may be encouraged to explore the three-dimensional potential of the cube. If the process is mysterious to the Luddite, the spectacle of total theatre is captivating.

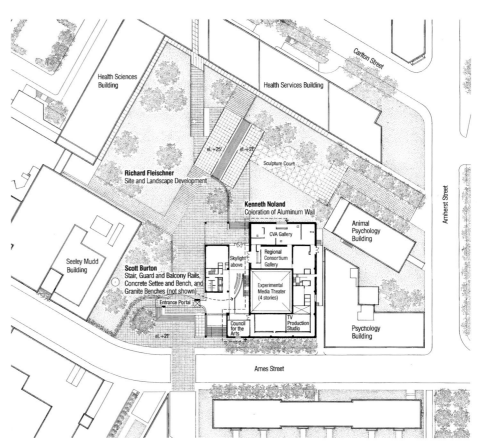

Aerial view of site with
waterfront developments
towards Back Bay

Kendall Square
Master plan: Moshe Safdie and
Boston Properties, 1981–

Cambridge Center is an enormous public/
private mixed-use development rising on
the site of deteriorating warehouses, abandoned factories, and vacant lots. It is
sponsored by the City of Cambridge Redevelopment Authority, Massachusetts
Institute of Technology and the Massa-
chussetts Bay Transportation Authority.
Ultimately, two million square feet will
form a modern complex composed of
offices (largely high-tech research and
development), restaurants, hotels, residences, public plazas, and mass transit
facilities. Although the development is
recent, its history reverts to 1969, when
NASA dropped its plans for an electronics
research center. At that point the Transportation Systems Center took over buildings under way, but most of the site
remained an urban wasteland. Throughout the seventies a series of master plans,
community projects, and environmental
impact studies offered possible solutions.
Conflicts and compromises are recorded
between the Cambridge Redevelopment
Authority, the MBTA, and Monacelli
Associates. As urban design consultants,
the latter studied land use controls,
changing markets, and design proposals,
and prepared *Public Sector Design
Improvement Guidelines*, a manual that
established design criteria for comprehensive streetscapes in the Kendall
Square Urban Renewal Area. Thus, all
the street accoutrements such as pave-
ments, lights, plantings, signs, and furniture and major design elements such as
private ways and public squares would be
subjected to rigorous review processes.

If we approach Technology Square from
the west along Broadway, the skywalk connecting the Draper Labs and their parking
garage acts as a gateway to the complex.
In the vicinity of Kendall Square, and bordering on the outer reaches of MIT, a thir-
teen-acre triangular site, known as Parcel
Four, bounded by Main Street, Broadway,
and Sixth Street, has been designated for
mixed-use development – office and
research space, hotel, parking and the
renewal of the subway station. Buildings
thus far erected constitute only part of the
24-acre site to be redeveloped with access
to the Longfellow Bridge leading to downtown Boston.

Now in the works is Parcel Three,
whose boundaries are Main Street, Sixth
Street, Broadway, and Galileo Way.
A blueprint for this plot has been drawn
up by Kohn Pedersen Fox. Further
development scheduled for the early
nineties is being planned by the Cambridge Redevelopment Authority on a site
belonging to the US Department of Transportation.

An important node of the center is *Point
Park*, near the entry to the Longfellow
Bridge. Situated at the junction of Main
Street and Broadway, once a traffic rotary
in Kendall Square, the landscape is being
designed by a group of artists, architects,
and engineers in accord with an overall
plan by Otto Piene that focuses on a five-
foot high stainless-steel earth sculpture.
Named *Galaxy*, it features a spherical
kinetic fountain in the midst of seating
and greenery about a paved open space,
its theme the earth, the stars, and light.

Buildings completed include *Five Cambridge Center*, a thirteen-story structure
that opened in 1981, and the research centers and hotel noted below, which are indicative of the whole complex.

Eleven Cambridge Center (1984) is a
high-security computer research and
development building, the corporate
headquarters of Symbolics, Inc. The red
brick structure contains a three-story setback glass atrium above its entry. On each
side, a row of piers is connected to the
building proper by a wooden trellis.

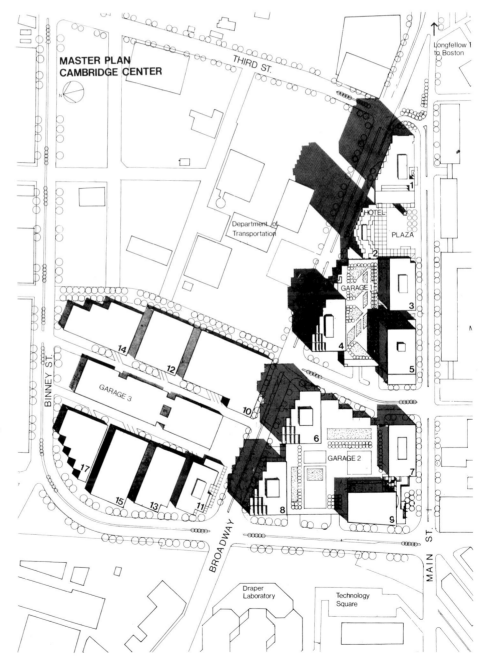

Marriott Hotel

tecting extant property rights, to promoting development than to heeding environmental issues. Cambridge Center is a disproportionately mammoth project, whose fortunes would seem to depend on those of the high-tech industries it harbors.

95
Bulfinch Square

47 Thorndike Street
Graham Gund Architects, 1986

The courthouse complex of East Cambridge, the county seat, had, like the surrounding district, fallen into blight and decay. Saved from the wreckers' ball in 1974, the Middlesex County buildings include the old courthouse of 1814, whose original design has been attributed to Charles Bulfinch (1763–1844). The handsome restoration has created a new urban area three blocks long, largely occupied by offices grouped about an open rectangular space named Bulfinch Square. Forming a backdrop to the square at the south end is the New Superior Court Building. Bulfinch's courthouse faces the old Clerk of Courts Building (Old Superior Courthouse), while the Registry of Deeds with its imposing brick Ionic portico stands at the north end. Completing the configuration on the outer periphery of the square are five newly restored three-story brick houses on Third Street known as Quality Row (1836–39), once owned by merchants. Despite the name, little of Bulfinch survives around the square, for the early courthouse was enlarged with two symmetrical wings by Ammi Young in 1848.

Only a series of fortuitous circumstances halted the demolition of the old courthouse buildings for a proposed parking lot. A newly appointed aggressive building commission to reform corrupt business practices came into being concurrently with the creation of tax incentives for rehabilitation through the Tax Reform Act of 1976 and the formation of the Cambridge Multicultural Arts Center in 1977, the latter to assist community groups and to provide facilities for artistic organizations. At this point Graham Gund took charge of the restoration and

Entry by auto to the *Marriott Hotel* (1985) is on the Broadway side, while the Main Street facade of this L-shaped 25-story red brick building is dominated by a large plaza, distinguished by its Persian-carpet like pavement and the subway headhouse, the entry to the Kendall Square station. A sloping glass atrium masks the entry, while the upper stories contain all the trappings of a luxury hotel – health club, pool, meeting rooms, and terrace gardens. Together with One and Three Cambridge Center the hotel enframes the plaza, which is animated by cafés, fountains, and a tower crowned by a kinetic octahedron that masks an emergency staircase. The success of the plaza was assured when the Tech branch of the Harvard Coop, containing the bookstore, moved to Three Cambridge

Center. Still, the multiple setbacks of the hotel appear to be awaiting a context.

Four Cambridge Center (1983) is a twelve-story mixed-use high-tech office building, with a bank at ground level. Reinforced concrete alternates with bands of brick veneer and glass, set above a colonnade. A parking garage is directly adjacent.

Planners' statements and project descriptions set forth admirable goals, specifically to link nearly a score of buildings by careful siting, massing, and materials, and "to create a sense of harmony and identity for the project as a whole." What we see is a missed opportunity on a grand scale, for despite the rhetoric more attention seems to have been given to parking garages than to pedestrian movement, to attracting new capital than to pro-rehabilitation of the group of buildings, and proceeded to negotiate with the bureaucratic governmental agencies. Using an 1848 lithograph as the basis for reconstruction, unsightly additions were torn down, whereas the more authentic elements were solicitously restored. An historical preserve has been created harboring elegantly appointed offices with the latest twentieth-century appurtenances.

The architects' respect for the past is indicated in the design of the whole, and even more in the secondary parts. This is particularly evident in the precision with which the building materials are matched, for the tinted cast concrete echoes the earlier brownstone, while the finely mortared new brick is almost at one with the old. Extraordinary care has been taken in restoring such details as the cast-iron trim, copper cresting, plaster medallions, exposed trusses, carved woodwork, and original moldings. The renovation here is perhaps a bit too faithful to a late Victorian aesthetic, as seen in the courtroom converted into a theatre, with its plaster ceiling décor, stenciled walls, ornamental balustrades, fanciful lighting appendages, and rich polychrome. Somehow, the verisimilitude of the restoration and the meticulous archival research on which it was based breathes the frozen culture of antiquarianism. Innovations are viewed in terms of precedents, creating a copy rather than a dialogue between the two principal defining cultures and all the intervening ones which have left their mark on the space.

Bulfinch Square represents a new, significant urban space that is acting as a catalyst in the development of the Lechmere Canal area. If much has been transformed, the gilded cupola of the courthouse with its scales of justice continues to remind us of the building's original function.

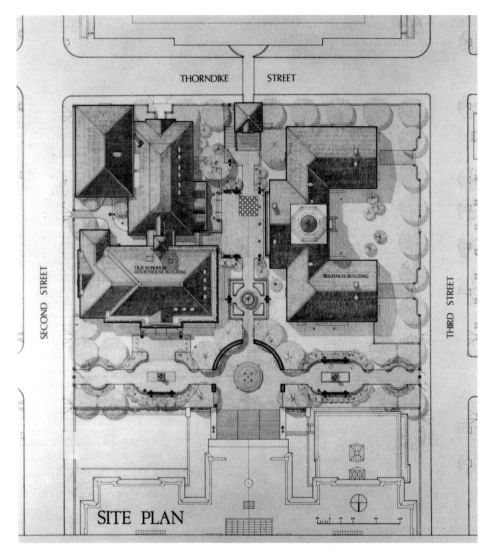

SITE PLAN

96
East Wing Addition,
Museum of Science

Science Park, Charles River Dam
The Stubbins Associates Inc., 1987

Installed in 1862 in the Back Bay (in the building now occupied by Louis), the former New England Museum of Natural History moved to its present site in 1949. The primary function of the most recent addition is explicit in the cylindrical form of the Mugar Omni Theater, which dominates the red brick exterior. Limestone stringcourses stress the horizontality of the three-story facade, whose surface is punctured by a huge oculus designating the atrium and the line of ground floor windows that light the museum shop. Entry through the high, recessed glass doorway leads to the main lobby, the public space that joins the east and west wings (the latter built in 1972). The lobby is also accessible from the parking garage, which occupies an inordinate

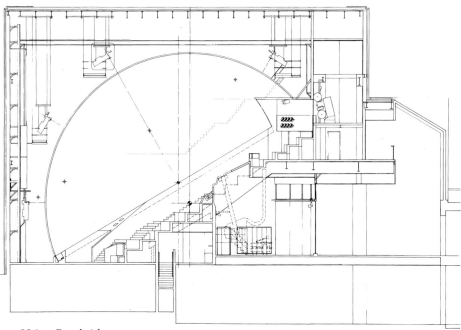

amount of the total square footage. Logistics are carefully designed, so that the theatre wing has its own entry, convenient in terms of admission and scheduling. From the central space overlooking the Charles River, Science Street, a vaulted concourse leads between the science shop and the café to the atrium.

With its soaring proportions, the atrium functions as a forecourt to the theatre and an exhibition hall for scientific sculpture (such as *Human Connections*, a "polage," or polarized collage). The space itself is animated by a curvilinear balcony and staircases in dynamic opposition. Here

too are provisions for scientific presentations and performances, whereas the floors above are designed as galleries for temporary exhibits. The keystone of the new wing is, in the interior also, the hemispherical dome of the theatre, which features a near spherical screen and intricate sound systems creating maximum illusionistic effects.

The new addition lends a more unifying aspect to different building phases in the museum's history. If the general composition of the exterior with its focus on the symbolic tower vaguely recalls the formal configuration of F. L. Wright's headquar-

ters for the Johnson Waxworks in Racine, Wisconsin, the interior is dictated by practical concerns. Education rather than design appears to be the principal motivating force, as it was from the museum's inception in 1832. That the museum purports to serve both as a laboratory of science and as an introduction to current technology is explicit in a statement of its theme: "To explore new advancements in science and technology; to expose people to new ways of seeing our world; to serve an adult market and foster public awareness of science issues."

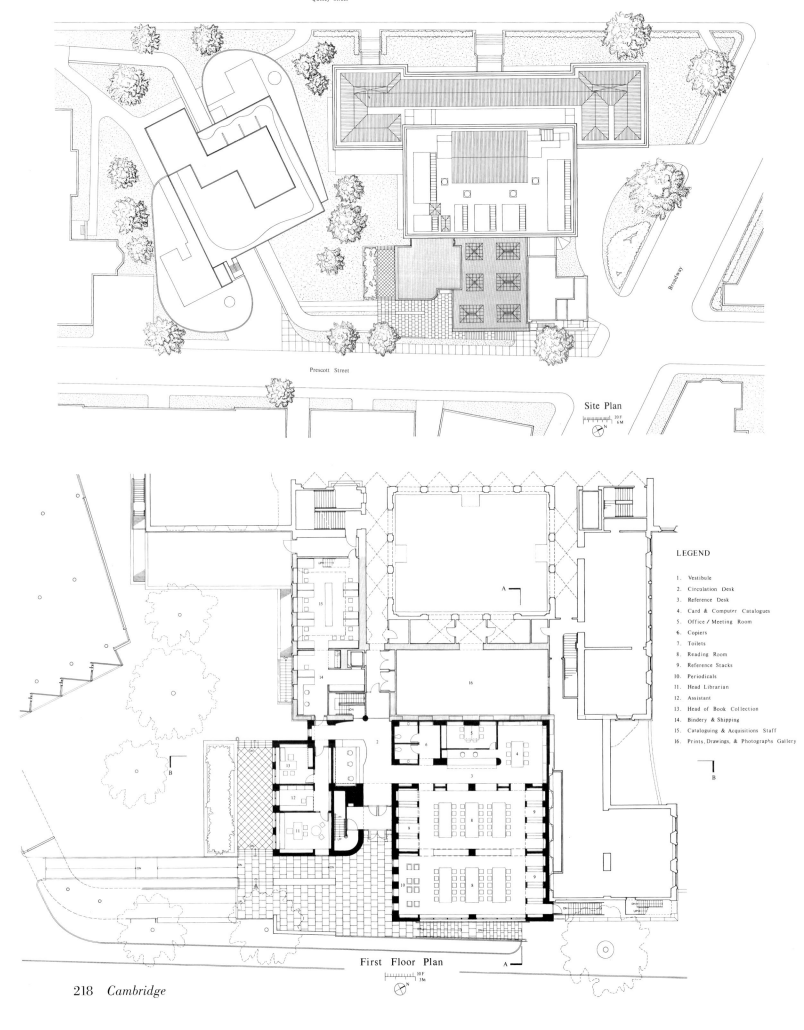

Quincy Street

Broadway

Prescott Street

Site Plan

20 F
6 M

LEGEND

1. Vestibule
2. Circulation Desk
3. Reference Desk
4. Card & Computer Catalogues
5. Office / Meeting Room
6. Copiers
7. Toilets
8. Reading Room
9. Reference Stacks
10. Periodicals
11. Head Librarian
12. Assistant
13. Head of Book Collection
14. Bindery & Shipping
15. Cataloguing & Acquisitions Staff
16. Prints, Drawings, & Photographs Gallery

First Floor Plan

10 F
3 M

97
Busch-Reisinger Museum, Harvard University

Prescott Street
Gwathmey Siegel & Associates,
Architects, 1990–

Shortly after the opening of the Sackler Museum with much fanfare, the original Busch-Reisinger relinquished its functions as a museum to become the Center for European Studies. Hence, additional space was needed for the art collections. The new building will also provide more spacious quarters for the Fine Arts Library.

The site is quite impossible in terms of size and shape: a rectangular plot abuts the rear of the Fogg Art Museum that faces Prescott Street, and its northern side confronts the irregular contours of Carpenter Center. The program is hardly less difficult, for the building must provide that the library, as also the collections and archives, be accessible from the Fogg Museum.

Addressing itself to the eclectic surroundings, the building's exterior is a sophisticated essay in contextualism. Indeed, it is refreshing to see how the architects have created a sparklingly modern work, whose three-story facade manages to interact with Le Corbusier's highly complex building, even visually incorporating the ramp as a circulatory element. At the same time a two-story structure forms a logical extension of the original Beaux-Arts building of the Fogg Art Museum.

According to current plans, the exterior will be of granite, porcelain, metal panels, and slate. Considering the red brick of the Fogg and the concrete of Carpenter Center in addition to the cacophony of shapes, the conversation may become a bit raucous.

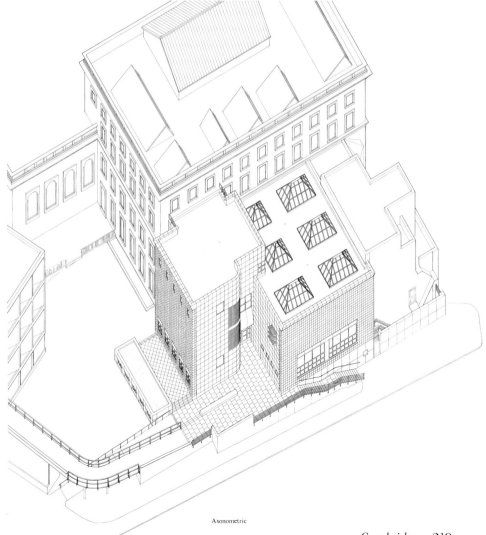

Axonometric

Fenway and Longwood

[The Fens] is a direct development of the original conditions of the locality in adaptation to the needs of a dense community. So regarded, it will be found to be in the artistic sense of the word, natural, and possibly to suggest a modest poetic sentiment more grateful to town-weary minds than an elaborate and elegant garden-like work would have yielded.

Frederick Law Olmsted, *Report of the Landscape Architect Advisory,* 1880

Somewhere within the incredible disorder of the area bounded by Brookline and Huntington avenues, Francis Street, and the Fenway, lie the classical white marble buildings that constitute the Harvard Medical School (Shepley, Rutan & Coolidge, 1907). By now the dignified aspect of this axially symmetrical complex is almost lost among the surrounding hospitals – independent, but all owing much to the eminent institution. If there is a master plan, it is hardly evident to the layman.

Drawings deceive, and few more so than those of urban planners. A study of *Framework: Master Programming for the Longwood Medical Area*, published in 1981, together with the reports of MASCO (Medical Area Service Corporation), has little to do with our experience of this 174-acre compound with its twenty top-flight medical and cultural institutions.

Granted that some of the goals of the Framework program to initiate "area-wide strategies" and provide a context for planning are welcome, the path from the drawing board, with its preference for bird's-eye views, to the site is unclear. As the area is a major traffic hub, problems connected with local and regional parkways and circulation systems have not unexpectedly been given priority.

Upon arrival at this grand medical and educational center the patient, visitor, staff member, or student is often confronted by difficult and even disorienting access. Confusion is magnified by the eclectic aggregate of institutional buildings, whose growth has been haphazard, largely dictated by immediate needs and new technology. Clarification, or in architectural parlance "a sense of place," is almost entirely wanting. Hence, the most promising of the plans is the "open space framework," a proposal to improve the entire environment. Attention must be given to both the restorative benefits and the aesthetic aspects of parkland: enhancement of the physical ambiance is as commensurate with medical goals of healing as is a beautiful landscape, like the Fenway and Riverway in the vicinity of art museums. Most promising is the decree that provisions for open space and such amenities for pedestrians as pathways, bus shelters, plantings, public art, etc., be incorporated in the planning process from the very beginning. A favorable outcome is reasonably predicted for the future.

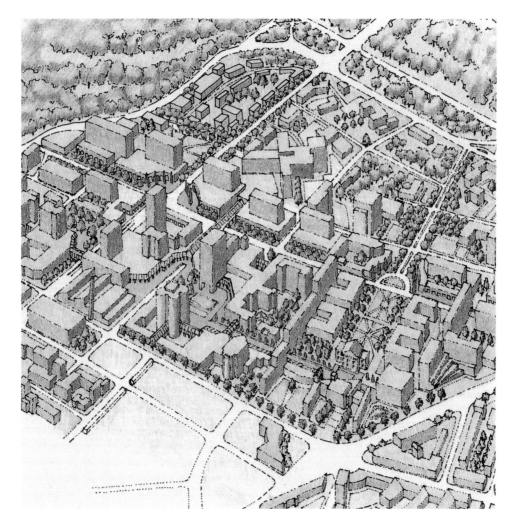

98
Power Plant

Francis Street and Brookline Avenue
Benjamin Thompson Associates and
United Engineers, 1979

Within the dense complex of amorphous buildings, this tall tapering cylindrical tower constitutes a welcome compositional element, virtually a landmark in the Medical Area Total Energy Plan. The envelope, comprising the lower red brick facade on concrete piers, encases the concrete-faced structure, whose roof bears circular vents. Across a recessed area a dialogue ensues between the angled and the curved brick walls. It is with the latter that the concrete stack, enclosed by metal framing, forms a distinct vertical node, thereby giving some cohesion to a disparate whole. At ground level, plantings and slatted wood benches, directly opposite the parking garage, seem to mollify the strength of the mammoth machinery within.

Enormous controversy greeted this plant at birth. Its present operation has been designed to meet new requirements, such as monitoring devices for air control and computer programming, elements not necessarily functional or in accord with the original scheme.

the framework

Improving the appearance of the Longwood Medical Area (LMA) has long been recognized as a vital component to the growth of the LMA as a world-class medical and educational center.

As building development in the LMA continues at a rapid pace, we must allocate space for open areas as well as for buildings. Most visitors get their first image of the LMA from the streets and sidewalks as they arrive here, not from the hospital's interiors. Without an open space philosophy or framework, the LMA will continue along a development path leading to concrete environments of high density with little consideration for amenities of a smaller, human scale.

The goals of the Open Space Framework are to:

- Improve the visual and physical environment of the LMA.
- Focus on the well-planned use of the LMA's open space, rather than the leftover areas between buildings.
- Provide restful and restorative outdoor spaces for patients, visitors, staff, and students.
- Make pedestrian areas more attractive, useful, clean, and safe.
- Contribute to a sense of common identity and place by standardizing certain built elements.
- Provide a framework for better planning and development.
- Encourage incorporation of open space into future projects.

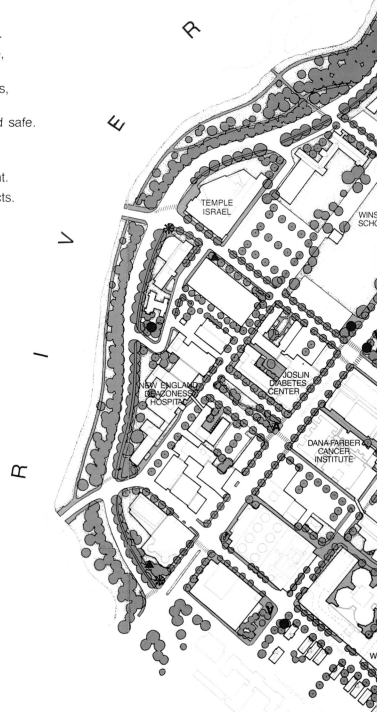

legend

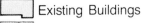

	Existing Buildings
	Existing Trees and Major Green Areas
	Important Pedestrian Circulation Areas
◉ ◉ ◉	Proposed Tree Plantings
	Proposed Bus Shelters
	Proposed Pedestrian Amenities
✳	LMA Gateway Improvements
▲	Outdoor Exercise Center
●	Mini-Park Opportunities
V	Potential Vendor Location
A	Proposed Public Art

riverway-fenway

The greenbelt of parkland known as the Riverway and the Fenway surrounds much of the Longwood Medical Area (LMA). These two links of the "Emerald Necklace" were designed by Frederick Law Olmsted and completed in the late 1880s. These greenbelt areas have become very important to the LMA. The Riverway and Fenway provide an opportunity for patients, visitors, staff and students to enjoy a walk in a country setting. These areas significantly expand available open space. Improved linkages with the Riverway and Fenway are important to the LMA.

0   200   400   800

scale in feet

LONGWOOD MEDICAL AREA
OPEN SPACE FRAMEWORK
MASCO/CDM BOSTON, MASSACHUSETTS 1986

99
West Wing Addition, Museum of Fine Arts

465 Huntington Avenue
I. M. Pei & Partners, 1981

I. M. Pei's addition to the overall classical plan of the museum, designed by Guy Lowell in 1907–09, both respects and enhances the extant geometry. Whereas the driveway immediately before the entry, with its windowless wall, might recall the approach to an elegant suburban bank, the plan, in model or aerial view, reveals the circular road to be a perfect complement to the curved "carriage entrance" from Huntington Avenue and the elliptical vehicle area facing the Fenway. Even the space allotted to parking conforms perfectly to the boundaries of the street. Although the Deer Island granite sheathing of the outer facade of this rectangular structure is like that of the older building, its austerity speaks a different language. Only a concrete lintel and an unadorned black column of the type associated with minimal sculpture relieve the bare exterior.

Plans for renovation and expansion began in the 1970s, following the addition of the White Wing and courtyard by Hugh Stubbins (1966–70). Essential to the program was the installation of climate and humidity controls and the provision of space for new mechanical equipment. Pei's East Wing extension of the National Gallery in Washington, DC (an exemplar of Beaux-Arts architecture designed by John Russell Pope in 1935), must have been top recommendation for the Boston commission.

In many ways, the West Wing is the paradigm of the "new museum": one-sixth of the three-story building is devoted to art galleries, whereas the rest comprises spaces for new facilities – three restaurants, hierarchically arranged with lower, middle, and upper levels, the latter overlooking the sculpture terrace and open court. Additionally, areas are provided for a museum shop, auditorium, lobby, and information services. Administrative offices and research and conservation laboratories are located on the two upper levels.

Organized about a skylit space, the core of the new wing is the 220-foot long, 53-foot high reflective glass barrel-vaulted "galleria," with a screen of aluminum tubing to regulate the effects of daylight. The decidedly bright and cheerful indoor "street" on the ground level is lined on one side by a café sited before the glass enclosed bookstore. Tables separated by ficus trees in planters, opposite white paneled walls, enhance the light and lively quality of this street-level concourse.

At the heart of the West Wing is the Graham Gund Gallery, which has become the principal exhibition space for temporary installations and the grand blockbusters. Its coffered ceiling, based on a fifteen-foot square grid module, has grooves for the installation of partitions, and the area can thus be subdivided to conform to the specific requirements of different exhibits. A similar flexibility animates the skylights in the center of each coffer, where the combination of natural and artificial light can be controlled and manipulated by means of attachable fabric screens.

Notwithstanding the air of classical monumentality that adorns the Huntington and Fenway facades, the new wing has become the principal entry to the entire museum, and the turnstiles keep clicking. A new culture conscious consumer is being attracted, a predominantly suburban client who travels by auto. Accessibility on arrival is matched by provisions for dining and shopping, making the West Wing completely responsive to the changing requirements of a once hallowed urban institution. If the total experience is less grand and uplifting than in those earlier "palaces for the people" enclosing musty treasure-filled halls, the new museum is finely attuned to its contemporary patrons, young and old. Once again, Pei proves to be a master of

site planning, an architect who works with
modernist clarity and precision to achieve
a classical harmonic balance. Not only is
this wing brilliantly scaled in proportion
and siting to form imperceptible passages
to the original building, it is, like Pei's
East Wing at the National Gallery, a
delightful and vibrant "place to be."

Tenshin-en (The Garden of the Heart of
Heaven), designed by Kinsaku Nakane of
Kyoto, Japan, opened in 1988. Entry to
the walled garden is on the Fenway side of
the parking lot through a roofed gate made
of Japanese cypress. Dedicated to a Oka-
kura Kakuzō, author of *The Book of Tea*
(1906) and a curator of the Department of
Asiatic Art, it is a "dry mountain water
garden." In the words of the architect,
". . . this landscape is the re-creation of
the essence of mountains, the ocean, and
islands in a garden setting, as I have seen
them in the beautiful landscape of New
England."

Opposite: View towards original building

George S. and Ellen Kariotis Hall and Thomas E. Cargill Hall, Northeastern University

360 Huntington Avenue
Herbert S. Newman Associates, 1982

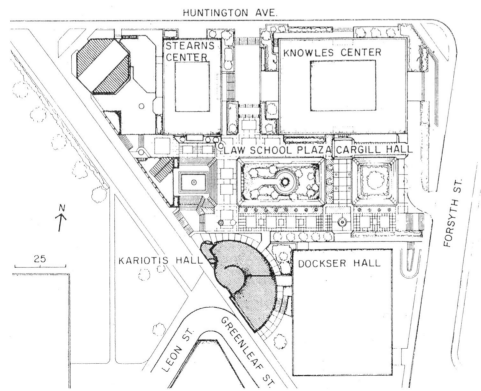

Situated on a frequented stretch of Boston's "cultural mile" between the Museum of Fine Arts and Symphony Hall are the largely undistinguished neoclassical buildings of Northeastern University (Shepley, Bulfinch, Richardson & Abbott, begun 1934). Hence, the circular form marking the Huntington Avenue corner of Cargill Hall – in reality, the case study and lecture-room of the new law school buildings—appears as an odd and intrusive element. So it cannot be denied that it has added visibility to an expanding professional school. The focus of the competition design became a partially sunken landscaped plaza, with provision for greenery and seating at the junction of a popular pedestrian route between the main campus and the newly restored nineteenth-century warehouse, now the seat of the university's administrative offices.

Much of Cargill Hall is straightforward, quite attuned to the standard gray brick Northeastern buildings. The severe rectilinearity of the brick-clad main facade is only relieved by the projecting overhang and its columnar forecourt, interspersed with curvilinear stone seats. Kariotis Hall, on the other hand, is overly complex, both inside and outside. Its semicircular plan is divided into pie-shaped classrooms, while a bridge joins the convex curve of the building to the older Dockster Hall. Gridded glass-enclosed stairwells and an overarching projection add to the intricate articulation of the corner facade, characterized by the irregularity of concrete bands on red brick, the corner quoins, and the concave overhanging cornices. With its standard modernist quotations, from the elliptical glazed corner stairwell to the contextual bow to its late nineteenth-century neighbor, the buildings are striving to produce significant statements.

However, despite the eclectic aggregates, the halls have, theoretically at least, by their very massing created a much needed "place" on a rather amorphous campus. Other problems are raised by the actual configurations of these new spaces, and the building forms that shape them. Surrounded by high walls, Cargill Hall is divided into three depressed areas with domed skylights, thus diminishing the possible integration of the building with the campus. The lack of stability, clarity, and order in these buildings seems to be especially inappropriate for a law school.

Top: Kariotis Hall from courtyard of Cargill Hall

101
Medical Area Service Corporation

333 Longwood Avenue
Jung Brannen Associates, Inc., 1982

Set apart from its surroundings, this rusticated red granite and brick building is outstanding in color and in scale, both outside and inside. The six-story medical office and commercial building (with the Harvard Coop and the BayBank at ground level) is distinguished by its intricately patterned facade—rough and smooth stones are laid horizontally and vertically, in alternate tones of rose and pink. Most impressive are the large tondos between pairs of narrow rectangular windows. On the four upper stories window bands alternate with patterned brick, reinforcing the horizontality of the whole. The entry is prominent but functions somewhat awkwardly, with its arched piers standing before a glass door and its inexplicably narrow lateral openings.

However, the real surprise is reserved for the fourth to sixth stories with their skylit coffered atrium. Walls in shades of pastel pink with white trim are punctuated by a large clock with a blue face. Aqua-toned balustrades and concave balconies (echoing the exterior facade) form interior viewing points of the luxurious palm court, whose four rose velvet settees are geometrically placed about a rose marble table, the whole resting on a lush grid-patterned carpet of deep rose and green.

Despite the high fashion so apparent here, the relatively modest size of 333 Longwood, with its finely wrought details, makes this building welcome on the streetscape. A matching garage lies just behind on Binney Street.

102
Museum School,
Museum of Fine Arts

230 The Fenway
Renovation and expansion:
Graham Gund Architects, 1986–87

As part of the long-range capital development of the Museum of Fine Arts and its
adjacent properties, Graham Gund
designed an addition and renovated the
original building (Guy Lowell, 1927) of the
Museum School on the Fenway. The earlier building set the scale and the character for the new structure. The two-story
original building, with a high-pitched roof
concealing skylights, became the leit-
motiv for the similarly massed new three-
story building. The two buildings are
joined by a cross-gabled public space set
back from the Fenway elevations and providing a common entrance. Within this
bright, open space, a monumental, indus-
trial-looking staircase and elevated walkway take on the character of public
sculpture. To the right, the new brick
structure is wrapped with limestone
bands and squares and punctured with
studio, office, and gallery windows. The
addition contains a gallery, marked by a
large arched window looking out on the
Fenway, an auditorium, classrooms, and
offices. Outside, a bronze rhinoceros by
Katherine Lane Weems (modeled 1935,
cast 1987) whimsically guards the entrance.

In 1988, as an amenity for students and
visitors to the Museum of Fine Arts, Di
Giorgio Associates constructed a parking
garage adjacent to the Museum School on
Museum Road in a compatible brick
vocabulary. The segmentally arched openings and the articulated stair and elevator
towers at each end of the building dis-
guise its function – creating a possible
conflict with the West Wing of the
Museum of Fine Arts.

The revitalization and expansion of the
school, the construction of the garage,
and the various internal and external alterations to the museum further consoli-
date the importance of this neighborhood
as the major arts district of the city – especially considering that the Massachusetts
College of Art, the Gardner Museum, and
the expanding Wentworth Institute are all
within the radius of a few blocks.

103
Children's Inn Extension and Longwood Galleria, Children's Hospital Medical Center

350 Longwood Avenue and
400 Brookline Avenue
Ayers/Saint/Gross and LEA Group, 1987

The public needs of major urban medical institutions are served by this complex of hotel, office and retail space begun in the 1960s and increased in the 1980s. A post-modern wraparound and expansion of poured concrete buildings, the complex is a fascinating commentary on the service facilities that may be required in the modern hospital. Founded in 1869, Children's Hospital is the country's largest pediatric health care center and the primary pediatric teaching hospital of Harvard University. In the 1960s, Children's recognized the necessity to provide residential accommodation for the families of patients by adding a hotel, called The Children's Inn. In 1985, the popularity of this facility encouraged expansion: eighty new hotel rooms were built, and the services of the complex were extended with the construction of a shopping mall, conference center, and additional office and retail space. The Longwood Galleria, as the shopping corridor was named, was created in the former open space between the inn and a research tower to the south, both of which were expanded with additional levels. The L-shaped, three-story galleria is the focal element for a complex of doctors' offices and related service enterprises, such as cafés, travel agencies, bakeries, hair salons, and the like. At lunchtime the six fast-food restaurants in the atrium feed a throng of hungry denizens, making the site seem like the Quincy Market of the Longwood hospital district. The excitement of people-watching, however, is offset by the constricted nature of the interior street and the unmitigated noise. The entrance to the galleria from Longwood Avenue is confusing, bringing the pedestrian to the second-level shops by a circuitous route, whereas the Brookline Avenue access is more generous and direct.

Longwood Galleria. Interior

Inpatient Facility, Children's Hospital Medical Center

300 Longwood Avenue
Shepley Bulfinch Richardson & Abbott,
1987

A skywalk bears the name of the hospital on the main Longwood Avenue entrance. If the semicircular driveway of the Inpatient Facility with an arched walk behind bears a resemblance to an airline terminal, this is reinforced by the reception-area, where travel brochures are available at the information desk. On the exterior of the concave facade, rose granite is trimmed with white precast panels. The gridded-glass pavilion projecting from the tower dates this addition in the late eighties.

Divided into circular seating areas, the spacious lobby is varied and lively, a fun place. Would you like to be near the giraffe family, or would you prefer the lions beneath colorful banners, or perhaps the walk-in dog house — or how about the open-air café replete with clusters of birch trees, visible through the glass-brick doorway? Blue and pink col-

umns are dispersed informally through-out, and a glass-enclosed elevator leads to the "entertainment" center, its fittings scaled for tots, its atmosphere ever cheerful. Light colors and forms also appear at the rear entry on Binney Street. No hint is given here that indicates the actual working of the hospital. Back on Longwood Avenue, we cannot but note the original building of Children's with its Corinthian portico and copper-domed roof, especially in contrast to 320 Longwood, the concrete tower of John Enders Pediatric Research Laboratories, and the rising new Research Facility Expansion.

Aerial view of Medical District with Inpatient Facility and hemicycle courtyard in center

105
Medical Education Center

260 Longwood Avenue
Ellenzweig Associates, Inc., 1987

The reticence of the four-story building
and its complete conformity with the
Beaux-Arts Longwood Avenue facade of
the Harvard Medical School building are
signs of its elevated status, a feeling sec-
onded by high security upon entry. Pro-
longing the gray granite base of the old
medical school (Shepley, Rutan &
Coolidge, 1906), the education center
reflects the articulation of its marble
facade — specifically, the six bays and the
three-story piers projecting between windows and spandrels, as also alternating
cast stone and concrete forming striated
patterns. A rose granite post-and-lintel
portico leads to a modest vestibule,
hardly sufficient preparation for the glass
domed space-frame atrium within, whose
size seems out of key with this small building. Here are potted ficus trees and tables
and chairs on a red and black diamond-
patterned floor, more suitable for intense
dialogues than for dining. Known as the
Commons, the central skylit space serves
as an informal meeting place for faculty
and students. Constituting a facade of the
courtyard, the exterior wall of the old
school reinforces the illusion of an outdoor plaza, transferred indoors. Scores of
white marble busts depicting famed
physician-educators from the eighteenth
century to the present — founders and pro-
fessors of anatomy and surgery and the
like, arrayed in togas like Roman
emperors — communicate the important
function of the building. Oliver Wendell
Holmes (1847–82), merely suited, guards
the entry to the headquarters of a society
bearing his name. With all this pomp, it is
somewhat surprising to note the elevators
clad in the conventional gray and rosy
hues of postmodernism.

To implement the introduction of new
programs, the building includes a variety
of flexible spaces — work stations, skill
areas, case study classrooms, amphi-
theatre lecture halls, small senior rooms.
All these innovations are designed to
update medical education by creating a
more interactive environment and by providing opportunities for high-tech experi-
ments and humanistic discourse.

Exterior view with original Harvard Medical
School building at left

Courtyard

106
Louis B. Mayer Research Laboratory, Dana-Farber Cancer Institute

440 Brookline Avenue
Shepley Bulfinch Richardson & Abbott,
1988

This seven-story medical research building with minimal, taut exterior sheathing in rose and gray granite veneers hardly suggests the level of theatricality that one normally associates with the name of Louis B. Mayer. Indeed, the movie mogul and benefactor of the laboratory is only represented by a modest photographic portrait in the elevator lobby. The Mayer building is the most recent addition to the meandering complex of research laboratories and hospitals that make up this comprehensive cancer research center, founded in 1947. The thin granite and glass facade encloses a functional slab for research, containing two levels of parking and five floors of laboratory space. On the exterior, the monochromatic colors allow the building to merge gently into its surroundings.

107
Ambulatory Services Building, Brigham and Women's Hospital

45 Francis Street
Kaplan, McLaughlin and Diaz with Tsoi/
Kobus & Associates, 1989

Both inside and out, the Ambulatory Services Building is the most welcoming and friendly of the recent additions to the Brigham and Women's complex. The materials, scale, and colors project an anti-institutional structure more like a motel than a hospital. When contrasted with the concrete fortress of the patient tower at 75 Francis Street, the Ambulatory Services building makes one doubly glad to be up and about. Although only one of three major entrances to the Brigham and Women's complex, 45 Francis Street is the most comprehensible and accessible. The two-story exterior format of bay windows continues into the building, where a surprisingly large skylit lobby provides both direction and repose. Like an enclosed street, the lobby is defined by bay windows and balconies that suggest the compartmentalization that the doctors' offices here represent. The basement-level seating area, with ficus trees shading comfortable chairs, brings to mind the contemporary Atrium Pavilion at University Hospital. Here, however, space is more generously allocated, and the overall environment is a cheerful, calm one. The building is truly an oasis in the otherwise chaotic Brigham and Women's plant.

Transportation

But the notion that the private motorcar can be substituted for mass transportation should be put forward only by those who desire to see the city itself disappear, and with it the complex, many-sided civilization that the city makes possible.

There is no purely local engineering solution to the problems of transportation in our age: nothing like a stable solution is possible without giving due weight to all the necessary elements in transportation – private motorcars, railroads, airplanes, and helicopters, mass transportation services by trolley and bus, even ferryboats, and finally, not least, the pedestrian. To achieve the necessary overall pattern, not merely must there be effective city and regional planning, before new routes or services are planned; we also need eventually – and the sooner the better – an adequate system of federated urban government on a regional scale. Until these necessary tools of control have been created, most of our planning will be empirical and blundering; and the more we do, on our present premises, the more disastrous will be the results.

In short we cannot have an efficient form for our transportation system until we can envisage a better permanent structure for our cities. And the

Even if Boston turned towards the mainland with the advent of the railroad in the mid-1830s, the city remained a leading seaport until the late nineteenth century. Intracity transportation changed radically in these years. At mid-century horse-drawn street railways ran through the town, and in 1889 the first electrified streetcar service accelerated the growth of suburban areas. Rapid mass transportation in the U.S. began in Boston with the building of the first subway (under Boylston and Tremont streets) in 1897, and was soon followed four years later by the elevated train over Washington Street.

The problem is our transportation systems and infrastructures. We have a 19th-century infrastructure as we go into the 21st century.

John Burgee, cited in *The New York Times*, 14 May 1989.

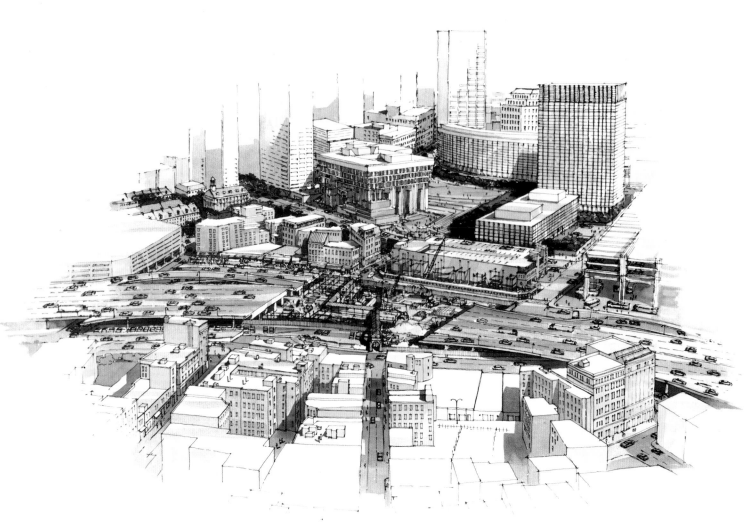

A revolution in transportation came after World War II, when the auto precipitated the move of urban dwellers to the suburbs, and highways like Route 128 encouraged the rise of industrial developments on the periphery. The townscape changed too. Storrow Drive traversed the course of the Charles River, the Mass Turnpike roared into the Back Bay and the Central Artery smashed through downtown Boston connecting the Northeast and Southeast expressways. When in the early sixties the movement to revitalize the city was underway, bureaucrats and planners found it expedient to consider transportation as an integral part of redevelopment. Joint efforts between the Boston Redevelopment Authority and the Committee for the Central Business District together with massive federal grants led to the improvement and expansion of public transportation. The subway station modification program that began in the 1970s was enhanced in 1978 when the Cambridge Arts Council received a grant from the Urban Mass Transit Administration and the Massachusetts Bay Transit Authority for the "Arts on the Line" program. Subway lines were extended to outlying districts, new bus terminals were opened, and old interstate railroad stations were rebuilt. Pedestrian nuclei or traffic-free zones and water shuttles to Logan airport and commuter boats from Hingham may create an illusion of a new order. Withal, the Bostonian's passion for the auto has not abated and traffic has increased to such a degree that the depression of the Central Artery and the construction of the Third Haror Tunnel are now in progress. Problems abound. Growing realization of such potential disasters as the Charlestown termini and further environmental pollution renders the entire undertaking controversial.

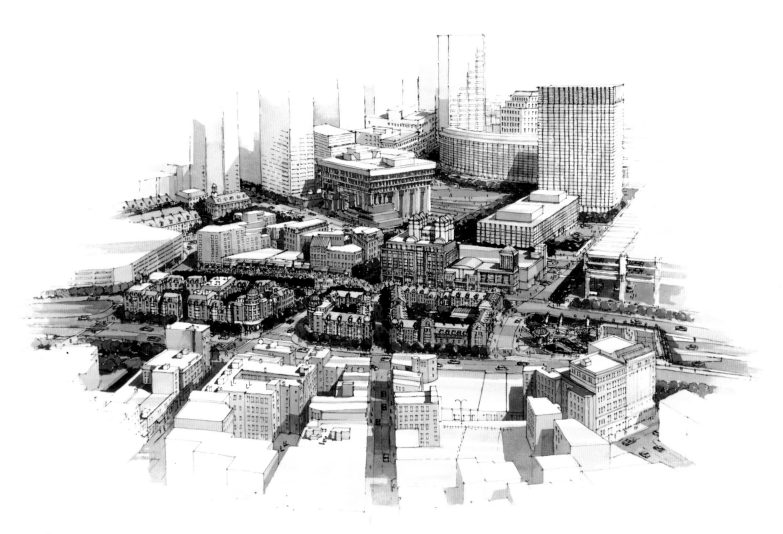

Southwest Corridor Park

Engineering: Kaiser Engineers, Inc./Fay,
Spofford & Thorndike, Inc.
Land development:
Charles G. Hilgenhurst &
Associates, Inc.
Landscape architecture:
Roy Mann Associates
Urban design and station architecture:
Stull and Lee, Inc.
Community participation and planning
and educational training program:
Ellenzweig Associates, Inc.
1987

Among the most exemplary of recent
urban designs, the award-winning Southwest Corridor Park is also a model of participatory planning. Its very existence is a
product of the watershed years of the late
sixties, when protests led to the defeat of a
highway project for this deteriorating site
along the tracks of the railroad lines
separating the South End and the Back
Bay.

Designed in 1977, the 52-acre urban
park was a decade in the making, for it
involved taking into account the needs of
distinct socio-economic communities –
the Back Bay, the South End, and Roxbury. Like Olmsted's nineteenth-century
transformation of marshy flats into the
Southwest Corridor Park forms a welcome
and varied connective link along a 4.7-
mile tract, a veritable green belt joining
formerly separate districts. Particularly
attractive is the three-quarter mile long
park above the transit tunnel, which
extends from behind Copley Place in the
Back Bay to the Massachusetts Avenue
T-station, the latter designed by Moriece
and Gary. Nine new Orange Line stations
reinforce communication, and even paved
roads appear and disappear along parts of
the corridor. Its winding pedestrian paths
following the old rail tracks are lined with
trees, while cross-walks reveal an impressive variety of plantings – hardy
species, flower beds, and community
vegetable gardens. Provisions for
cycling and play, for solitude and meeting
are thoughtfully interspersed throughout.
Renewed admiration surges for the old
mews-like streets in the shadow of modern
compounds, or a blue-surfaced basketball court, or a tennis court adjacent to a
church lawn, or the ventilator ducts along
the south side, disguised as town houses.
New vistas of well-known skyscrapers
emerge against a backdrop of the old
brownstone and red brick of both gentrified neighborhoods and streetcar suburbs. A sense of community has been fostered in the maintenance (by adjoining
properties such as Copley Place) and use
of the park, which is patroled by Metro
Police. In terms of its present state and
future projections the Southwest Corridor
appears to be a perfect antidote to both
high-density development and urban
parking wastelands.

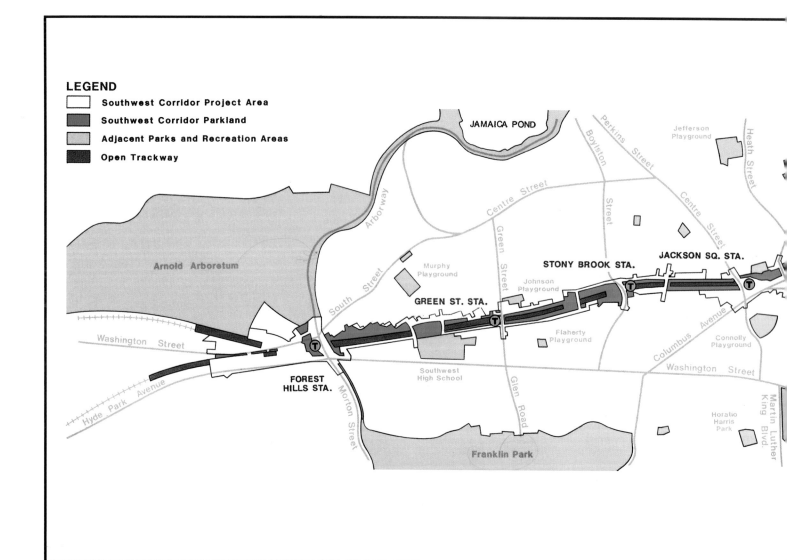

Subway Stations, Massachusetts Bay Transportation Authority

Orange Line

Coordinators: Stull and Lee, Inc., 1971–88

In lieu of the projected Southwest Corridor, proposed in the 1960s as a link in the interstate highway system, the city recently celebrated the opening of the new Orange Line. A victory for mass transportation, this line replaced the elevated Washington Street rail, built in 1901; its only vestige, the Victorian copper and wood Dover Station at the intersection of Berkeley and Washington streets, will disappear shortly. Beginning at Back Bay, the eight-station line runs 4.7 miles along a sunken railroad bed across town and parkland to the terminus in Forest Hills. An effort has been made to rehabilitate the areas bordering on the stations by discreet landscaping and facilities for local communities.

Thus far, each of the color-coded MBTA lines has a different character. The Blue and Green line stations, refurbished in the 1960s–70s (begun by the Cambridge Seven), are dominated by brickwork and photomurals relating to the areas of the individual stations.

The Orange Line follows a more sculptural aesthetic: surfaces are tough, practical, cold, yet with a certain machine-age beauty – witness the high-tech Massachusetts Avenue Station with its steel truss canopy and aluminum facade.

Ruggles Street Station

Stull and Lee, Inc., 1988

The tubular-framed high-tech structure stands on the edge of a large parking garage, with a covered pedestrian concourse at street level. Its proximity to the Massachusetts Avenue Station may be justified by its function as a transfer point, with nodes for stairs, escalators, and elevators providing links to commuter rails and buses. In fact, its strategic position between the South End and the Back Bay, especially convenient for Northeastern University, may well serve as a point of communication as well as passage.

→

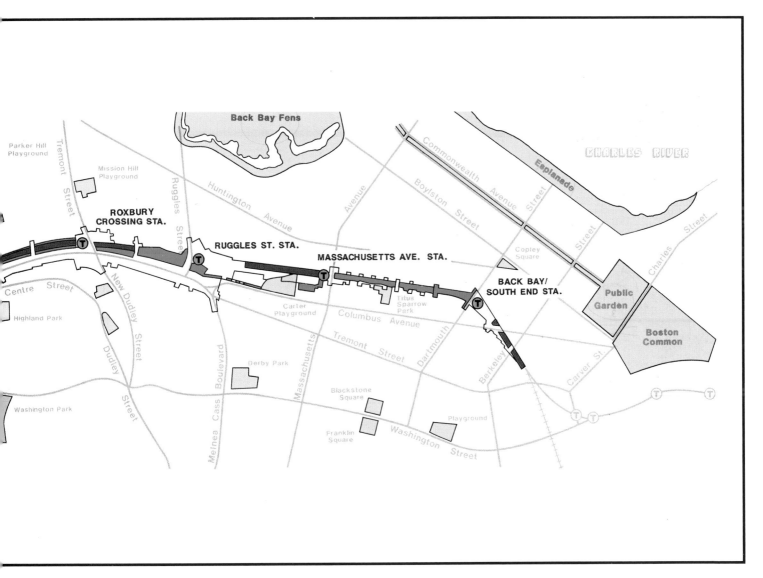

Ruggles Street Station, Roxbury end

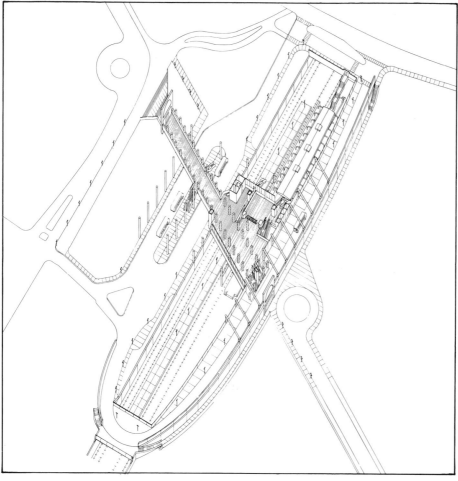

Forest Hills Station

Cambridge Seven Associates, Inc., 1988

Exiting from the subway at Forest Hills, the southern end of the Orange Line, an urbanite will probably be overwhelmed by the change in scale. This huge station serving as the center of a public and private transportation network is comparable to those suburban depots on the Washington (DC) Metro. Its white metal space-frame clock tower, looming 120 feet above the station, has become a highly visible marker for the entire neighborhood. Does this skeletal frame harbor the memory of an earlier structure? Composed of a series of hip-roofed glass pavilions, the station itself is supposedly designed to relate to the destination of many riders to this terminus, the Arnold Arboretum and adjoining Franklin Park. The greenhouses of the Botanical Gardens are anticipated in the glass-enclosed structures of the subway station.

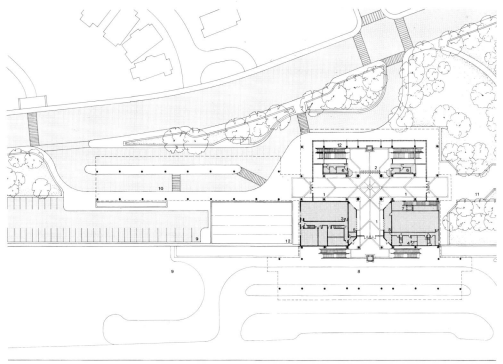

FOREST HILLS STATION
Main Lobby & Upper Busway Plan

0 20 40

Plan Key
1. Main Lobby
2. Paid Lobby
3. Station Service
4. MBTA Police Facility
5. Concessions
6. Public & Staff Toilet
7. Commuter Rail Access
8. Lower Entry & Busway Below
9. Public Parking
10. Upper Busway
11. Park & Surface Transit Acces
12. Open to Tracks Below
13. North Headhouse
14. Inbound Surface Transit
15. Outbound Surface Transit

The Red Line Expansion

Alewife Station and Garage

Ellenzweig Associates, Inc., 1985

Part of a program to extend metropolitan transit to outlying surburban areas, Alewife Station and Garage is a vast complex serving as an intermodal transfer hub northwest of Cambridge. Viewed as an alternative to increasing highway construction, this enormous station is one of the MBTA projects designed to encourage further use of public transportation.

The complex, which seems to stand in a pedestrian no-man's land, forms a glass-enclosed atrium designating the central aisle of the garage – the beginning and end of the journey – between double-helix ramps. Arts on the Line has provided artworks to enliven the interior space.

Arts on the Line

In 1978, in accord with a policy of the US Department of Transportation concern-

Alewife Station

ing design criteria for transportation systems, the MBTA and the Cambridge Arts Council created the Arts on the Line program for the Red Line rehabilitation and expansion. The administrators commissioned works of art as part of the subway system's modernization program, focusing on site-specific work that resulted from collaborations between artists and architects.

At Harvard Square Station (whose slurry wall construction pioneered a technique, now widespread, whereby a mud-like mixture is used as temporary soil replacement during excavation to prevent the collapse of the surrounding earth), tile murals by Joyce Koslof and Gyorgy Kepes spread joyful notes through the vastness of the brick and concrete concourse and bus terminal. Other notable works may be found at Downtown Crossing Station, where L. Simpson's *Situations* (1988) is composed of heavy-duty polished granite seats. Even more inventive is Paul Matisse's *Pythagoras from Kendall Band* (1988), an aluminum, teak, and steel kinetic sculpture that is activated in concert performance, appropriately enough at Kendall Square/MIT

Station. Graphics and photomurals celebrating the history and technology of the famed institute further enliven the station. The modernized Central Square Station features abstract tile murals on underground walls, but the most welcome additions are to be found at street level, where circular rose granite seating areas are placed beneath metal-framed glass overhangs that serve as bus shelters and waiting posts.

Central Artery/Tunnel Project

Design, construction and management:
Bechtel/Parsons Brinckerhoff, and
Wallace Floyd Associates, 1989–

Built in the late 1950s for an average of
75,000 vehicles per day, the Central
Artery now deals with almost three times
that number. Hence, the current master
scheme was dictated by a set of circumstances that threatened to bring traffic to a standstill in the near future. As
dirt and rubble were once transferred
from Needham to provide landfill for Back
Bay, excavation has now begun for the
largely underground ten-lane highway
between the Southeast Expressway and
Charlestown, the third harbor tunnel, and
the connecting extension of the Massachusetts Turnpike. At present, the dirt
to be carted away by barge to Spectacle
Island is destined to transform a garbage
mound into a harbor park. Messages conveyed by this colossal project are ambigu-
ous – to prevent gridlock but at the same
time double highway capacity, to open up
vistas of a newly rehabilitated downtown
waterfront but make the motorist spend
more time underground, whether en route
to South Station or to Logan Airport. This
prompts the question: does the vast undertaking promote the use of public transport, or, by enlarging the highway system,
does it not contribute to further environmental pollution? Whereas the opportunity to employ new technology in replacing the old utility lines is surely in the
minds of the project's coordinating teams,
they appear to be amazingly shortsighted
as regards long-term ecological problems,
generated, for example, by the huge ventilation stacks required for underground
traffic and by the changes that would be
wrought by the design of a 1,200-foot long
four-lane tunnel beneath the harbor – not
to mention the continued encouragement
of vehicular traffic.

At present more than forty different
agencies are attempting to meet the
requirements of more than fifty environmental regulatory boards. Aside from
technological matters, questions also
arise concerning the 22 acres of land that
would be created by depressing the Central Artery. Would the sense of urbanity be
obliterated by the development of a park
recalling the Emerald Necklace? Would it
be better maintained by the construction
of low-rise mixed-use developments?

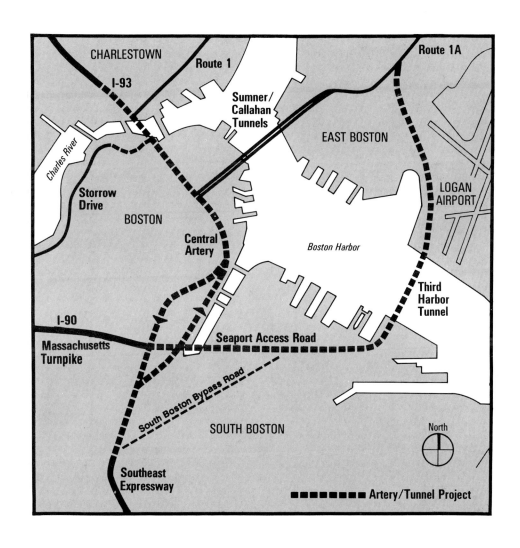

Appendix

List of Architectural Firms and their Projects

Dean Abbott with Clarke + Rapuano, Inc.
Copley Square, 1989   no. 71
Anderson Nichols & Co.
Wang Laboratories, 1985   no. 27
Anderson, Notter, Finegold
Constitution Quarters, 1978–81   no. 81
The Architects Collaborative
– 855 Boylston Street, 1986   no. 60
– Copley Place, 1980–84   no. 57
– Fiduciary Trust Building, 1977   no. 3
– Heritage on the Garden, 1988   no. 65
– Neworld Bank, 1976   no. 4
– Shawmut Bank NA, 1975   no. 2
The Architectural Team
– Building 34 (Parris Building), 1987   no. 83
– China Trade Building, 1987   no. 30
– Lincoln Wharf Condominiums, 1987   no. 31
Arrowstreet Inc.
– CambridgeSide Galleria, 1990   no. 90
– Massachusetts Archives, 1986   no. 88
– Mystic River Bridge Building, 1987   no. 78
– St. Cloud Building, 1987   no. 78
Ayers/Saint/Gross and LEA Group
Children's Inn Extension and Longwood Galleria,
Children's Hospital Medical Center, 1987
no. 103

Bechtel/Parsons Brinckerhoff, and Wallace
Floyd Associates
Central Artery/Tunnel Project, 1989–   no. 110
Boston Properties   see Moshe Safdie
Bruner/Cott
20 and 21 Custom House Street, 1989   no. 39
John Burgee Architects with Philip Johnson,
Architects
The New England, 1988   no. 63

Cambridge Seven Associates, Inc.
– Charles Square, 1984   no. 91
– Forest Hills Station, 1988   no. 109
Cannon Associates
Parkside West, 1989   no. 42
CBT/Childs Bertman Tseckares & Casendino,
Inc.
– 399 Boylston Street, 1982–84   no. 54
– Grant-Hoffman Building, 1987–89   no. 69
– 116 Huntington Avenue, 1990   no. 70
– Louis, 1988–89   no. 68
– Shipyard Park, 1981   no. 82
Clarke + Rapuano, Inc.   see Dean Abbott
Comunitas
Paul Revere Housing Cooperative, 1988   no. 86
Cossuta & Associates
Long Wharf Marriott, 1982   no. 17

Ellenzweig Associates, Inc.
– Alewife Station and Garage, 1985   no. 109
– Medical Education Center, 1987   no. 105
– Post Office Square Park, 1989–   no. 48
– Southwest Corridor Park, 1987   no. 108

Earl R. Falnsburgh & Associates, Inc.
– Angell Memorial Park, 1982   no. 13
– Boston Design Center, 1988   no. 33
Wallace Floyd Associates   see Bechtel/Parsons
Brinckerhoff

Frank O. Gehry Associates with Schwartz/Silver
Architects
Tower Records, 1987   no. 66
Goody, Clancy & Associates, Inc.
– Harbor Point Apartments, 1988–   no. 89
– Paine Webber Building, 1984   no. 20
– State Transportation Building, 1985   no. 59
– 99 Summer Street, 1986   no. 29
– Tent City Leighton Park, 1986–88   no. 80
Graham Gund Architects
– One Bowdoin Square, 1989   no. 37
– Bulfinch Square, 1986   no. 95
– Church Court Condominiums, 1983   no. 56
– Deutsch House, 1983   no. 73
– One Faneuil Hall Square, 1988   no. 36
– Institute of Contemporary Art, 1975   no. 50
– Museum School, Museum of Fine Arts,
1986–87   no. 102
– 75 State Street, 1988   no. 38
Gwathmey Siegel & Associates, Architects
– Busch-Reisinger Museum, Harvard University,
1990–   no. 97
– 37 Newbury Street (formerly Knoll International),
1980   no. 51

The Halvorson Company, Inc.
Post Office Square Park, 1990–   no. 48
Hoskins Scott Taylor & Partners, Inc.
– 101 Arch Street, 1989   no. 43
– Atrium Pavilion, University Hospital, 1987
no. 77
– Inpatient Towers, Massachusetts General
Hospital, 1989–[93]   no. 47

Carol Johnson
Lechmere Canal Park, 1988   no. 90
Philip Johnson, Architects   see John Burgee
Architects
Philip Johnson & John Burgee Associates
International Place, 1985   no. 24
Jung/Brannen Associates, Inc.
– One Exeter Plaza, 1984   no. 55
– 160 Federal Street, 1988   no. 35

– One Financial Center, 1985   no. 23
– 125 High Street, 1989–[92]   no. 46
– Medical Area Service Corporation, 1982   no. 101
– One Post Office Square/Meridien Hotel, 1981
no. 12

Kallmann, McKinnell & Wood Architects, Inc.
– Back Bay Station, 1987   no. 62
– John B. Hynes Veterans Memorial Convention
Center, 1985–89   no. 67
Kaplan, McLaughlin and Diaz with Tsoi/Kobus
& Associates
Ambulatory Services Building, Brigham and
Women's Hospital, 1989   no. 107
Kohn Pedersen Fox Associates, P. C.
– 75–101 Federal Street, 1988   no. 34
– 125 Summer Street, 1989–90   no. 44

LEA Group   see Ayers/Saint/Gross

Mintz Associates Architects/Planners, Inc.
The Bostonian Hotel, 1980–82   no. 10
Mitchell/Giurgola Architects
Lafayette Place, 1985   no. 25

New England Development
East Cambridge Riverfront, 1978   no. 90
Herbert S. Newman Associates
George S. and Ellen Kariotis Hall and Thomas
E. Cargill Hall, Northeastern University,
1982   no. 100
Notter, Finegold + Alexander, Inc.
– Berkeley Building, 1988   no. 64
– Burroughs Wharf, 1989–   no. 45
– 2 Clarendon Square, 1988   no. 79
– 303 Congress Street, 1984   no. 21
– Pier 7 (Constellation Wharf), 1988   no. 84

John Olson
Royal Sonesta Hotel, 1984   no. 90

Payette Associates, Inc.
Wellman Research Center, Massachusetts General
Hospital, 1981–84   no. 14
I. M. Pei & Partners (now Pei Cobb Freed &
Partners)
– John Hancock Tower, 1968–75   no. 49
– John Fitzgerald Kennedy Library, 1977–79
no. 87
– West Wing Addition, Museum of Fine Arts, 1981
no. 99
– Wiesner Center for the Arts & Media Technology,
Massachusetts Institute of Technology, 1985
no. 93

List of Buildings and
Urban Projects

Photographic Acknowledgements

Images not specifically cited below were provided by the architects.

Aerial Photos of New England, Inc.   p. 50 bottom
Joe Aker Photography/Houston, TX   pp. 132, 153
American Architect and Building News (June 9, 1888)   p. 40 top
Arrowstreet, Inc.   pp. 196
Christopher Barnes   pp. 180, 186
Beacon Properties   p. 43
Boston Athenaeum   pp. 21, 28, 29, 33 bottom, 34 bottom
Boston Redevelopment Authority   p. 45
Bostonian Society   pp. 18 bottom, 39 bottom, 44 top, 58 bottom
Richard Cheek, Belmont, MA pp. 26 bottom, 30 bottom, 36 bottom, 39 top, 42 bottom
F. M. Costantino, Architectural Illustrator p. 152
Mary C. Crawford, Old Boston Days & Ways (1909) p. 18 top
Culver Pictures   p. 22 upper right
Robert Damora   p. 134 top
Joe DeMaio   p. 161
[Charles W. Eliot], Charles Eliot, Landscape Architect (1902)   p. 38
FAY Foto/Boston   p. 126 top
Isabella Stewart Gardner Museum   p. 40 bottom
General Services Administration   p. 45
Paul Gobeil   p. 174, 175
Anton Grassl   p. 147, 199
David Hewitt/Anne Garrison   pp. 114, 157

Ralph Hutchins   p. 184
Ed Jacoby   pp. 78, 79 bottom, 172
Warren Jagger Photography, Inc.   pp. 84, 103, 213, 216, 217
Kimberley Shilland Collection   pp. 32, 33 top, 41 bottom
King's Handbook of Boston (1878)   pp. 22 lower left, 31, 34 top, 35 top, 41 top
Peter Lewitt   pp. 102, 127
Library of Congress, Map Division   front end-papers, p. 17
Nathaniel Lieberman   pp. 194, 195, 219
Alex S. MacLean/Landslides   pp. 128 bottom, 183 bottom, 187, 192, 200, 212 top, back endpapers
Richard Mandelkorn   pp. 91, 112, 229
Bruce T. Martin   pp. 106, 107
Massachusetts Bay Transportation Authority   pp. 236, 237
Massachusetts Historical Society   pp. 20 top, 30 top
Massachusetts Institute of Technology News Service   p. 49 upper left
The Massachusetts Magazine, 1789   pp. 23, 25 bottom
The Massachusetts Magazine, 1794   p. 26 top
Naomi Miller   pp. 27, 49 upper right, center right, lower left, lower right, 54, 57 top, 58 top
National Park Service/Frederick Law Olmsted National Historic Site   p. 37
New England Survey Service, Inc.   pp. 48, 50 bottom, 51, 53
New York Public Library   p. 20 bottom
New York Public Library, Stokes Collection   pp. 24, 25 top

Cymie Payne   pp. 10, 73 top, 149
Richard Payne, AIA   p. 99
Jack Pottle   p. 100
Cervin Robinson   p. 111
Steve Rosenthal, Auburndale, MA   front cover, frontispiece, pp. 55 bottom, 60, 66, 69, 82, 83, 86 upper right, 88, 89 top, 94 bottom, 96, 97, 101, 109 top, 110, 116, 117, 118 bottom, 120 bottom, 122 top, 135, 136, 137, top, 142, 143 top, 144, 145, 147 bottom, 151, 154, 159, 160 top, 166 bottom, 167 top, 171 upper left, 179, 182, 183 top, 189, 207, 210, 211 top, 215 bottom, 224, 225 upper left, 228, 231, 233, 239 bottom, 240
Irving Salsberg & Assoc., Inc.   p. 138
John Sharratt   pp. 75 bottom, 166 top, 170
William T. Smith   p. 185
Society for the Preservation of New England Antiquities   p. 120 top
Rick Stafford   p. 208
Ezra Stoller, c Esto   p. 70
Sam Sweezy   pp. 80, 86 upper left, bottom, 87, 105
Peter Vanderwarker   pp. 77, 81, 118 top, 160 bottom, 168, 176, 177, 197, 238
Nick Wheeler   pp. 71, 72, 76, 85 top, 92, 93, 95, 108, 109 bottom, 113, 129, 139, 140, 141, 148, 162, 173, 204, 226, 227
Franklin Wing   p. 56 top
Justin Winsor, Memorial History of Boston (1882) pp. 22 upper left, bottom left, 35 right, 36 top
George Zimberg   p. 50 top

Legend for Boston Map

The numbers refer to the entry numbers.

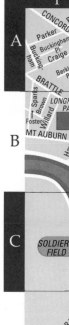